RING OF FIRE

LIVERPOOL INTO THE 21ST CENTURY
THE PLAYERS' STORIES

SIMON HUGHES

CORGI BOOKS

TRANSWORLD PUBLISHERS
61–63 Uxbridge Road, London W5 5SA
www.penguin.co.uk

Transworld is part of the Penguin Random House group of companies
whose addresses can be found at global.penguinrandomhouse.com

First published in Great Britain in 2016 by Bantam Press
an imprint of Transworld Publishers
Corgi edition published 2017

A CIP catalogue record for this book
is available from the British Library.

ISBN
9780552172738

Typeset in 11/14pt Sabon by Falcon Oast Graphic Art Ltd.
Printed and bound by Clays Ltd, Bungay, Suffolk.

Penguin Random House is committed to a sustainable
future for our business, our readers and our planet. This book is made from
Forest Stewardship Council® certified paper.

MIX
Paper from
responsible sources
FSC® C018179

1 3 5 7 9 10 8 6 4 2

For Rosalind (again)

CONTENTS

FOREWORD

There was a practice match at Melwood. Two sides of eleven, made up of kids like me and a few older pros not away on international duty, were scheduled to play against each other so that the new manager, Gérard Houllier, could form some opinions about the players he had to work with.

I was desperate to be involved. Change was in the air at Liverpool. The partnership between Roy Evans and Gérard had failed and, with Roy resigning, Gérard was in sole charge.

It felt like an opportunity. I'd only featured in a few games for the reserves but in each one I'd felt comfortable.

The problem was I'd broken my wrist and it was in a plaster cast. Phil Thompson was Gérard's assistant and he stopped me. 'Look, you can't play – it's the rules.'

I was very frustrated. Fortunately, one of the other players, Richie Partridge, caught Gérard's eye that morning. Richie was an Irish winger and he was flying at the time. Lots of people spoke about him as a potential first-team player.

Gérard decided to watch Richie in an under-19 fixture at the academy in Kirkby. It was one of my comeback games after the wrist injury. I didn't know Gérard was going to be there but then I saw him on the side of the pitch before the match kicked off. My dad had always told me from my first day at Liverpool that football was about matching opportunities with performance. I knew this was my chance. Thankfully, I took it and a few weeks later I made my debut for the first team.

The following twelve months proved to be a transitional period at Liverpool. When 1999 turned into the year 2000, I was nineteen years old. I did not foresee success being just around the corner under Gérard but only because I was too young to really understand what it took to create a successful football team at senior level. At that age, you only think about yourself, not what is in store for the club.

I felt a long way from being a regular in the side. Gérard had sat me down and explained that I needed to strengthen my body and change my lifestyle to suit the modern game. I knew straight away that Gérard had visions for the club and wanted to restore a winning mentality. Even though I was young and trying to establish myself, I could see something special was happening and that the manager was a winner who would do anything he thought was necessary to improve the situation of the club.

A few years earlier, I had been an apprentice at Liverpool and I was aware of the Spice Boy image. There was a drinking culture and things throughout the club were perceived as not being quite as professional as they should have been.

Gérard quickly set about clearing out the players he thought weren't prepared to do what he was asking for on and off the pitch.

For us young lads, he made it obvious early on in his reign that if we were not prepared to ride with the changes he was implementing – and come into work with a winners' mentality – then we would not find ourselves involved in his project moving forward.

He promoted young lads into the team who he thought had the required hunger and talent, and then used more experienced professionals he believed would set the standards for everyone else.

I would watch Patrik Berger, Vladimir Šmicer, Sami Hyypiä, Jamie Redknapp and Robbie Fowler – the way they acted in games, in the dressing room and on the bus. I asked a lot of questions and tried to learn from their experience. You see professional players who do the right things and you see professionals who don't. You learn from both.

I was fortunate in that I was in and around the scene at a time when attitudes were shifting because of Gérard's will. The mood not only presented a chance for me to impress but it also made me realize which was the right path to follow. Had I emerged a few years earlier, I could have gotten involved with the wrong crowd and been exposed to things that were to the detriment of my career rather than my benefit: going out more, eating bad foods, listening to the wrong people.

The weight of expectation at Liverpool is enormous.

Whether you are a player or a manager, the shadows of the past loom over you. When Gérard was appointed, Liverpool had not won the league for eight seasons and yet the demand for that to happen remained – and that's the way it should be at Liverpool.

Gérard revolutionized the club in terms of the way it operated and hauled it into the twenty-first century quicker than anyone could have imagined. The 2000–01 season will be remembered by all of those involved, player or supporter. Jamie Carragher speaks about it as his favourite season in a long career but he was a little bit older than me and probably appreciated more what it all really meant.

In the treble season, I felt young and naive. I felt like I was still learning and that I was nowhere near being the finished article. I was still coming to terms with being a first-team player.

The campaign ended with three trophies in a few months and qualification for the Champions League for the first time since it ceased being the European Cup. If you think about how difficult that would be to achieve for any team now, you realize just what a brilliant story it was. I don't think the feat will be matched for a long time.

The following season we finished second in the league – the strongest performance since 1990. And yet this period of success fell between a few fallow years and the immediate glory achieved under Rafael Benítez in 2005 with that amazing night at the Ataturk Stadium, winning the most important trophy in European competition for the first time in twenty-one years.

Gérard's contribution probably doesn't receive the credit it deserves because it gets diluted by what happened in Istanbul. On a personal level, I know what Gérard did for me. If you're a proper football person and analyse what Gérard achieved, it was incredible.

Take the trophies away and what did he do for the football club? It was in a far better position when he left than when he joined. He rebuilt the team and installed a mentality that Rafa was able to develop. Rafa would not have immediately achieved what he did at Liverpool had Gérard not created a much more professional set-up first. That's not a criticism of Rafa, it's just something that's impossible to ignore.

It became more difficult for us to win trophies as the decade progressed. Liverpool were still competing on the highest stage but Chelsea had emerged from the pack and Manchester City were gradually becoming a force too. On top of that, Manchester United and Arsenal were there. The competition at the top arguably became more ferocious than ever.

Not many people seem to recognize it but I think Gérard and Rafa were very similar managers in terms of the teams they created, which were compact, very aggressive with the ball, no spaces between the lines and had a solid defence. There were also match-winners within the line-up. Both were so thorough in their preparation, and that, when married with good, determined players, always gives you a chance.

The difference was their personalities. Both personalities got the best out of me. Gérard was a strong man-manager. He acted as a father figure. He looks out for your family and checks on what you are doing away from the game, putting in a lot of time and effort to work on personal relationships. When you go out to play for him and you don't perform, you feel like you are letting a family member down.

Rafa went the other way. He tries to inspire by provoking reactions. He leaves you searching for praise and that drives you on. There is a distance and a coldness with him. In every training session and game, I needed to prove myself to try to earn love from him. Looking back now, he was good for me. He helped me reach my peak as a footballer.

By the end of the 2000s, Liverpool was barely recognizable in comparison to the club that began the decade. Hundreds of players had come and gone, with new managers came new staff and, meanwhile, the owners had changed as well.

When I first broke into the team, David Moores was in charge, a local man who cared deeply about the success of Liverpool as a football club. By the end of the decade, we were in American hands. Whereas before, Liverpool felt like it was a family-run institution, as 2009 became 2010 it had turned into more of a business. Liverpool was not alone. Most clubs have experienced similar stories.

Gérard had made a big decision to make me captain as a twenty-three year old and it was the position I held until I left when I was thirty-four.

The captaincy of Liverpool is a duty you have to enjoy and embrace, otherwise it will drag you down. It was sink-or-swim time when I was appointed, because I was still developing as a player and probably not quite ready for it as a person.

I was lucky that I had a leader behind me in Jamie Carragher, who was my eyes, my ears and also my voice. Even though I had the armband on, Carra's influence was enormous. My relationship with him became very strong.

At any big club, the captaincy is a huge responsibility. At Liverpool, I recognized quickly it wasn't just about leading the team out once a week. It's a 24/7 job every single day. As a person, you have to develop and if at any point you feel like the responsibility is too big, too heavy or too pressured, you're not made for it.

The decade was not without its problems. There were some difficult times, especially towards the end. As captain you have to find a way to rise above them and power on.

Steven Gerrard

INTRODUCTION

On the third afternoon of January, Liverpool travelled to London to play Tottenham Hotspur in their first game of the new millennium. Chris Armstrong's goal meant a 1–0 defeat for Gérard Houllier's team.

A week later, Blackburn Rovers from the Championship – the second tier of English football – visited Anfield and, again, Liverpool were defeated, tumbling out of the FA Cup after Nathan Blake's lone strike with six minutes to go.

Fewer than thirty-three thousand spectators turned up to watch on that blustery day, more than ten thousand short of the stadium's full capacity. Liverpool were fifth in the league and Houllier's sweeping changes had not yet inspired trust.

Jamie Carragher was continually being compared to Merseyside-born legends from Liverpool's past and many doubted he was capable of becoming one himself. Steven Gerrard was a shy teenager who came alive on the pitch, charging about, trying to put his stamp on everything, but, though hopes were higher for him, concerns over his physical capacity remained. Houllier had not yet found the best way to manage Gerrard's developing physique, which was being challenged by the tough new fitness demands of the Premier League.

Ten years later, as they made their way to Birmingham in the snow for the last game of the decade against Aston Villa, Liverpool were seventh in the league and Houllier's replacement, Rafael Benítez, was halfway through his final season as manager, one that would end in disappointment and uncertainty – just as the decade had begun.

By then, Carragher had cemented his position as the foundation of the defence and he would finish his career second on the club's all-time appearance list. Gerrard, meanwhile, was regarded as one of the club's greatest players. He was the player who seemed to be able to do everything after all and the person who carried the burden of the supporters' hopes and dreams over so many seasons.

Carragher and Gerrard were in the eleven that beat Villa 1–0 when Liverpool's goal was scored late into that December night by Fernando Torres – someone who, like Gerrard, would capture hearts. Unlike Gerrard, however, Torres would also break them with his subsequent career decisions.

The 2000s had been an era where Liverpool became serious about winning again. Having lifted only two major trophies in the 1990s, there was one for each year in the subsequent decade if you include two Charity Shields and as many European Super Cups. With Houllier in charge, there was a cup treble in 2001, and then the Champions

League title against all the odds in 2005 when Benítez had taken over, before another FA Cup a year later.

The football from Houllier's teams was powerful, quick and disciplined. And discipline was one of the main reasons he had been appointed at Anfield. In the 1990s, society had begun to view footballers more negatively due to the excesses their newly inflated wages afforded them. Liverpool's Spice Boys had been a high-profile symptom of this change and there was a feeling that the dressing-room culture at the club had to be addressed. Houllier was seen as someone with the ability to restore order.

Houllier saw the way football was going and in the 2000s the expectations on the footballers of Melwood were as clearly defined as the expectations on footballers across the rest of Britain. Wide sections of society and the majority of the media demanded they be normal while simultaneously placing them on pedestals as role models due to their influential reach, not to mention their new-found wealth.

Football raced into a new era of heightened professionalism, where nearly all players attempted to do the right things, say the right things and appear to be the most right-minded people. The obsession with them as well as the inability to separate the sportsman from the celebrity created a very unhappy environment, and in writing this book I was conscious of that and wanted to select individuals who would speak honestly about their experiences rather than giving some sanitized, prepared-for-the-media version.

The 2000s was the decade where, at Liverpool

especially, it became a dangerous policy to deal only in outcomes, as if they were the definitive answers. Through technological advance, the world became smaller than it has ever been but just because it was the most-talked-about period in the club's history, this did not necessarily make it the most understood.

The football from Benítez's teams was similar to Houllier's but more sophisticated. He trusted creative players, those who could 'play in-between the lines', though always with tactical awareness. Under him, Liverpool went as close as they had to winning the title in any of the previous nineteen seasons, but in 2009 frustrating home draws against lesser opposition proved to be critical.

And yet there is a belief that it is impossible to discuss modern Liverpool without mentioning the name Rafael Benítez. Few divide opinion like him: the person who earned the loyalty of Liverpool supporters by providing as magical a night as any in the club's history in Istanbul, while also, apparently, being misunderstood – as Liverpool people often feel they are.

Benítez was the first person of influence to publicly expose the troubled times under the co-ownership of Tom Hicks and George Gillett after they had taken control from David Moores, and yet throughout the corresponding years – like all obsessives – he was accused of losing touch with reality.

From 2008 to 2010, there was civil war at Liverpool. Conclusions about the causes of the problems in that period may have seemed black and white according to which person you listened to. Objectively the evidence revealed the failed relationship between Hicks and Gillett was the root and yet at boardroom and management level the problems were nuanced. I hoped this book might shed new light on the situation.

I was told by readers of *Red Machine* and *Men in White Suits* that the strengths of those books were the meetings with the more curious types: individuals that perhaps made less of a contribution at Liverpool compared to others but retained more information because their experiences were briefer. For *Ring of Fire*, however, I decided for a step up in profile with the interviewees, aware that it might contribute towards a more serious book.

The 2000s were also the period in which I entered professional journalism, and this enabled me to appreciate that the better players usually had more exciting things to say, revealing that – although it might seem otherwise, and though certainly not always the case – in many instances the game's most influential characters are the footballers with the most engaging and forceful personalities.

And yet I determined there should be a few notable absentees. Steven Gerrard released his second autobiography in 2015, covering many of the issues I might have spoken to him about. Maybe it was a big call to leave out Liverpool's greatest modern player but in the end I decided it would be better for him to do the foreword, looking over the book like the protective guardian he became for so many at Liverpool for so long.

He would be a presence throughout the narrative anyway, just like Benítez, who similarly to Gerrard remains active in football. This complicates things because active sportsmen have more to lose by being unguarded. Benítez realizes he divides opinion and I had never seen an interview with him where he discusses his innermost feelings. After reading his autobiography, for example, I was left with the impression that he might believe that most football outcomes are a consequence of tactics rather than relationships.

Active players and managers have a habit of telling you more when the Dictaphone has been switched off. They hope their thoughts are presented as undisputed fact, thus blurring the lines of truth. I didn't want *Ring of Fire* to be that sort of book, especially when the success of the others was based around the accountability of the stories.

I met with Benítez's representatives to try to establish what might happen if we met and I left wondering about the benefits of including him. I arrived at the conclusion that, although Benítez's name counts for something, in terms of core material – strong content – he might be best left alone, in the same way Kenny Dalglish was left alone in *Red Machine* or Robbie Fowler in *Men in White Suits*. Then within twenty-four hours Benítez was appointed as Newcastle United's manager and a meeting became impossible due to his newfound responsibilities.

I had turned to Jamie Carragher first, because he seemed like the most sensible starting point. His Liverpool career stretched across three decades, cover-ing the whole of this one. He released his autobiography in 2008 and so much has happened since then I hoped I might establish a different reflection on the period now he is older and maybe a bit wiser.

Carragher was incredibly generous with his time, sitting down with me on three occasions across successive weeks. These meetings required the least amount of travel. We live in the same area of Liverpool, so it involved me opening my door and walking three minutes to a modest restaurant around the corner where we sat and talked mainly about what drives him on the most, what fuels that insatiable appetite that kept him at the top of the game for so long.

Carragher is such a humble and entertaining person it is easy to forget just how much people revere him. At the end of the third interview, upon discovering a parking ticket on his car because his time had elapsed in the throes of our conversation, he returned to the restaurant, where I was organizing myself, to tell me of his frustrations, joking that I should pay the fine. 'But you have the freedom of Sefton,' I reminded him. 'If you wanted to graze wild horses on the roundabouts, nobody could stop you.'

I went to see Houllier in Paris. Like Carragher, he was kind, insisting on picking me up from my hotel during rush hour. Houllier was magnificently French: intelligent, expressive, reflective and occasionally abrupt. As Liverpool's manager, he prided himself on his accessibility, being there for the players if they needed it, no matter the hour of day. I wondered whether this had a detrimental effect on his health, never being able to switch off from work. He recognized I had flown out specifically to meet him and after realizing I was not leaving France until the next day, he invited me to his office the following morning in case there was anything I'd missed in the initial interview.

More time with a subject is an offer no journalist refuses, so naturally I went along, regardless of the fact I was pretty happy with the initial outcome. Upon arriving at his hidden office on a dusty side street off a road that leads up towards Montmartre, Houllier greeted me ambivalently. 'You came then?' But after five minutes or so, he returned to being intelligent, expressive and reflective. Later, as I walked away back towards the banks of the Seine, I realized I quite liked him and began to understand why players did too.

When I met with Phil Thompson, he sat with his gym bag next to him and talked for hours, reminding me of his traditional values and connecting this book with Liverpool's past by reaching back into the 1960s and offering a description of what made the club great in the first place.

In the book Thompson is followed by Danny Murphy, a midfielder who proved you can score three match-winning goals for Liverpool at Old Trafford and still not be remembered fondly; similarly there was Michael Owen, who proved you can score hundreds of goals for Liverpool but this will count for very little if you later sign for Manchester United.

The chapter with academy graduate Neil Mellor is shorter than the rest because I wanted it to reflect his snapshot Anfield career and his brief but significant contribution to the first team. After Mellor is Dietmar Hamann, the untypical German midfielder – and an untypical footballer – yet someone who is more serious and perceptive than he lets on.

From there, I thought a flavour of Spain was essential to try to explain why Benítez divides opinion. Hamann had spoken so positively about him, and Mellor had too, so I went to see Xabi Alonso and Albert Riera, players who in 2016 find themselves in very different places.

For a change, I thought it wise to speak to someone with great influence who did not play and was not a manager. The role of the chief executive emerged as a significant feature of football in the twenty-first century and Rick Parry revealed to me the reality of what it was like running Liverpool day-to-day, week-to-week, month-to-month, year upon year. His story is a reminder that although supporters might have an opinion on the work of someone like Parry, ultimately the only opinion that gets tested is his. After I spent nearly six hours with him, Parry joked that I must have felt like Anthony Clare from the radio series *In The Psychiatrist's Chair*.

I arrived finally at Fernando Torres, realizing it is impossible to think about his breathtaking contribution towards Liverpool without considering the circumstances of his departure. You cannot divorce Torres the centre-forward who streaked across boxes and dashed past defenders as if they were not there from Torres the traitor, the one who signed for Chelsea.

Torres had never given an interview to anyone where he detailed the reasons why he left Liverpool, so I consider his inclusion as a coup. He recognized this was a unique opportunity for self-justification, because he did not want to do it through the papers, where news headlines might detract from his reasoning. He understood there is greater room for context in a book and hoped that this might make Liverpool supporters understand why he made the ultimate decision to go somewhere else.

It was only when Torres took breaks to compose himself, as his sentences became shorter while he spoke about his acrimonious exit from Liverpool and what happened in his career thereafter, that I realized the Spanish star is more complex – and certainly more vulnerable – than I ever really appreciated. It forced me to conclude that his expressed fondness for Liverpool and its people had always been genuine. I also discovered sadness in him, maybe even loneliness.

Torres had flourished at Liverpool with a great midfield and Steven Gerrard pulling the strings behind him, and though he was sharing pitch space with lesser talents like Milan Jovanović and Paul Konchesky by the end of his time at Anfield, Xabi Alonso and Michael Owen had proven before him that legacies are only protected by selecting the timing of your exit and your next destination wisely.

Liverpool had fallen some distance very quickly. In 2010, for the second successive year, the auditors KPMG expressed 'material uncertainty' about the club's ability to continue as a going concern. The new chairman, Martin Broughton, appeared before the Premier League to give a guarantee, which had to be backed up by the banks, that Liverpool would be able to fulfil their fixtures.

The seismic split between Hicks and Gillett had created a power vacuum, inspiring only a culture of paranoia at

Liverpool, where the best interests of the club were not being served first by anyone consistently.

If one story sums up the mood at Melwood by the end of the decade, it is this. It was late in the afternoon and the training ground was almost empty. Bunkered in his office up on the second floor, Rafael Benítez was looking at some papers from behind a desk. An unfamiliar member of staff knocked on the door, picking up letters to be delivered in the final post of the day.

Benítez seemed surprised by the sudden company.

And then he is said to have asked, 'Whose side are you on?'

CHAPTER ONE

cultzeros.co.uk

PHIL THOMPSON,
MR LIVERPOOL

IT WAS THE SECOND WEEK IN NOVEMBER 1998 AND LITTER
from the fast-food kiosks inside Anfield whirled across
the pitch in strange formation. The floodlights shone,
lighting up a squally winter's night, but the gloom on
the terraces intensified as the temperature and the mood
plummeted. Wisecracks were made about the cardboard
plates, hotdog wrappers and drink cartons forming a
more effective barrier than Liverpool's defence. The
famous stadium seemed quiet and lonely, the only loud
noise coming from the Anfield Road End, where the

few away fans stood in a pack for warmth. 'Are you Tranmere in disguise?' came the muffled chorus. 'Bye, bye, Evans,' they continued cruelly, knowing that a 3–1 victory for their team, Tottenham Hotspur, was likely to mean the end for Liverpool's joint manager, Roy Evans, who had served the club for more than thirty years.

The main stand was silent, aside from the commentary area where Graham 'Beeky' Beecroft, an experienced presenter, was describing the scene in front of him, where John Scales had scored – a player sold by Evans to Tottenham because he was deemed past his best almost two years earlier.

Phil Thompson was the match analyser for Radio City. When the visiting team's third goal went in, he leaned his elbows on the table in front of him and held his head in his hands, cursing to himself. Thompson – a European Cup-winning captain with Liverpool – eventually looked up and stared at the dugout where Evans and Gérard Houllier, the person he shared a job with, were positioned at opposite ends of the seating arrangement.

'I was thinking to myself, *What the fuck is happening? Where the fuck is this all going?* I was looking at Roy, I was looking at Gérard and between the two of them you couldn't feel anything. Neither of them seemed to want to take control.'

Thompson remembers the moment he picked up the microphone and began to speak, glowering dead-eyed at Beecroft, who was reduced to the role of listener for the next five minutes.

'My frustrations erupted on the radio,' Thompson continues. 'I've learned over time it's about how you say things rather than how angry you get. But I went into a rant about how I saw my football club. There was no relationship between the managers, the players and the supporters. I said that things needed to change. They needed to change right away.'

Thompson drove home in a bad mood that night and went straight to bed without saying anything to his wife, Marg. The following morning, it was back to the day job. Pine DIY was one of his businesses in Kirkby. Upon opening the back door he found a letter left with only his name scrawled on the envelope. It was from a Liverpool fan who, after hearing Thompson the previous evening, had decided to write to him straight away, delivering the message to his door. Thompson was humbled by what he read.

'It was four pages long and it began something like, "Phil, your time has come to return to Liverpool FC; your calling has arrived. We need passionate people like you; people who will set those players straight."'

In the afternoon, Thompson arrived at the Pitz five-a-side football facility not far from Anfield, down the hill in Kirkdale, where he was to prepare for a forth-coming masters tournament with other former players. Thompson says his trousers were 'literally around my ankles' when his mobile phone began to ring and on the other end of the line was Peter Robinson, Liverpool's secretary, inviting him to a meeting at the mansion of chairman David Moores in Halsall, Lancashire.

'Straight away, I thought I might have been getting a dressing-down for what I'd said on the radio – that kind of thing happens,' Thompson admits.

'But on the way to Halsall, I spoke to my brother Owen and the wife. Marg's a teacher and she was still at work. I told her, "Love, you've got to get out of the classroom. It's possible that I've had *the* call from Liverpool . . ."'

In Halsall, Thompson was greeted by a sombre atmosphere.

'David has a lovely house but it was like a funeral parlour, with everyone sitting around in silence. Peter stepped forward and explained that Gérard was going to be the manager in sole charge and that it was unanimously agreed that he needed someone by his side that was disciplined and someone who could stand up to the players and rescue the club from the Spice Boys era. They wanted a big voice. Tom Saunders stood up and began to speak: "There's only one person we need – and that person is Phil Thompson."

'After what happened with Graeme Souness, it was a lovely moment – they were coming for me.'

Thompson had been sacked by Souness and Liverpool seven years earlier for supposedly being too aggressive with the club's reserve-team players, swearing at them too much. Thompson reasons he was only following what Ronnie Moran had done two decades earlier when Thompson was a teenager and Moran was coach.

'It did no harm to my career,' Thompson thinks. 'I moulded my reserve team on Ronnie's. He barked orders, so I barked orders. I didn't care if I was popular or not. My satisfaction came from getting results and seeing young players get pushed into the first team. When Graeme sacked me, he said I shouted too much at the young lads in the reserves. My attitude was, if you couldn't handle me shouting at you in front of a couple of hundred people at a reserve match, you wouldn't have a chance with the first team, where everyone, especially the crowd, wants to have a pop at you.'

Having dismissed Thompson's authoritarian approach on the advice of Souness, Liverpool's board now deemed it to be the key ingredient missing from the dressing room. Thompson didn't leave Houllier's home near Sefton Park till the early hours of the following morning, marking the end of what he considers the most remarkable twenty-four hours of his life.

'I'd only met Gérard once before and I didn't know the fella at all. But I said to him that evening, "Listen, mate, I'm going to be different to anything you've ever worked with. I'm a nark. I'm brash. I'm aggressive. I'm a moaner. But Gérard, I'll give you 100 per cent loyalty and trust to bring the success back.'

The mission facing Houllier and Thompson was enormous.

'There was indiscipline at the club,' Thompson says. 'Gérard and Roy had been dragged apart by the players who had too much power. Re-instilling the discipline was a big responsibility and it was going to be an arduous task.

'I became the Bob Paisley of the duo. Gérard was going to be the Shanks – the good guy. I went in there and I was like a whirlwind. I loved it. And everybody hated me, every player.'

Before Thompson's return was made public, he turned up at Melwood unannounced. He concedes that to some of the players it must have been like an old fearsome guard returning to the asylum after the lunatics had taken over.

'I bumped into some of the lads that played under me for the reserves. Jamie Redknapp and Steve Harkness were there.

'"What are you doing here, Thommo?" they asked.

'"I'm your new assistant manager, lads," I told them.

'Their faces, you should have seen their faces – they dropped on the floor. Straight away, Harky warned me, "You can't be the way you were with us, Thommo – it won't work."

'"Oh," I said. "In any walk of life – no matter how much money you're being paid – you've gotta have discipline."

'"Mmmmm," he goes, dismissively. "We'll see . . ."

'I thought to myself then, *I've got to get into these straight away*. So I did.'

Houllier and Thompson quickly concluded that the presence of Paul Ince, the club's captain, was the biggest problem at Liverpool. Ince's influence when Evans was in sole charge was so considerable that he'd persuaded the manager to switch from an effective 3–5–2 formation to a standard 4–4–2 because it suited his qualities more and it was what he was used to at previous clubs Manchester United and Inter Milan.

'Paul was a good player, don't get me wrong,' Thompson says. 'But he wasn't what we wanted or where we wanted to go or be. So our development was going to be at his expense.

'Everyone called Ince "the Guv'nor". He was the big

man, running the dressing room. A lot of the young lads looked up to him. So I made it my point to make it difficult for him. And he hated me. He hated Gérard too, writing a massive two-page article in one of the tabloid papers when he left for Middlesbrough, saying that we would drag the club down.

'A couple of years later, in 2001, Gérard thought it was time to reply and he admitted that Ince was right. We had dragged the team down – to Cardiff, not once, not twice, not three times but four – winning all of those cups!'

A smile begins to slowly spread across Thompson's distinctive-looking face towards the end of this particular story, his eyes twinkling. It satisfies him that he was able to bring down those he thought acted like they were more important than Liverpool, the club he'd grown up supporting, the club he ended up playing for and winning a European Cup with as captain all those years before.

Thompson admits he relished cracking heads.

'If you ask any of the lads that played with me or any of the ones I coached, I know what they'll say about me,' he says, making a slitting gesture across his throat. 'There was a passion burning inside of me. It was uncontrollable. It's still there, I think. I'd say I'm a perfectionist. Others would say something less flattering.'

Thompson reasons that his quest for perfection stems from a desire to make up for what he sees as disappointments in the past, in that he was not selected to play for Liverpool's youth teams until he was fifteen.

He wasn't even in the Kirkby boys' district side until the age of fourteen. His passion for Liverpool and for football became greater because his struggle to get there was greater than that of others.

'Liverpool was the Holy Grail for me. It was something to reach for. I dreamed of nothing other than being a Liverpool player from the age of eight. It meant that I was able to enjoy my football club and support them as a child. I went through the process of the standing boys' pen. These kids now, they feel as if they belong at Liverpool from birth because they're being signed up too early. They're still fans but they're fans in a less fervent way because they are having to think about their own standing within the club too soon. Maybe it erodes the love.

'The clubs – all of them, not just Liverpool – have encouraged elitism,' he continues. 'It's not healthy. Kids can't have proper childhoods. One or two do because their parents know the score but many slip through the net. Those who don't have the family support behind them, they let the status go to their heads. Rather than receiving the right guidance, they get over-coached and as a result few of them are able to figure out solutions for themselves. The instinctive footballers have disappeared. How many kids have come out of Kirkby in the last ten years? Not many.'

The building of Liverpool's academy had already been commissioned by the time Thompson and Houllier became assistant and manager. He thinks the site's separation from Melwood hasn't really worked out.

'There's a desire in the modern world to compartmentalize everything. I was fortunate that at fifteen I could see the reserve-team players, those younger professionals. I was in the B team and I wanted to be in the A team. When I was in the A team, I wanted to be in the reserves. When I was in the reserves, I wanted to be in the first team. I could visibly see my career in front of me. I knew the standards that I needed to meet because they were obvious around me.

'In 1998, when the academy was built here in Kirkby, it became elitist, because all the responsibilities a young player used to have disappeared. There was no more cleaning baths, boots, balls and changing rooms. The young players had people there to do that for them and it made them precious.

'When I was fifteen, I loved being there at Melwood. I was going to enjoy my time at Liverpool no matter how short or long it might be. Just being near my heroes, my idols, was the biggest thrill. I wanted to be the best boot polisher at the club, my baths were cleaner than any other apprentice, my floors were done with warmth and love, and the training kit, although it was crap, was put out as neatly as possible.

'When I was twenty-four or twenty-five, I sat down with Ronnie Moran and all the others. It was one of those moments where you realize how far you've travelled. I asked Ronnie what he saw in me, a skinny kid from Kirkby. I was rake-thin. "We could see you could play, Thommo," he told me. "That's why we always picked you on the staff team for the famous five-a-sides."

'It wasn't because they knew I could run all day – I was a cross-country runner for the county as a kid

– it was because I didn't want to be beaten at all. "We watched you every day doing those meaningless jobs and you didn't cut corners. You did them to perfection. That tells us, as staff, you'll go all the way on the pitch to make sure the backs of your teammates are covered."'

Bill Shankly – the man who transformed Liverpool from Second Division also-rans to First Division and FA Cup champions – was Thompson's hero. But Moran was his mentor, the former player whose career at Liverpool followed the same path as Thompson's: from B team to A team to reserves before making the most important step of them all – to the first team. Before Thompson could drive, Moran used to give him lifts to training in his Morris Minor.

'I'd get the 44D bus to the Crown pub in Norris Green and Ronnie was always there on time, as promised,' Thompson recalls. 'Ronnie had more influence over me than anyone else at Liverpool. He was the biggest moaner I've ever met. He complained about everything. He would not rest. Even if we'd won 5–0 on the Saturday, he'd arrive for work on the Monday morning screaming at everybody. He treated us like school kids and if he wasn't happy, he'd have us doing shuttle runs as a punishment, no matter what the previous result had been. Kenny Dalglish, Graeme Souness – he didn't care how great you were, he'd be bawling at you, the moaning bastard. It's only when you stop and analyse it that you realize Ronnie was the driving force behind a lot of the success. He made sure there was no rest for us. He made sure everybody remained grounded. Ronnie got praise for his work but not as much as he should have done.'

I meet Thompson one morning in November at the bar of the David Lloyd health and fitness centre in Kirkby. He lives a fifteen-minute drive north into Lancashire but he returns to the facility in his home town pretty much every week day because he knows most of the people here, a community spirit exists and he enjoys connecting with his past.

'Where we are now is the site of the old Kirkby Town FC,' he informs me. 'I played here for Kirkby School Boys when I was a lad.'

The David Lloyd centre is next door to Liverpool Football Club's aforementioned youth academy. 'You can see wonderful pitches there now but back in the day it's where I used to run my Sunday league team from when I was playing for Liverpool. The area has played a big part in my life. It's religious ground for me, this.'

Thompson was twenty-one years old and in his prime when he took charge of the Falcon Sunday league side for the first time. By then, he was already well established in Liverpool's first team, having helped win a league title and a UEFA Cup double. He was also the owner of an FA Cup-winners' medal.

'I was obsessed by football, bloody obsessed,' he grins, rubbing his hands together. 'I couldn't get enough of it. That's why I took charge of the Falcon. The best-known Sunday league team in Kirkby was the Fantail and people often got us confused with them. We were probably a step down in terms of football ability but we were a proper team with a proper spirit from a proper pub.'

Thompson managed the Falcon for twelve seasons. On Monday mornings, he'd arrive at Anfield and while he was getting changed, Ronnie Moran and Roy Evans, the first-team coach and reserve-team manager, would ask the same question separately.

'"How did you get on yesterday?" they'd say – not even mentioning the Liverpool game on the Saturday. Wherever we played – even if it was Southampton – I'd be on Arbour Lane on a Sunday morning by 11 a.m. with the kits, the balls and the sponges in the boot of my car. It was blowing a gale every week. The lads would breathe alcoholic fumes all over you. You'd be driving around Kirkby trying to get some of them out of bed to come and play. But they were fantastic times. As much as I loved playing for Liverpool, some of my greatest football moments were with the Falcon.'

Surely all the other teams in the league must have wanted to beat a side managed by a Liverpool player?

'Of course they did,' he laughs. 'There was expectancy on us every week. It got harder for us after an administration error meant we had to leave the Kirkby and District League, where we were comfortable, and join the Kirkby New Town League. Because our application was late, there was only one place left in all of the divisions and it was in the top one. Oh my goodness, it was tough. We got kicked all over the place. These teams, they were good anyway but they upped the anti a notch or two because I managed the Falcon. In the dressing room after one game, I told the lads if they wanted to pack it in, they should discuss it in the pub and I'd understand. They were getting booted everywhere and I appreciated they had to go off to work on a Monday morning as labourers. Many of them were self-employed. I didn't want to be responsible for an injury; they needed to work to support their families. My older brother Owen, who also played, later came to me and said that the lads wanted to continue. They didn't want to duck out and let the bigger fellas win. It was typical of the attitude you get from lads in Kirkby.'

The Falcon went on to win everything there was to win in the New Town League. Thompson created what he calls a 'no-excuse culture' by putting pressure on himself to attend all games. His commitment was as great as anyone else's.

Liverpool had not yet won a European Cup in the spring of 1977 but having beaten FC Zurich in Switzerland during the semi-final first leg that year, he was ruled out of the return through injury and decided to attend a final the Falcon were playing in at Prescot Cables instead. He remembers driving down the M57 and seeing the floodlights of Anfield shining in the distance and then the celebrations afterwards back at the pub after finding out that Zurich had been brushed aside. The Falcon had also won.

'We trained every Thursday night where the old Kirkby Stadium used to be, on shale all-weather pitches. It was twelve- or thirteen-a-side; you'd get lads who weren't good enough but came along for the craic anyway. It was cut-throat stuff. But I'd train too – even though I had a game for Liverpool on the Saturday. Nobody at the club knew.'

It was only when Thompson was given the job as

Liverpool's reserve-team manager after retiring that he resigned as manager of the Falcon. Sunday morning was a busy part of the working week for Liverpool's backroom staff, as they used the time to clean kits, treat injuries and discuss what had happened the day before. That Thompson was able to lead a double life for so long – his entire playing career – reflects his mania for football.

'I think it all started with my mum rather than my dad,' he says. 'My mum was a big Liverpudlian and she went to Anfield all the time. She used to go in the main stand during the 1950s, right by the tunnel. One of my earliest memories was going with her along with my auntie and brother Owen to the Inter Milan European Cup match in 1965. I was eleven years old and how she got tickets for it, I'll never know. It was the biggest game in Liverpool's history and beforehand Gerry Byrne and Gordon Milne walked around the pitch holding the FA Cup, which had been won a few days before. We were sitting on the front row of the Kemlyn Road and I could reach out and almost touch it. God, I get goosepimples just thinking about that night.

'Mum was really passionate, so when I started playing she couldn't have been any more proud. My dad was an Evertonian and he worked at sea; a lot of men in Kirkby did. Whenever he came home from America, he'd bring us gifts from New York and try to make me and my brothers turn towards Everton. It was never going to happen. I was still standing on the Kop when I was seventeen and playing in the reserves. I was Liverpool mad.'

Thompson's terrace education began in the infamous boys' pen.

'There was a lad from school, Tommy Heaton, and we used to go together. It was a shilling to get in. The environment was a tough one. There was a drainpipe in the corner and I used to try to scale it to get in the Kop, because that's where you aspired to be. Being in the Kop was a sign of maturity.'

Although he grew up in Kirkby, Thompson was born in Kensington, the inner-city area of Liverpool known affectionately by locals as 'Kenny', which has given the world a series of famous musicians, including John and Mick Head from Shack, as well as Ian McNabb. Thompson was one of seven brothers and sisters who lived in a Victorian terraced house on Ling Street under the watchful eye of his mum, May, whose sister, June, was never far away, helping her control the young boys.

'Kenny's only a mile away from Anfield. On match days, you knew a game of football was happening because everyone seemed to be heading in the same direction. My mum applied to the council for a bigger house. Kirkby was an overspill town being built because of the baby boom, so we were shoved out there on Stonehey Road.'

The three-bedroom new-build was opposite the old Brookfield High School and backed on to St Joseph's juniors. Thompson was surrounded by football pitches and such access eventually helped nurture skills that invited an opportunity to trial at Melwood, Liverpool's training ground, aged fourteen. Thompson missed his end-of-year school exams to make sure he was there. John Gidman, who later played for Everton and both Manchester clubs, was also in attendance, along with Kenny Pritchard, whose goals at junior levels had marked him out as the one to watch over the six weeks they spent together.

'The other lads signed apprentice forms before me,' Thompson says, underlining the fact that his career was not mapped out from a young age. 'Liverpool kept me waiting. It was coming towards the end of the trial and we had a game against Bury at Melwood. I was too scared to ask the people at Liverpool what was going on. I wanted it so much, so I asked my mum to come along and speak to Tom Bush, who was the youth development officer. We won and I played really well but as we walked home, past where the Bill Shankly Playing Fields are now, I was struggling to find the courage to ask her what Tom had said. "Did you speak to him then?" I asked. She delayed her response. "What's the matter – it's bad news, isn't it?" Then she told me Liverpool wanted me to sign, though Tom had told her not to tell me because he wanted to deliver the news the following day. I was so emotional. I feel it now. I gave her the biggest hug ever.'

Of the fifteen players who signed apprentice forms that summer, Thompson was the only one to emerge as a professional. And this was despite the fact that midway through his two-year apprenticeship Tom Bush died and Tony Waiters was appointed as his replacement for a brief period.

'I left Brookfield School without any qualifications. I

threw all my eggs into one basket. So I had to make it happen,' he reasons. 'Maybe Tom dying unsettled a few of the others. I know Giddy [John Gidman] and Tony didn't see eye to eye. Sometimes that happens in football and your career is sent spinning on a different path. I liked Tony, though.'

Thinking about this period in his life, Thompson still gets excited now.

'It was a fascinating time to be an apprentice,' he explains, racing through his thoughts. 'Can you imagine going into a dressing room and Roger Hunt is sitting there? He was a knight of the realm to Liverpool supporters like me. I'd stand there open-mouthed, looking at him like an idiot. I've met Pelé and Eusébio; I've played against Diego Maradona. But Roger was the greatest to me. I had photographs of him behind my bed and posters all over the walls. When I think that I won more than Roger did at Liverpool and eventually achieved what Bill Shankly did in managing the club, even if it was only for three months, I have to stop and take a moment. It's weird.'

Thompson trained on Tuesday and Thursday nights at Melwood, sometimes under the supervision of Reuben Bennett. A former goalkeeper, Bennett once completed a game for Dundee with a broken leg. He later joined Liverpool's coaching team under Phil Taylor. Obsessed by fitness, Shankly put him in charge of physical conditioning. In Liverpool's Boot Room, he was known as Sherlock because he often patrolled the grounds of Melwood in a deerstalker hat.

'Reuben was a hard, rash Scotsman from Aberdeen. He was mysterious – Shanks's right-hand man. I know

Bob Paisley was Shanks's assistant but Reuben was the one Shanks confided in. His bark was bigger than Ronnie Moran's. He didn't live far from Melwood, so he would turn up for training and stand on the side of the pitch in his long raincoat. You felt in awe when you saw him; you were honoured.

'Later, when I joined the first team, Reuben was over sixty but played as the goal-hanger in the five-a-side games. No matter what the weather was like, he'd wear a pair of trainers rather than boots. Even if he scored the first of seventeen goals, he'd celebrate it as if it was the FA Cup final. He'd wind up the young lads and you were desperate to beat him because his passion was so clear.'

Thompson remembers meeting Shankly for the first time, bumping into him in the corridor outside his office at Anfield. He describes the moment as 'an audience with the Pope'. His outstanding memory of those early years is of the way Shankly used to ignore players who were injured, ostensibly because they were of no use to him but the deeper reason being that he thought of injuries as diseases that would contaminate his squad if acknowledged.

'It was purely psychological,' Thompson thinks. 'Nobody wanted to get injured, because the loneliness was humiliating. I can see him popping his head into the treatment room and letting on to Bob [Paisley] and Joe [Fagan] but ignoring the fella lying down on the table. It could have been Roger Hunt or Ron Yeats but he wouldn't have wished them good morning if they weren't available to play for him.'

Thompson describes Anfield as a 'workplace'.

'We'd be in every day doing long hours. I can still smell the bleach now, the way we'd clean the floors using a scrubbing brush, then a mop and a bucket. Ronnie and Joe would come along and inspect your work and you couldn't go home if the baths weren't sparkling. It was a labour of love. Anfield held a sense of belonging. I'm convinced it had an impact on results too because, come a match day, we felt comfortable.'

Shankly had transformed Melwood from a run-down weed-infested playing field into sacred earth by introducing the five-a-side games that defined his 'pass-and-move' philosophy. Shankly raised the club from the lower reaches of the old Second Division to become champions of the First in less than five years, before Bob Paisley's team went on to dominate Europe. Outsiders struggled to figure out Liverpool's secret, believing mystical forces were at work behind the walls of the training ground. Thompson thinks the success was based on simple repetition and working by a set of unwritten rules enforced by tough men like Ronnie Moran.

'As a kid, you were told not to hold on to the ball for too long, particularly in midfield or at centre-half; you had to get it, you had to give it. Ronnie would drill us. It was only when you got around the opposition's 18-yard box that you were allowed to express yourself.

'If I close my eyes and think about training at Melwood as a teenager, my thighs begin to hurt because Ronnie had us down on our haunches, jockeying an opponent back and forth. I don't think anyone knows what jockeying is now. It's such a basic skill and learning how to do it properly improves your understanding of timing.

'A lot of the success was a consequence of repetition. Getting it, giving it – it became a natural act. When I stepped up to the reserves, all I could hear from the touchline was Ronnie screaming, "Give it early!" I was a midfielder originally but I remember shouting back to Ronnie, "I haven't even got it yet!" Ronnie wanted things to happen before it was humanly possible. Ideally, it was done in one pass, without the need for a controlled first touch.

'We didn't have a term for it but it was this simplicity that I believe formed the Liverpool way. Others tried to complicate it. When the lads later got together for former players' games, it was as though we still had Ronnie on the touchline. Someone would pass it to me and straight away I'd shift it to Phil Neal. The Everton and United players, they'd try to do tricks and run through the middle of the pitch, holding on to possession for too long. At Liverpool, only the wingers – Steve Heighway, Cally [Ian Callaghan] and Peter Thompson – were allowed to run with possession. Everyone else – get it, give it.'

Thompson evolved into a central defender, having spent his teenage years in midfield.

'By the time I reached the reserves, I was more of a holding midfield player but I still scored seven or eight goals a season. My biggest asset was being able to read the game and be in position at the right time, before things happened. I knew what was going on.'

An injury to the hulking Larry Lloyd presented an opportunity for Thompson but not before others were selected first, reflecting again that Thompson's route to the top was not an automatic rite of passage.

'There were other boys rated higher than me at the time. It disappointed me that I was behind a few of them but I took it on the chin and cracked on with it. You see so many lads sulking when that happens now.'

In the second half of the 1973–74 season, Shankly began to regularly pair Thompson with Emlyn Hughes in the centre of defence. Thompson considers this decision to be the making of a 'modern' Liverpool, where defenders, rather than merely being stoppers, were expected to take on extra ball-playing responsibilities.

'Emlyn and myself were very similar. He was more of a rampaging midfield player but was a good reader of the game and could play in most positions. In our first game together, we beat Coventry City 2–1 at Anfield and we were 2–0 up. They scored a consolation late on and I remember feeling absolutely gutted. After that, we went seven games without conceding a goal.

'People say the 1974 Dutch team at the World Cup were the first to play so-called "Total Football". No they weren't. We started it. Holland played with two smallish centre-backs in Arie Haan and [Wim] Rijsbergen. As we know, the Dutch were great observers of the game and I think they saw Liverpool and thought, Wow. Me and Emlyn were the first to prove that you didn't need a monster at the back. We could play. I'll argue with anyone that Liverpool invented "Total Football", not the Dutch.'

Thompson's first cup final came a few months after his first game in defence. Even at twenty years old, he did not suffer from nerves and in the hours before the 3–0 victory over Newcastle United, he remembers lying on the couch watching the BBC's *Road to Wembley* programme while teammates like Brian Hall were 'biting their nails'.

'The confidence came from the fact it was what I wanted to do and knowing that Liverpool seldom lost. The bigger the game, we'd win it. I didn't lose a Merseyside derby for seven years, for example. In my time at Liverpool, we lost just one cup final and that was the FA Cup final of 1977 against Manchester United. And I was injured that day by the way . . .'

Thompson's supreme conviction led to two European Cup final appearances, and Liverpool won both. In the second, in Paris in 1981, Thompson was the captain. He marked the achievement of beating Real Madrid by taking the trophy back to the Falcon in Kirkby, allowing all of his friends to drink from the prize.

'It was the greatest night of my professional life,' Thompson smiles. 'When I lifted the cup, I could see the Falcon lads across the Parc des Princes with the Kirkby flags. There was a gang from the Kingfisher pub as well.'

Earlier in the season, after winning the League Cup in a replay with West Ham United at Villa Park, Thompson was told off by Peter Robinson, Liverpool's secretary, for leaving the trophy in the coach after travelling home from the Midlands. On that occasion, his plan to take it back to the Falcon was disrupted by his wife-to-be, Marg, who, having drunk so much on the open-top-bus parade around Liverpool, needed to use the toilet at a house on Utting Avenue near Anfield. The distraction meant Thompson had to catch up with the bus by hailing a ride in the back of an ice cream van.

'When the parade was over, I hid the European Cup in a red velvet bag and, despite being intoxicated, to my shame, I raced off in my Ford Capri to the Falcon with Marg. I walked in with the cup above my head. The place was bouncing. There was a queue for the public phone box and the whole of Kirkby seemed to turn up. What a night.'

Thompson still lived in Kirkby at the time in a modest two-up, two-down semi-detached house. The next morning, Peter Robinson called.

'He goes, "Phil, do you happen to know where the European Cup is?" My eyes were so blurred, I saw five European Cups standing there on the mantelpiece. Peter told me that the cup was expected at Anfield at eleven o'clock for a press shoot but I'd promised everyone at the Falcon they could bring their kids down and have a photo with it. In the end, I took it to the Falcon. The press could wait. They weren't very happy when I eventually arrived – the faces on them!'

The responsibility of Liverpool's captaincy was soon taken away from Thompson after a poor start to the 1981–82 season. Recalling the period clearly still hurts him now.

'It was awful,' he says flatly. 'Things weren't going great. Bob had decided to sell our goalkeeper Ray Clemence, who for such a long time acted as my eyes and ears. Clem was a great talker and his focus was fantastic. Bruce Grobbelaar came in and he was a completely different animal. It was difficult for everyone – for Bruce and the whole defence, especially me.

'December came around and we were mid table in the league. We were travelling back from Melwood on the bus after training and Joe Fagan wanders over: "Phil, the boss wants to see you." I was sitting next to Terry McDermott as always. "I wonder what that's about," I said. Over my shoulder, Ray Kennedy enters the conversation and goes, "I know what it's about – you're going to have the captaincy taken off you." Something had been said behind my back obviously. I asked Ray who was going to get it. "Graeme Souness."'

It is widely agreed amongst those that played under him that Paisley was not comfortable in confrontation.

'I was his longest-serving player and, yes, I was proud – prouder than anyone – to captain Liverpool. He reasoned that taking the responsibility away would help me focus on my game. But I was fuming. "Who are you giving it to? Wouldn't be Graeme Souness by any chance, would it?" He was spluttering then. "We'll see how it goes, then maybe give it you back." I knew he was trying to fudge it. I stormed out. From then on, my relationship with Graeme Souness was very frosty to say the least. It felt like I'd been stabbed in the back.'

It is painful for Thompson to recall his first game not as captain, standing at the very back of the line as the players prepared to pass through the tunnel at Swansea City's Vetch Field.

'Joe Fagan tried to speak to me and I told him where to go. Afterwards, I still had the hump and I didn't speak to anyone. But low and behold, we won the game 4–0.

I'd never let feelings get in the way of a performance. Never.'

Thompson can now admit the decision to remove him was the right one, considering Liverpool ended up winning the title that season, having trailed by some distance until the big decision was made. The disappointment of the experience was valuable decades later when Gérard Houllier decided to swap the responsibility between Sami Hyypiä and Steven Gerrard. Like Thompson, Hyypiä responded in the right manner and eighteen months later his presence was crucial as Liverpool won the Champions League in 2005.

The antipathy from Thompson towards Souness has never really gone away, though.

'I blanked him for weeks and weeks afterwards until he came to me claiming that he hadn't done anything wrong. It broke the ice but things were never the same between us.'

Thompson left for Sheffield United in 1984 before returning to take charge of Liverpool's reserve team after Kenny Dalglish became manager. When Souness succeeded Dalglish in 1991, one of his first acts was to remove Thompson.

'I was later told by other ex-players that he thought I lacked trust in him because of what had happened over the captaincy and therefore I wasn't trustworthy myself. If that's how he thought then I find that absolutely incredible. If he felt that, why didn't he have a word with me? Apparently he'd heard that I'd said at the time that he was changing things too quickly. I honestly don't know whether I did or I didn't all those years ago. But what I do know is, he's admitted it himself since leaving Liverpool that he attempted a revolution when only evolution was required. The trustworthy thing still gets me. Because it's not me.'

Thompson says the hardest part of his second departure from the club was telling his two boys that he wasn't going to be taking them to Anfield every other Saturday any more, 'an afternoon they loved'.

'They were broken-hearted, sobbing their hearts out,' Thompson says. 'That day, I thought that I cannot and will not speak to Graeme Souness again. I was devastated.'

When Sheila Walsh, the secretary of every Liverpool manager since Bill Shankly, died in 2008, Thompson and Souness met at the funeral and, according to Thompson, relations have since been cordial. He recognizes that Souness's shortcomings as a manager between 1991 and 1994 led to a chain of events that contributed to his own return in 1999. He stops to think about Souness's abilities as a player.

'Graeme was a typical Liverpool footballer: aggressive, two good feet, quick-thinking, streetwise. But he wasn't that way before he came to Liverpool. The intensity of the club spurred him on and he rose to the challenge of playing, at the very worst, eight out of ten every week. He became one of the greatest centre-midfield players this country has ever seen. As a manager, you couldn't really say that. Graeme wanted too many players to be like him. And it didn't work.'

Thompson was thirty-seven years old when he was sacked as reserve-team manager.

'I believed that I did things the Liverpool way as a coach. I hoped there might be a way back. I was disappointed that I never got the chance under Roy [Evans – who succeeded Souness].'

In 1998, Gérard Houllier was appointed as joint manager with Evans, an ill-fated decision that culminated in Evans departing within three months of the season starting. Thompson met Houllier for the first time in a hotel bar while working for Radio City as co-commentator in a UEFA Cup game in Valencia. In the dressing room after the 2–2 draw, Houllier and Evans argued in front of the players, causing Evans to storm out, the pressure clearly showing.

'The night before the game, I was standing with Tom Saunders and Ronnie Moran and their wives. Tom asked me whether I'd ever consider getting back involved in front-line football again. I was happy with my working life – doing newspaper columns and the radio – but I was honest with him. If the right offer came along, I'd jump at it.'

Houllier is widely credited with turning Liverpool's defence from one that was made out of goo to one that was made out of granite. Yet it was Thompson who worked the hardest on this issue.

'In our first few months in charge, we played Man United at their place in the FA Cup. Michael Owen scored early for us and we held on to the lead until the last two minutes when Dwight Yorke equalized before Ole Gunnar Solskjaer snatched a winner. We played three at the back that day and the three were Steve Harkness, Jamie Carragher and Dominic Matteo. That told you

47

where our problems were, because you can't forget that the jury was out on Carra at that time.

'Listen, defensive coaching isn't the most fun part of training,' Thompson continues. 'In fact, it's the most miserable, the most tedious, the most repetitive. It can be very boring but it has to be done over and over and over again.

'It was basics: positioning collectively and individually, and learning when to push up and squeeze the play at the right time. I did all of the defensive coaching, making the reserve wingers cross balls all the time, getting in the right positions until it becomes second nature.

'I had good lads, particularly Carra. Remember, Carra wasn't everybody's cup of tea if we're being honest. The crowd would moan about him, letters appearing in the *Echo* – that sort of thing. But Carra would do exactly what you wanted week after week, time after time, game after game. We'd put defensive sessions on, crossing balls in from different angles, and he'd head them out all day long until it was going dark without complaining. He'd head it away then yell at the other boys to push out, repeating the drill in the pissing rain.

'We needed fellas like Carra, your Stéphane Henchozes, your Sami Hyypiäs, your Markus Babbels: a calibre of people that were able to maintain standards. Carra had a burning passion to be a winner. That's why Gérard loved him. He knew how much he wanted to be better than everyone else. He had challenges, Carra: [Christian] Ziege coming in and then [John Arne] Riise. But he practised and practised and listened to the coaching, improving his left foot all the time, which was his weaker foot. We saw Carra a bit like Denis Irwin at Man United because of his desire to remain.

'Out of the six seasons Gérard and I were in charge, we had the best defensive record in the league in two of them. For me, that was the proof in the pudding.'

Although Thompson and Houllier didn't know each other before beginning a working marriage, the relationship blossomed. The decision made between Tom Saunders and Peter Robinson was a master-stroke.

'It was based on 100 per cent trust,' Thompson says, reminding me of why Souness had supposedly sacked him. 'I'll admit, I was abrasive. Sometimes I'd fly off the handle in the dressing room and Gérard would let me do it. I'd give them hell. I'd carry on for two minutes, then he'd go, "That's enough, Phil." He'd let me have my say, then he'd move in and be calm and composed.

'We'd been beaten at Anfield in one game and I went against him. I was furious but Gérard came in afterwards and said, "Boys, I want you to go away from here and I want you to forget everything that has happened today. We've got to look forward and focus on the next game." I was boiling inside. "Forget it?" I went. "I hope that you go home and think about it so much that you can't sleep all weekend. You all need to have a good look at yourselves . . ."

'Gérard never said anything in that moment but straight after the last player had left the dressing room, he pulled me to one side. "Phil, can I have a word?" he asked. "I appreciate you and often I agree with the things you say. But don't cut across me again. When players hear that, they see it as a division between me and you.

I've said one thing; you've said the opposite. They'll use it as an excuse for failure; they'll use it against us."

'Gérard was bang-on. Dead right. I was too battle hardened to realize the best way sometimes. The emotion would take over – this was playing for Liverpool for fuck sake! We're striving for that nine out of ten minimum every week. When it didn't happen, it hurt me. It hurt Gérard too but he was better at rationalizing his emotion. Gérard was an educator. It wasn't just the players that learned from him.'

The good times rolled again at Liverpool. After winning a League Cup, an FA Cup and UEFA Cup treble in 2001, Thompson was trusted enough by Liverpool's board to be asked to take over from Houllier while he recovered from a heart operation having been taken ill inside the dressing room at half-time of a game against Leeds United. The date is imprinted in Thompson's mind.

'It was incredible, 13 October 2001. Gérard's heart stopped on the operating table – he literally died. But they brought him back to life.'

The pressure on Thompson was immense. While his friend and closest colleague was in the operating theatre, Thompson had to organize the team for an away game against Dynamo Kiev in Ukraine, a country where no British team had ever won.

'I went to the Royal [hospital] to see him only to find he'd been sent to Broadgreen. Doc Waller [the club doctor] and Norman Gard [the long-serving players' liaison officer] were there too, along with Isabelle [Houllier's wife]. The specialists told us there was a massive problem with his aorta. I held Gérard's hand and told him that he'd be OK as they wheeled him past to the operating theatre. He didn't look at all well.'

On the flights for European away games, Houllier and Thompson took up a row of three seats between them and spent their time discussing tactics while eating wine gums.

'The next morning, I was sitting by the window of the plane and nobody was next to me. I suddenly felt very lonely. Gérard always used to bring the wine gums.'

The task of performing the pre-match duties expected of a manager preyed on Thompson's mind.

'Gérard's team talks were famous: two flipcharts, the team on one, which I would normally write for him; then another where he would note down the key tactical points that he wanted to make. The responsibility of taking this on was daunting because his speeches were almost presidential. He'd start off very softly but by the end it was like reaching the finale of a horse race. The players would get really pumped up. Gérard was a calm and measured person but when the talk needed to be passionate, he could deliver it.

'As soon as we reached Kiev, I told the doc [Waller] that he had to explain to the boys the basics of the technical stuff related to Gérard's illness, although we didn't want to give them everything because it might worry them and cause them to lose focus on the game.

'Gérard had already selected the team before the Leeds game, so that bit was sorted. We wanted to go there and give a classic Liverpool away performance in Europe – maybe nick a 1–0 win or a draw. We wanted to set up as a block and quieten the crowd. And then I flipped the chart over and it read simply: "Do it for the boss" in big letters.'

Thompson believes Houllier's illness inspired the players. A 2–1 victory was followed by just one defeat in Liverpool's next twelve matches and that came against Barcelona in the Champions League. While Thompson shuffled along with his responsibilities, so did first-team coach Sammy Lee, who took on assistant-manager duties.

'I told Sammy, "Listen, you're the one who'll have to give out the bollockings from now on." I needed to keep a clear head, especially if I was making substitutions. I couldn't be standing there on the touchline having arguments. Because that was my instinct.'

Thompson says one of his proudest moments was being asked by chief executive Rick Parry to attend a board meeting on the flight home from Kiev.

'I thought to myself, *Fucking 'ell, Phil Thompson, Kirkby lad, missed his fourth-year exams – I've got to go to a board meeting as Liverpool's manager.* The circumstances couldn't have been worse with Gérard's illness but I couldn't have been any prouder considering Souness had me sacked because of trust issues. Now here I was, back at the place I loved most, doing the most important job in the world. I stood before all of the board members, realizing a lot of people, especially amongst the press, were questioning whether I was the man to take on Gérard's responsibilities because of my temperament. "Gentlemen," I said, "I know some of you may have doubts about whether I am good enough to see us through this period. I know some ex-players are touting other names around." And then I told them I knew exactly what was needed to keep the club moving in the right direction. "I've had a great teacher in Gérard," I said. "Nothing else needs to change. We will be fine."

'David Moores responded by telling me that they trusted me and that I would be able to run it as I saw fit. I'd have their full backing. It makes me quite tearful thinking about this moment.'

The records reveal that Houllier is the most successful Liverpool manager in a quarter of a century. Yet by the time he left the club by mutual agreement in 2004, many supporters recognized it was time for him to go.

Criticism of Houllier stemmed from his decisions in the transfer market after returning from illness to lead the team again. His signings from the French league proved to be particularly disappointing, with Bruno Cheyrou, Salif Diao, El Hadji Diouf, Florent Sinama Pongolle and Anthony Le Tallec not meeting the standard consistently enough or not at all. The fact that Houllier missed out on signing Cristiano Ronaldo around the same time, when he could have been taken from Sporting Lisbon for £4 million, only for him to move to rivals Manchester United for three times that fee before emerging as one of the game's greatest modern attacking players, might explain Houllier's downfall to some degree.

Thompson can describe the pursuit of Ronaldo because he was at the forefront of it. He says both he and Houllier were 'hounded by guys who work for Paul Stretford and Jorge Mendes', the agents that represented the player towards the end of the 2002–03 season.

'A fella called Tony Henry was on the phone every other day saying that this boy is available for four million quid. "You should take a chance on him, he's a decent player."

'I went to see Ronaldo for Portugal's under-21s. Sporting Lisbon were trying to get a buyer for Ricardo Quaresma as well and he really impressed me too. It was a contest of who could do the most step-overs and normally I wouldn't go for that type of thing. The difference with these two was, there was an end product.'

Thompson made a second trip to watch Sporting play FC Porto, who'd won the UEFA Cup with a controversial victory over Celtic the week before under José Mourinho.

'You could see Ronaldo had great ability and afterwards I was invited to dinner with Tony and Jorge Mendes. They were really pushing for £4 million spread over four seasons at a million a year. Then I asked about his salary and they were quoting a million quid a year net. "A million pound?" I said, surprised. "We've just signed Le Tallec and Pongolle and they're on nowhere near anything like that."

'I went back and had a word with Gérard and told him that Ronaldo was a very good player. The problem was, we hadn't received our budget yet for the following season. Gérard then went to Rick [Parry – the chief executive] to try to find out what it was.

'I think we had £12 million that summer. Three million went towards the French lads [Pongolle and Le Tallec], £3.5 million on Steve Finnan and another £5 million on Harry Kewell. The idea was to go for Ronaldo but to try to negotiate the price down and then probably leave him in Lisbon for a year because he was only eighteen years old.'

It was in August when Thompson, sitting in the canteen at Melwood, saw the breaking story on Sky Sports News. Manchester United had recruited their target for £12.2 million.

'I couldn't believe it, mainly because of the fee,' he says. 'It was a huge price to pay. It had rocketed over a short period of time. He was being touted around everywhere for £4 million.

'When I look back, I think the problem was the circumstance. We'd committed a third of our transfer budget on two young foreign players already. The team needed an injection of experience. I know we know how good Ronaldo is now but how would it have gone down if we had spent so much on three untried foreign teenagers?'

Houllier's departure from Anfield was a long one. Liverpool finished second in the league in 2002, seven points behind champions Arsenal, fifth in 2003 when Manchester United were the champions nineteen points ahead, and then fourth in 2004 – only this time there was a thirty-point gap. Performances led to criticism from former players like Ian St John.

'I went into his office one day and Gérard had written down the names of twenty-two ex-players who were working in the media. He said, "These are the ones we have to put up with – they're all against me . . ." I told him they weren't. I'd been in the media and obviously I'd been critical of the regime towards the end of Roy's spell in charge. I was just doing my job – it wasn't personal. But Gérard took it personally. Some of them went overboard because everyone is different, but Gérard put them in the same pot. Comments that were constructive were seen as destructive.'

Alan Kennedy, who scored goals that secured two European Cup wins for Liverpool in 1981 and 1984, was banned from Anfield briefly after first annoying Houllier by a jokey remark made on the *Soccer AM* magazine show on Sky Sports. Houllier then refused to give interviews to Century Radio – where Kennedy worked on their nightly phone-in show – before and after the matches because of the row. Thompson says there is more to the story, linking the feud to a tackle by Blackburn Rovers' Lucas Neill, the tenacious Australian full-back, that broke Jamie Carragher's leg.

'Al knew people at Liverpool, including Sammy Lee, myself and others. In the aftermath of the tackle on Carra, Al found out about what was said inside the Liverpool dressing room and told Graeme Souness, who was Blackburn's manager. It was an error of judgement and he was full of apologies afterwards to Gérard. I told Gérard that Al was one of the nicest guys out of all my former colleagues but was sometimes not the brightest. He was the butt of many a joke and probably didn't think about what he was doing, if I'm being totally honest. He was sincere in his apologies. But Gérard wouldn't let it go.'

Despite the distractions and frustrations of the last few years, Thompson believes he and Houllier left a better club than the one they joined. 'It was certainly a more disciplined one, because the lunatics were running the asylum back then,' he insists.

Thompson says he is tied to Liverpool and will never work for another club. He does not have an agent representing him and although he's had offers – including one to join his old friend in Birmingham when Houllier became Aston Villa's manager in 2010 – the opportunity did not motivate him.

'It didn't seem me. It didn't seem right, because Villa are not my club,' he reasons. 'Some people have said to me when the times were bad at Liverpool under Rafa Benítez, Roy Hodgson and Brendan Rodgers, "Phil, you should go back there and sort the egos out." But I think my time has been. I've done my bit.'

He recounts one last story, when Liverpool were beaten 1–0 by Sheffield Wednesday at Hillsborough in May 1999, six months into his and Houllier's reign.

'Wednesday were a really poor side and we were crap, so I had one of my famous rants,' he recalls, grinning. 'Brad Friedel had played in goal and he fronted me up. It got quite aggressive.' Thompson bares his teeth to imitate Friedel's anger. '"You, Thommo, you," he says, "You're having a go at us all the time – you think we don't care but we do!"

'"Whoa, whoa, whoa, Brad," I goes back. "You're bang on – I know you care. I know every player wants to win and wants to go out and do well. But it's how far you will go to achieve that, how far you will push yourself to make sure it happens – and how much it hurts you when you get beaten."

'And then I went to him, "But I'll tell you something, Brad: a lot of you don't care enough. There's a fucking difference, Brad. There's a big fucking difference."'

cultzeros.co.uk

DANNY MURPHY,
Versatility

'IT WAS BETTER THAN ANY OTHER NATURAL HIGH,' DANNY Murphy reveals, his expression remaining serious.

'Even sex?'

'Oh yeah, even sex – an out-of-body experience. Indescribable.'

Murphy is attempting to convey the sensation of scoring a match-winning goal for Liverpool against Manchester United at Old Trafford, a feat he achieved three times.

'The first one was a free kick past Fabien Barthez,'

he remembers, citing how silence fell across the stadium as he approached the ball to strike it. 'They were the champions and we needed to prove ourselves under Gérard Houllier, prove that we could compete with them.

'I'd given possession away a few minutes earlier and I was really angry with myself,' Murphy continues. 'I needed to make amends. I took quite a straight run-up, to try to deceive the keeper. Barthez stood still. It curled right in the bottom corner. I could see the faces of the United supporters in the Stretford End. Closing my eyes, I can see a fella with a black hood with his mouth open going, "Oh no!" After that? There was white noise. A blur of colour. Look at my arms right now – you can see the hairs standing on end.

'A lot of people have tried to put into words the euphoria of scoring a winning goal. None of them do it justice. You lose yourself. There's a huge adrenalin rush of emotion that takes you to a place you didn't know existed. Afterwards comes the contentment. When you're sitting on the bus in the car park, seeing all the United fans walking home with glum faces, hearing all the Liverpool supporters in the distance, still locked inside the ground. Only then does it sink in – what it means to you personally.

'I used to drink in the Oaklands Pub on New Road in Chester. Normally, my brother and a couple of mates would be there after the game. We'd have a pint, a chat and unwind. This time when I walked in, there was uproar. The place was packed. It went off. It was mental. It was brilliant. Loads of singing. Only then did I really realize the impact a goal and a win had on everyone else. It defines weekends. It can define seasons.'

Liverpool completed a cup treble that year. A second clinching moment against Liverpool's greatest rivals came the following campaign, though circumstances this time were different.

'Some Liverpool supporters cheered in the game before against Southampton when I was substituted,' Murphy explains, frowning, reflecting his difficulty with the memory by blowing out his cheeks. 'It was only a few of them. But hearing that negativity – god, it was probably the lowest point of my career.

'Phil Thompson was filling in as manager for Gérard Houllier, who was recovering from his heart problems. Thommo called me into his office and tried to reassure me. "I know you must feel a bit shit. I trust you. I'll play you all day long. Don't worry about it – I know the Liverpool supporters better than anyone."

'But I did worry about it. Never believe a player who says they don't hear the heckling. It was like a dagger through the heart. I felt like crying. When you care about the club you play for, you crave acceptance.

'So the following Wednesday night at Old Trafford, Steven Gerrard gets the ball. What a pass. What. A. Pass. It gets overlooked just how good that pass was – maybe it was the pass of the decade.'

Murphy saw Barthez again. This time the French World Cup winner had strayed a few yards from his line.

'So I chipped him. It was a difficult one to execute, because Stevie's pass was as forceful as

61

ever and it had some curl on it. With the chip, I had to change the trajectory and slow the pace of the ball down, otherwise it wouldn't have gone over the goalkeeper.

'How did I feel when it went in? Initially, there was joy. Then there was a bit of relief. Then the feeling of *fuck you* came along, if I'm being honest. A *fuck you* to the doubters.

'At the end of the game, I ran from the Stretford End towards our supporters with Stevie and Thommo. I don't know where Carra was. Five thousand of them were singing my name. The turnaround in just a few days. Here, see my arms again . . . uncontrollable.'

The instinct to get into position to score was down to Murphy's own ability, yet he believes the platform to perform confidently and not buckle under the immense pressure was given to him by Thompson, the temporary manager.

'Thommo changed immensely when he took over the reins from Gérard,' Murphy says. 'Six months before, maybe he wouldn't have been capable of being so subtle, knowing how to deliver a boost, knowing exactly what was needed. On the touchline, he was a raging bull. He'd have argued with his granny, probably. Some of the foreign players weren't used to it. They thought he was mad. But I didn't mind a kick up the arse. I'd grown up around that type of aggression at Crewe. I reacted well to it. I benefited from it.

'Suddenly, Gérard became ill and a Zen-like quality took over Thommo. He wasn't shouting and screeching in training any more. Sammy Lee became the enforcer.

Thommo became the observer. Bob Paisley had to change when he got the job from Bill Shankly in unexpected circumstances, didn't he? Thommo had witnessed this when he was a player.

'Thommo was in charge for a lot of the 2001–02 season when we came second: the highest in the league Liverpool had finished in more than a decade. People saw him as the aggressive number two. But I think he would have been a bloody good manager if he'd tried elsewhere. He had more managerial qualities than I think he realized. We had our moments where we rowed – he rowed with everyone. Sometimes, though, I think he was just playing a role: the sergeant major.'

Murphy dispatched a third winning goal away at United in April 2004.

'Michael [Owen] was the team's penalty taker. He was the best penalty taker I've ever seen in training. He never missed. He'd drive the keepers crazy. One after another. Then the games came along and he'd shit his pants! Before United, he'd been on a bad run, missing quite a few. So he picked up the ball and went to me, "Go on then . . ."

'I meant to put it lower. Instead, I leaned back a bit and it flew in the top corner. It looked *cool as*. I couldn't believe I'd done it again. You shouldn't be blasé about scoring the winner at Old Trafford. It was the third time!'

It is coincidental that I meet Murphy less than a mile away from Old Trafford, the site of his greatest moments in a Liverpool shirt. It is a typical day of weather in Salford when he walks through the revolving doors of a hotel next to the BBC studios having driven through the morning from his Surrey home, with the rain beginning to batter his car windows both vertically and horizontally as soon as he got near Greater Manchester.

Murphy is small and stocky, wears jeans, trainers and a heavy black jumper. He is two hours away from the start of his working day as a pundit on *Match of the Day*. Having lived in London since leaving Liverpool a decade ago, his accent has strayed curiously south. He grew up in Chester but can vividly remember watching his first game at Anfield.

'It was against Man United in 1985 and Frank Stapleton got the winner,' he recalls ruefully. 'It was a present for my eighth birthday. Liverpool were way off the pace behind Everton in the league that season. None of that bothered me, though. It was £1.80 to get in and kids had to go through different turnstiles to adults. It was absolutely rammed outside with people queuing to get in.

'You know when people speak about how a football club grabs you? Well, Liverpool really got me that day. Everything about it: the Kop, the green pitch, the noise. I'd never experienced anything like it before. It got me.

'My dad came from a big Irish family in Cork. They'd settled in Chester. Although my mum and dad were separated, he was a huge Liverpool fan and that filtered down to me and my brothers. I was the youngest and smallest of them. I always had something to prove.'

Murphy joined Crewe Alexandra when he was twelve years old.

'I'd already been to Wrexham's academy for eighteen

64

months, I'd been up to Liverpool to train a couple of times, I'd been down to Aston Villa in the school holidays, I'd gone to Sheffield Wednesday too. I never felt particularly comfortable at any of them, although they'd all asked me to sign schoolboy forms.

'I was in demand and started to realize I was a decent player. I was selected to play in the district side a year above my own age group – that's when it really started to hot up, with scouts knocking on my door. One of them was a fella called Alex Gibson and he was really persistent, asking me to go to Man United, god forbid. Suddenly, Alex moved jobs and went to Crewe.

'The first training session there was on the old AstroTurf pitches under the floodlights beside Gresty Road, Crewe's ground. Dario Gradi, Crewe's first-team manager, took the session. I'd never met a first-team manager before at any of the other places. The session was different to anything I'd experienced. Dario was years ahead. The standard was also a lot higher. I looked at the other players and thought, *Wow, these are good*. Everybody made me feel welcome. I wanted to be at Crewe.'

Since arriving there in 1983, Gradi had transformed the small club from the small Cheshire town famed for its railway station. Milanese, Gradi had been born in Italy during the Second World War, moving to live in London with his English mother in 1945. He combined a career in non-league football with grammar-school teaching before turning to coaching, where his most significant break came as an assistant at Chelsea, aged just twenty-nine. Wounded by relegations at Wimbledon and Crystal

Palace, Gradi arrived at Crewe when it was lodged in a rut, with the club's future hinging on whether it could secure re-election to the old Fourth Division.

Gradi's vision was for Crewe to develop its own young players, sell the best of them to earn the finances necessary to survive and then produce some more players through academy investment, in a continuous virtuous circle. Before Murphy's introduction to the system, Gradi had proven that he possessed the talent-spotting and coaching genius that his proposed strategy required to be successful, with David Platt, Geoff Thomas, Robbie Savage and Neil Lennon all securing lucrative moves away while the club simultaneously rose up the leagues.

Murphy says the atmosphere was key to his emergence.

'Because of the small pool of players compared to the bigger clubs, each player had the intimacy of knowing everyone who worked for the club and, similarly, the first-team manager – Dario – knew which fifteen year olds were doing well and which ones were falling behind, which ones needed attention,' Murphy says.

'I remember going to Melwood to train aged twelve and fifty kids were there; many of them had signed forms for the club already. I might have made it at Liverpool but the system at Crewe felt better to me. The club wasn't being greedy, recruiting aggressively. They recruited selectively and made the small details count with the players they had.

'Dario was a pioneer. He had similar traits to the two

other managers that had the biggest influence on my career: Gérard Houllier and Roy Hodgson. They were all a bit old-school in terms of their temperament, being gentlemen. Gérard wasn't a coach in the same sense as Dario and Roy but they were all teacher-like and father figures. I clashed with some of the younger managers I worked for because I can be gobby when I'm not happy. When my dad separated from my mum, Dario filled the void.'

Training sessions at Crewe were focused on developing technique.

'The emphasis was on ball-work, making you comfortable in possession. Sessions began with half an hour of passing drills. There was no running. As you got older and closer to the first team, it was more about developing game intelligence – common sense. Whereas Liverpool and Man United had had a first team, reserves, an A and a B team, at Crewe it was first team, reserves and a youth team made up of players aged sixteen and under. It meant that as a youth player, you were performing against older boys, sinking or learning how to swim very quickly.

'Dario had an influence on every decision at the club. He looked at the development of every player. For the reserves, Dario decided I should play as a sweeper when I was sixteen years old. Two big lads played at centre-half and they stopped me getting whacked because I was still at school and probably only 5 ft 6 in. tall. The idea was for the goalkeeper to roll the ball out to me and for me to build up play from the back. I could move forward into midfield and join in attacks. I had been a sweeper but now Dario told me I was going to play some games as a right-sided midfielder, then on the left wing, centre-midfield – where I wanted to be – and finally up front. It helped my understanding of all positions and in the end made me a better centre-midfielder.

'Dario was light years ahead of other coaches. I used to play against other teams in the lower leagues and wonder why they were so bad. I realized that, actually, we were so good. We worked on the basics like positioning. But it was the attention to detail that set Dario apart and gave us the advantage. The number of hours we spent on quick short corners and quick free kicks – getting the opposition on the back foot before they can settle. Throw-ins – oh my god, we spent hours on them. How many clubs have I been at since where players don't know how to take throw-ins and receive a ball? I watch Premier League games now and see players run fast at throw-in takers and close the space down. Did nobody ever teach them what to do?

'Dario was the first manager to use scenarios in training sessions. He'd say, "Right, it's eleven on ten, there's five minutes left, the team with ten are winning 1–0, let's go . . ." He wanted intensity and to see the players switch on straight away. If we couldn't figure out what to do, he'd let us know that he wasn't happy.

'I suppose Dario was fortunate in that he was working at a small club and his job was safe. He had a place on the board. It meant that he could follow his passion. He was more interested in player development than team development and success. Of course, he wanted success – and the fact that Crewe stayed in the Championship for so many years was a miracle, considering the size of the town, the size of the fan base and the money at the club. Work was never a chore and Dario made football enjoyable. We passed teams to death. It was really good fun.'

Murphy scored the winner as a substitute in his second appearance for Crewe, a 4–3 win over Preston North End. He was sixteen years old. Successive promotions were earned, taking Crewe into England's second tier. Murphy's presence in attack with Dele Adebola helped achieve the feat.

'Dele was a big lad and took a lot of my buffeting from the big centre-halves. I was playing a lot with my back to goal and I was better when the ball was in front of me. When I got smacked in one game, the lad told me he was going to do it; I'll never forget it. I'd nutmegged him in the first minute and set up the first goal. "I'm gonna do you," he said. And fair enough, he did. I was out after that for six weeks with a knee-ligament injury. When I came back, Dario decided to switch the system to a 4–3–3. I had more freedom in midfield. I could go and have a wander without being that disciplined.'

Gradi held a tight rein on Murphy's behaviour off the pitch. He peers back at his teenage self and cringes sometimes.

'I was precocious and there was a period where I'd answer back to anyone who was critical and have an argument with people that didn't agree with me. I had a tendency to be overdramatic whenever I misplaced a pass, throwing my hands up in the air and berating myself, cursing. It really annoyed Dario because he thought it was stopping me from going and putting it right, winning the ball back. It felt like months but it probably only happened for a couple of weeks where he'd stop training sessions. Dario would say, "OK, let's see the drama, everyone can stand and watch you throw your hands in the air . . ." Then he'd say, "How about when you give the ball away, you just bloody run back and don't let everyone know how disappointed you are? We all know it's a crap pass . . ."

'It took a while for me to get out of the habit.'

Had it not been for Gradi's guidance, indeed, Murphy wonders whether he'd have become a professional footballer.

'There was a spell before I went full-time at Crewe where I was late for training a lot. I was still at school. I remember calling Dario up, telling him that I wasn't going to make it in the following day for a youth-team match. I wanted to go to a party with my mates the night before and it would have meant getting up at the crack of dawn to get a bus before catching the train to Crewe. He said, "Danny, I'm not stupid, I know what's going on. You will get here. You'll be on time. If you make the effort to get here, I'll make sure you get home, whether I drive you myself or put you in a taxi."

'A lot of the lads at Crewe were being dropped off by their mums and dads. My mum was trying to look after four boys. I had to make my own way to Crewe and it was a bit of a trek and quite expensive. I wasn't a rebel but I was starting to experiment with things as you do when you're a teenager, drinking and chasing girls.

'In the end, Dario guilted me into showing up that

morning. I realized he was making such an effort for me. His attitude wasn't like, "You little twat, you get here," it was more, "I'm helping you here, come on and give me something back!"

'I had problems at home but I knew I could go to him. This isn't a violin story; it's just an example of Dario helping out. After I left school, Crewe put me on their YTS scheme and I was earning thirty quid a week. It meant that my mum lost her benefits for me, which were worth more than thirty quid a week. You'd get expenses for your travel to training but I was giving my mum a lot of my income so she could pay for food. She didn't have enough. I had a great relationship with my dad but he didn't have a pot to piss in either.

'I told Dario that I wanted to continue with my education and go to sixth form and play for Crewe at weekends. It worried me what might happen if I didn't make it all the way. It was the only option that I thought would work in the short term from a financial point of view. Dario said, "You'll fall behind if you do that. You won't make it as a footballer." Crewe had players before me who chose to do the same thing and had fallen behind. I suppose it makes sense, because if you're in training five days a week, you'll improve more than if you are there for just two.

'Dario's solution was to pay my mum dig money. It meant that my mum got forty quid a week for looking after me and then the thirty was mine. All along the way, any time there was a hurdle, Dario helped me cross it. He was a great judge of a situation. Gérard Houllier was very similar.'

71

Gradi trusted Murphy and gave him responsibility. One of his duties before he'd even made his first-team debut was to watch first-team games and offer opinions on what he saw.

'I'd sit in the stand and sometimes Dario would let me go in the dugout. He even asked me once during the half-time team talk to say something. "What do you think, Danny?" he asked in the dressing room when Crewe were losing. Can you imagine what the first-team players must have thought? *Who is this little shit?* Dario knew that I saw things that other lads my age didn't see. So he encouraged me to have an opinion on formation, performances and the way the game was going. When Crewe weren't playing, I'd go and watch Chester City because their ground wasn't far away from my house. Again, he'd ask me what I thought of rival players. Maybe he was thinking of signing them.'

Once in the Crewe first team, some of the more experienced players did not warm to Murphy due to his withering assessments.

'I figured that if Dario was asking me to highlight problems, I might as well go for it – let my voice be heard. The problem was, some of the older fellas saw me as one of Dario's pet projects. Looking back now, I can see why a senior player would have a problem with a youngster in this situation, especially when you consider that some of these players needed to play every week to earn their match bonus and the wages weren't very high anyway. They had families to feed, just like my mum.

'It meant that I had to grow up quickly and learn how to fight my corner. I took some shit. Luckily, there were some good guys there who realized I was a decent foot-baller and could actually help their financial outlook by playing well, scoring goals and improving the results of the team, therefore earning them a win bonus!'

Despite his own initial teething problems, Gradi was creating a culture based on collective responsibility.

'Every single player in that dressing room wasn't scared to give an opinion. If things weren't going right, each person would have their say and get issues sorted out pretty quickly. You couldn't afford to hide. That manifested itself on the pitch.

'If you're a manager who doesn't encourage questions and opinions, you're screwed,' Murphy continues. 'The best players have an opinion on the way the game should be played. If you don't allow these players to express themselves, they won't come to you. What happens then is, they talk behind your back and create a clique. Good managers know the trick: they listen without taking everything on board.

'Under Houllier in one pre-season, he set up a suggestion box. We had twenty-four players in the squad and he split us into groups of six, although not necessarily putting people with their friends. Each group would go into a room for half an hour and discuss the mood and atmosphere. Then, anonymously, we made suggestions on a piece of paper. If the same issue came up amongst the six, we'd then offer that suggestion to the manager. It was simple things like wearing track-suits over suits to away matches because we felt more relaxed in them. The biggest issue was staying behind in foreign cities after away matches in Europe. We usually waited to fly back until the next day and most of the players hated it. We wanted to fly home straight after the game.

'Houllier gathered us all together and discussed the merits of each suggestion. We reached the issue of staying in Europe – in Prague, Kiev, Moscow or wherever it may be. It turned out that every group had raised it. So surely he had to fold? Instead, Houllier produced a flipchart – he loved flipcharts – and he showed our points tally immediately after European trips compared to Arsenal and Man United. We were pissing it, performing something like 25 per cent better than the other two.

'Houllier wanted the Liverpool squad to have a proper meal within two hours of each match. He explained it was particularly important in UEFA Cup fixtures late at night. By flying home immediately, players would have resorted to unhealthy airport food, delaying the recovery process and possibly resulting in a more lethargic performance in the next game a few days later. Although players were still wired after a night match, a six- or seven-hour block of solid sleep was better than flying and disrupting natural sleeping patterns. It might sound boring but his was a bloody strong argument. There was no chance of anything changing. And the lads understood. Next . . .

'That's an example of good management: listening to the players' needs and concerns. Instead of going, "I'm the manager, it's my way or the highway," he addresses issues properly,' Murphy concludes. 'Someone like Martin Jol would have reacted a different way. I quizzed Jol on a pre-season trip when I was at Tottenham as to why some lads were doing more running while others were spending more time in the Jacuzzi and spa. It seemed a bit weird to me, so I asked the question. He seemed shocked and it really got his back up. It said to me that he wasn't equipped to deal with big-personality players. And there were certainly bigger personalities than me.'

Murphy did not originally sign for Liverpool from Crewe because of Gérard Houllier, however. The first option was to join Newcastle United, who were managed by Kenny Dalglish.

'Kenny was my hero. I had a Liverpool shirt and my mum ironed the old number 7 on to the back. I was desperate to go to Newcastle because it was him – the hero, Kenny Dalglish. I'm grateful to Dario, because it would have been easy for Crewe to take the money.

'Dario had already been having conversations with Liverpool and we were going for promotion. Dario said, as a matter of fact, "You're not going. I didn't want to tell you but Liverpool want you and I know they're your team. They're happy for you to stay here until the end of the season too and the other clubs that want you won't. So that suits us as well." He told me to relax and enjoy my football.

'I took a call at home the day after from someone claiming to be Kenny Dalglish. I put the phone down on him because I thought it was a wind-up. He tried again and I put the phone down for a second time. The next night, he finally got through and this time I listened to him. I couldn't believe it – I put the phone down on my hero twice and then I rejected him.'

Tottenham Hotspur were pushing hard to sign Murphy as well. Although he appreciated that competition at Liverpool would be the fiercest, it was an opportunity that ultimately he could not refuse.

'I knew Michael [Owen] and Carra from playing for England. Around the time I was making my decision, we all went to the Under-20 World Cup in Malaysia together. I scored twice against the United Arab Emirates and was on for my hat-trick when the referee gave us a penalty. Michael being Michael was desperate to take it – even though he was the youngest in the team – and we started arguing about it. In the end, Carra had to intervene and made Michael realize he was being unreasonable considering we were already 2–0 up. Michael was fuming. He was even gobbier than me!

'We had a great time over there in Malaysia, though. There were some real lads in the squad, including Kieron Dyer and Jody Morris, and others like John Curtis, John Macken and Ronnie Wallwork from United. Argentina beat us in the knockout stages. Juan Román Riquelme and Pablo Aimar were in their side.'

Riquelme would later become a legend at Boca Juniors. At Melwood, Murphy would train with one of his own legendary heroes.

'John Barnes,' Murphy says suddenly, as if the surname Barnes is awe-inspiring to him. 'Suddenly, I was around players that I'd worshipped for so long. It was surreal. John was on his way out. Newcastle were signing him. But he did the pre-season with us. I'd had a season ticket at Anfield. I wanted to be John Barnes. Now – briefly – he was my teammate. Weird. It took me a few months to relax and begin to enjoy it. I was a chirpy little character. But I struggled to express myself.'

Murphy remembers his full debut against Aston Villa, a game screened live on a Monday night by Sky Sports in September 1997. Robbie Fowler and Steve McManaman were at their best and Murphy felt 'ten-feet tall' being in such company. Yet he admits now the environment at Melwood was not conducive to sustained success.

'Although you don't realize that at the time when you're young,' Murphy interjects. 'Senior players, recognized internationals, boys like Razor Ruddock or Robbie [Fowler], were wandering out two minutes before training was due to start with a bacon sandwich in their hand. I'm sure that happened at many other training grounds. But the clubs like Arsenal and Man United – where they'd clamped down on player freedoms – were the clubs winning the trophies. Bacon butties never happened at Crewe, for example.

'The old ways were on the way out. That included training too: no more small-sided possession games, which were famous at Liverpool. They were all a bit too fun and not particularly relevant to the real games, which were becoming more about power and speed over touch and possession. Let's be honest, the intensity at Melwood was nowhere near where it needed to be for players to reach peak levels of fitness. I'm not saying it was easy, because we did fitness sessions that made you blow. The day-to-day stuff was quite lax, though.'

Roy Evans had signed Murphy for Liverpool.

'I got on well with him,' Murphy says. 'I thought he was a proper guy: very honest, straight and loved his football. But he came from an era when people did not know any better. Young people were changing, their motivations becoming different, not just in football but in society as well. It was only when Houllier started to achieve success by running the club a lot more professionally that everyone realized Liverpool had fallen behind because they hadn't moved with the times.

'In the late nineties, it was a joy for me to be at the club I'd dreamed of joining, experiencing things I thought were beyond me growing up in Chester: going to a Liverpool game in a team tracksuit, travelling abroad, being recognized in the street. But in terms of it being an environment that was really productive for young players? No.'

The Liverpool board's solution in the summer of 1998 was to appoint Gérard Houllier as joint manager with Evans. It proved to be an unhealthy compromise. Murphy made only four appearances during his second season at Anfield and one of them was in the last game where Evans was involved, the 3–1 home defeat to Tottenham Hotspur in the League Cup when John Scales, a player Evans had sold, scored for the visiting team.

'Even if you appoint two people who are great friends and have similar views on football to be in charge of a team, a decision still needs to be made and there will be disagreements. Everyone has different opinions on one player, never mind eleven players or sixteen players. So I can't imagine the amount of time Roy and Gérard must have spent picking a team or a squad. It must have been a nightmare. I could imagine Gérard saying, "Let's go defensive; we'll hit them on the break." Then Roy, "No; let's have a go here." It was an impossible working situation. Gérard believed in another way to Roy. That started with discipline, hard work and intensity. He didn't care what had happened at Liverpool in many ways. Yeah, he educated himself in the history of the club, but the way it worked previously? It didn't matter. It was only a matter of time before a split. The people running the club must surely have known that. They'd been in charge long enough.'

Houllier was left in sole charge. Things were about to change.

'There was a gentle approach when Roy was still around but as soon as he went, *boom*, Gérard was like a sledgehammer. "He's gone . . . he's gone . . . this is what we're going to do: we're training at these times, wearing these clothes."

'His methods were not particularly outrageous when you think about them. Quite often in football, common sense is the obvious route to success but people over-complicate it by overlooking the most basic things. In pre-season, we did two sessions: one in the morning and another at 5 p.m. Everyone was like, "What are we going to do in between?"

'"Rest!" Houllier would say.

'Gérard was a disciplinarian. You'd get fined for wearing the wrong clothes on match days. If you were meant to wear a black T-shirt and you wore a white one – even by accident – on the bus to an away game, it would be taken out of your wages. There were no mobile phones in the main building at Melwood. That became standard rather than a punishment. The same on a match day: no phones. It led to greater focus. And then the French lads would get fined if they spoke French amongst the British lads.'

Houllier's methods were met with resistance. David Thompson, a young midfielder from the tough Ford council estate on Wirral, found Houllier's methods punitive and admitted to relishing the challenge of pushing the boundaries as far as he could before he was offloaded to Coventry City. Robbie Fowler was installed as the team's captain but eventually Houllier became tired of his mischievous behaviour and sold him to Leeds United.

'No matter how big or important you appeared to be, Houllier would get rid of you if you didn't buy into his ideas,' Murphy says. 'He did it all for the benefit of the club. It was never personal. Paul Ince was the captain before Robbie, and Houllier got shot of him because he thought he had too much power in the dressing room even though he thought a lot of Incey as a player.

'Houllier gave a couple of lads a lot of opportunities to change, possibly more than other managers would have. Now they might say, "Danny Murphy – well, he's agreeing with Houllier because he played him." But there has to be some framework of discipline at a club. If a manager keeps allowing someone to step outside it – even if it's for daft things like turning up late – the indiscipline spreads quickly. Houllier was a fair man. There comes a tipping point. I disagree with some people who might claim they were pushed out of the door unfairly. They were pushed out of the door for a reason.'

At the beginning under Houllier, the progress made by Murphy at Crewe had halted at Liverpool.

'I was a young lad who didn't know any better: parties, drinking and girls. Carra would admit that he was the same, I'm sure. He turned that off, calmed down and became really professional quickly. It took me longer. I wish I had been as quick as him. When I eventually followed suit, I earned the rewards.

'I wasn't an important player when Houllier came in. I wasn't playing well enough and I wasn't fit enough. It was my second season as a Liverpool player and I'd got a bit comfortable. I was probably thinking without realizing, *Yeah, I'm a Liverpool player now; I'm made.* I've seen it happen to so many other players since. You think you're the man without having enough experience or ability to *be* the man. You forget that you need to continue to work. When you don't, you fall behind. Eventually, you begin to doubt yourself because a cold reality hits home if you're bright enough. I wasn't sure whether I was good enough for Liverpool. I wasn't sure whether I was good enough to even play in the Premier League.'

George Burley was in charge of Second Division Ipswich Town. He made Murphy a loan offer.

'I went to Gérard and told him that I wanted to go. Gérard told me about an opportunity to go back to Crewe. "Yeah, but they're bottom of the league, getting smashed every week," I said. "They're shit – how is that going to do me any good? I've already been there, done that."'

Houllier was insistent that Murphy move back to Crewe temporarily – and to the womb of Dario Gradi.

'He probably thought the value of a hard day's work and the strain of a relegation battle would show whether I was truly up for a fight at Liverpool.'

With Seth Johnson in midfield and Rodney Jack up front, Murphy helped Crewe stay up.

'Houllier told me the following pre-season that had I not agreed to go to Crewe, he'd have got rid of me. "I've seen your ability – you're a clever player, you see the bigger picture," he said. "I wanted to see that you still had the passion."'

Murphy was placed on a strict fitness regime. In October 1999, he was handed his first start in the league for Liverpool in more than eighteen months against Chelsea, helping the team to a 1–0 victory.

'Little Thommo [David Thompson], for example, had all of the passion in the world. But he channelled it in the wrong way. He kept having arguments. He'd argue with the manager, he'd argue with senior players, he'd argue with anybody – even himself. Houllier knew he was passionate about the club and was desperate to win. But he kept seeing red, kept getting sent off. In the end, Houllier probably came to the conclusion that he couldn't rely on Thommo to keep his cool. Ultimately, it was about ability and passion and harnessing the two to produce performances. That's why players like me and Jamie Carragher got along. We played all across the pitch. Sometimes we got frustrated filling in for other people, not playing centrally where we wanted to be. But we never let the frustration get the better of us. Thommo was like me and Carra: he wanted to play in the centre. We went through the same cycle of being the first player to be substituted. Whereas Thommo went mad – finger pointing at Houllier in the dressing room afterwards – I'd accept the decision because I appreciated it wasn't personal. It was only for the benefit of the team.'

Murphy relates Houllier's desire for controlled passion to results in the Merseyside derby, a fixture Liverpool had failed in previously. Under Roy Evans, despite Everton's clear inferiority in terms of talent and league placing, Liverpool had managed to beat them only once – a dire run stretching back to 1994. In the eleven derbies when Houllier was involved, Liverpool triumphed in six of them.

'In the dressing room before every derby – especially at Goodison Park – one of the last things Gérard used to say was, "Keep eleven men on the pitch and we'll win." Again, the message was clear: controlled passion. It felt like we scored a lot of winning goals late on, when Everton had someone sent off and they were tired. Everton wanted it to be a fight. We were up for the fight. But we became cleverer with our aggression, finding a way to wind them up.'

Steven Gerrard and Jamie Carragher later became the axis of the Liverpool team under Rafael Benítez and they developed a close bond. Under Gérard Houllier, though, Murphy was closest to Gerrard and the pair roomed together, while Carragher's best friend in the squad was Michael Owen.

'Because Houllier signed a lot of foreign players at the beginning, there was a perception on the outside that Liverpool's soul was being stripped away. There's no doubt the setting of standards was helped by the signing of foreign players like Sami Hyypiä, Markus Babbel, and Didi Hamann to a degree. But the heartbeat of the team was English: Stevie, Carra, Michael, myself, Robbie, Jamie Redknapp and Emile Heskey.

'Houllier realized that he needed British players. He realized that some sense of local pride is something any Liverpool manager needs to get into his side. Although the foreign lads were on board just as much and gave their all, because he bought well in the early years and they were the right type of characters, it still can't mean quite as much to them as it did to us. I'd been to cup finals as a kid and seen Liverpool win the league. I was desperate to emulate what I'd seen, absolutely desperate. I sometimes think the top foreign players get a team close to the line but the local ones help you cross it. Maybe I'm being too simplistic.'

During the 2000–01 season, which ended with Liverpool winning a cup treble, Murphy was often stationed on the left side of midfield, a role referred to by anyone who filled it as 'the graveyard shift'. A solid midfield four was Houllier's priority. It came at the expense of expansive wing-play; creative midfielders were required to be extremely disciplined, taking care of their defensive responsibilities first. Murphy believes that it was due to his education under Dario Gradi that he was able to perform the role without becoming irritated.

'At Crewe, we didn't have a big squad, so every player ended up filling in for someone else at some point. Young players got all the plaudits and the club sold them on but the real strength of the club was the collective mentality. For example, I learned quickly that if I was playing as a centre-forward, even though I didn't have the pace to beat defenders by running in behind them very often, I still had to make those runs because it created space for others behind me. Equally, I knew that if I played on the sides of the midfield, I wasn't Linford Christie. But sometimes I'd have to push out wide and get chalk on my boots from the touchline just to create the space for someone else to move into. Crewe helped me appreciate space: how to expand it, how to fill it.'

Though Murphy played plenty of times under Houllier on the right of midfield, the left defined him. When the team did not perform as well, he became a scapegoat for the crowd, the jeering after his substitution during the 1–1 draw with Southampton at Anfield in January 2002 ahead of the fixture with Manchester United being an example of the feeling towards him.

'On the right, I was able to get myself into a position where I could put a cross in with my right foot because it was a more natural thing to do. On the left, I became trapped, because I had to cut back on my right foot, slowing the game down. By then, Emile Heskey – the type of player who thrived on service from wide – was already marked. The crowd could see it.

'The reason why Houllier played me on the left more often than not was because he felt I offered more of a goal threat from that position. Houllier being Houllier proved this to me statistically. I was like, "Bollocks! He's got me again here!"

'First and foremost, Houllier was a defensive coach.

He wasn't adventurous and didn't encourage us to play a high-pressing game. We had Michael Owen, Robbie Fowler, Emile Heskey and later Jari Litmanen: four top-quality strikers he felt would score enough goals to win us games. Then there was Steven Gerrard, who was afforded more leeway in an attacking sense from midfield than anyone else. The rest of the midfield, the defence and the goalkeeper acted as a block. This isn't a criticism of Houllier in any way, because it was successful. But the reality was – as a right-sided midfielder, or especially on the left – my role primarily was to help the full-back defend. I was often asked to double up on a good wide player in the opposition. I remember playing the League Cup final against Manchester United in 2003 on the left and Houllier told me I was playing there to help John Arne Riise out, who was up against David Beckham and Gary Neville. I did very little going forward that day but played very well defensively and, ultimately, Liverpool won the game, so everyone celebrated. The same thing had happened in the UEFA Cup final in 2001. Carra was left-back and I was left-midfield. Houllier wanted to stop Cosmin Contra, the Alavés right-back, from raiding forward. Neither me nor Carra were left-footed and neither of us really wanted to play there but Houllier knew that both of us would die trying to stop him.

'The problems happened when Liverpool didn't win the game, especially against teams at Anfield who were lower down in the league. I could play well and execute the role Houllier was asking of me but if the team didn't win, my role became an issue. The crowd wanted to see flying wingers obliterate the opposition. Cristiano

Ronaldo was coming on the scene. I was diligent and tidy, but you'd never see me fly past a full-back. Likewise, flying full-backs were coming into vogue. Carra couldn't really do that, so he got stick as well.

'I was older when I played for Tottenham and Martin Jol used me on the left. The crowd got annoyed. As I had more experience then, I was able to reason with Martin and he let me play in the centre, and when I did I was able to influence the game positively. The difference at Liverpool, of course, was that I was just happy to be in the team. I wasn't Steven Gerrard. I was younger then; at the time, I couldn't do what Didi Hamann did and hold the midfield together, be that authority figure in the centre of the park. If it meant that in some games I'd have to sacrifice myself, I didn't really care because I knew one thing: I was playing for Liverpool, for god's sake. I had the best job in the world.'

Murphy emerged as a full England international, earning nine caps, with Houllier citing his versatility as a reason for his progression. Yet when Houllier left Liverpool, Murphy says his successor viewed such flexibility as a negative.

'When Rafa Benítez became manager, in one of his first training sessions he called me and Steven Gerrard over and said, "I've watched a lot of videos of you two." He pointed at Stevie and said that he needed to be more like me and then pointed at me and said that I needed to be more like Stevie. What he meant was, Stevie needed to be more tactically aware instead of bombing everywhere trying to do everything, while I needed to run about more because I appeared a bit too worried positionally. I would argue that perhaps I created that perception because of the players around me. When I played on the left at Liverpool and Stevie and Didi were in the middle, Stevie would attack and I'd fill in for him. Didi was an experienced guy and he'd shout over, "Oi, Danny – get in here . . ."'

On the pre-season tour of the United States in summer 2004, Murphy believes Benítez decided that Murphy, Gerrard, Carragher and Owen had formed a clique, which concerned the new manager.

'The four of us were quite strong willed. When I heard that Liverpool had hired Benítez, I was absolutely delighted. He'd won La Liga twice and played the type of football I like. Valencia had battered us in Europe.'

But now suddenly Murphy was told something he did not want to hear. Benítez was happy for him to leave Liverpool. He concedes it was a mistake that he agreed to do so.

'People who tell you they have no regrets are speaking bollocks. I regret leaving when I did,' Murphy admits. 'Even though Benítez made it clear that I wasn't going to be his first choice, I should have given it a year to prove him wrong. The problem was, quite simply, it is very hard going from playing for Liverpool – the club you love – to being told you are not part of the plans. You picture yourself being in the stands, not being involved at all. These are nightmarish thoughts. You think, *I'll lose my head here*. Carra was the same – that's why he retired [in 2013]. I wish I'd stuck it out, though. Maybe I'd have changed his opinion. Maybe I underestimated the strength of my own character.'

Murphy moved to Charlton Athletic. He signed for Tottenham Hotspur and then Fulham, where he became captain under Roy Hodgson. In 2010, Hodgson became Liverpool's manager, a move that Murphy backed publicly. Hodgson lasted six months in the role. His sacking was largely down to poor results but beneath that there was the joyless style of football as well as the perceived attempt to sink expectations at a time when the club was in danger of going into administration under American owners Tom Hicks and George Gillett. Hodgson described the challenge of Northampton Town from the lowest tier of professional football in England as 'formidable', before losing on penalties in embarrassment. Murphy, who had previously flourished under Hodgson, was considered as a Hodgson sympathizer in some quarters for his earlier commendation and, though no Liverpool manager endures such a dubious reputation, Murphy has not changed his opinion.

'Roy reminded me of Houllier in his methods and in the way he wanted the team to play,' Murphy maintains. 'He gave me a lot of responsibility and being straight with you even now – with what has happened since – I really enjoyed playing for him. Just because it didn't work out for him at Liverpool, it doesn't change the fact that at Fulham he took the club from the relegation zone to a European final in two years and made me a massive part of it.

'I look back on that period very fondly. It was more recent, for starters. When I achieved success at Liverpool, we played final after final. We got results at amazing stadiums like the Nou Camp. But when you're young, the experience passes you by. At Fulham, I realized I mightn't have too many chances left. I was also a central figure in the team and the squad. There was a tremendous satisfaction in what we achieved.'

Murphy recognizes that he continues to divide opinion amongst Liverpool supporters.

'My memories are positive, though,' he insists. 'The general feedback I get is good. I had more good games than bad. I contributed well when I was at my best. I look back and think about my dreams at the beginning, reflecting on what I eventually achieved: *Oh my god, seven years at Liverpool, trophies, goals – just give me one in front of the Kop, just one.* I scored the winner at Old Trafford three times. I scored the winner in the Merseyside derby at Goodison Park.

'These are the memories you take to the grave.'

CHAPTER THREE

cultzeros.co.uk

MICHAEL OWEN,
Boy Wonder

IT IS THE END OF AUTUMN AND MICHAEL OWEN PULLS TIGHTLY on his Canada Goose puffa jacket as he prepares to be photographed in front of his stables on the English side of the border, where Cheshire blurs into Wales. He requires no direction thereafter, a smile emerging as the camera begins to click. At thirty-five, he still possesses the youthful appearance of the boy next door.

An interview like this probably would not have been possible in 2001, when Owen was crowned European footballer of the year, winning the Ballon d'Or because his twenty-four goals for Liverpool that season contributed significantly towards a cup treble under Gérard Houllier's management. These were achievements that seemed to set him on a natural path towards legendary Anfield status. By then the 21-year-old was also one of England's most important players, having already played and scored in a World Cup and a European Championship.

'I'd receive sack loads of fan mail every single morning,' Owen remembers of the period where his working day was micro-managed between football bosses, coaches, agents and their assistants. 'The sacks would arrive at Melwood, my parents' house and my house as well. Some of the people would be really determined – they'd send the same letter to all three addresses. My mum, Jeanette, told me, because she went through them. She did at the beginning, anyway. After a while, it would have been impossible to keep up – a full-time job for anyone.

'It felt normal to me at the time, scoring goals for Liverpool and England in important games. It was the normal thing for me to do because I'd done it all my life. Being recognized was an extension of that. It was fine. My agent, Tony Stephens, dealt with all kinds of requests. You really wouldn't believe some of the proposals.

'It's certainly a lot quieter than it was back then,' Owen concedes. 'The fan mail hasn't stopped completely but most of it comes from the Far East. Not from England.'

Owen is a household name because he was a super-star of his profession. Owen was a cleansing antidote to the brash Spice Boy era at Liverpool, the pin-up boy of a new generation of footballer. With David Beckham, he became the first living person outside of the British royal family to feature on a postage stamp.

Owen justified his reputation by performance, rattling in 158 goals in 297 games for Liverpool: an average of more than one in two. His presence helped determine the outcome of league games, cup finals and entire campaigns and, to an extent, managerial reigns.

And yet, for many, Owen's name is not as revered as it might be. He realizes the decision to sign for Real Madrid in 2004, which meant he missed out on Liverpool's Champions League success a year later, as well as other subsequent career choices, determined how he is now remembered. Though he insists – and later explains at length – that the true account of his story is not quite what many imagine it to be: 'Because it never is in the mad world of football, especially the higher you go and when so many different people are involved.'

Owen was well on his way towards becoming a Liverpool great at the point of his departure. He chose to leave for Madrid mainly because of curiosity, with an intention to return to Anfield within a year. And yet he ended up coming back to play for Newcastle United before signing for Manchester United, Liverpool's greatest rivals. The decision was viewed on Merseyside as the ultimate betrayal.

I ask Owen whether he still recognizes the teenager that shot to prominence in a Liverpool shirt – when he looks in the mirror, what does he see?

'I've changed,' he says. 'Life makes you change. There are a few extra lines on my forehead for a start.

'You enter football as a closed book. You're naive. Naivety is sometimes a good quality, because it makes you fearless. You don't give a damn who you are playing. You just get at them without considering the consequences. As you get older, you think more. You worry more. You begin to agonize. You begin to appreciate what you have, what you've lost.'

Owen has all of this now: the magnificent Manor House Stables in the middle of nowhere, amongst the trees, the wide open fields, the horses, the sheep, the weathered cottages and the muddy lanes. The road signs in Malpas say we are thirty-one miles away from Liverpool. But it seems much further while out in the countryside where farms specializing in beef, pork, lamb, eggs and honey are the main source of trade, and the pungency of dung and fertilizer hangs in the air.

Owen splits his time between here, breeding horses; Hawarden, where he grew up and still lives; the television studio, where he works as a match analyser for BT; and an office, where he runs Michael Owen Management Limited, a player management company he shares with adviser and friend Simon Marsh, whom he met working for one of his old sponsors, Umbro.

'The general perception of footballers is bad and it annoys me,' Owen says, beginning to explain why he entered the agency business. 'Footballers need help, because not many people are born to be a role model, yet because of the media glare and the instant wealth, the public's expectations shift immediately. Fame is thrust upon them. It was thrust upon me, certainly. Footballers have to learn fast, probably faster than young people in

94

any other industry. Social media is an absolute minefield. You cannot prepare someone for becoming a millionaire overnight. My message is always the same: focus on the game and improve. The money will come.'

It's certainly true that plenty of people have preconceptions about Owen. Venal, taciturn, disconnected and robotic are recurring descriptions from those who have viewed him from afar, those who have resisted warming to his clinically matter-of-fact public persona. Meet others who have worked with him, and those who know Owen socially – like Jamie Carragher – and you would not believe they are speaking about the same individual.

It was Owen, of course, who raced into the limelight before Carragher and Steven Gerrard: a trio who emerged from Liverpool's centre of excellence under Steve Heighway. Heighway's greatest gift, perhaps, was not to be afraid to tell young players how great they could be. While Gerrard was troubled by self-doubt and Carragher's inner qualities became more obvious as time progressed, Owen did not need much reassurance.

Confidence was a continuous companion and yet it is not very British at all to display such a quality in public, never mind talk about it. Any sportsman who attempts to describe their self-belief risks being accused of arrogance. But scoring goals was a 'normal' or 'natural' act for Owen in the same way breathing or sex is to others. Yet Owen does not sentimentalize his ability and rarely resorts to embellishment when it comes to discussing his best moments.

'Because footballers have answers on the pitch, we

are expected to have answers off it as well and that's unfair,' he says. 'I would have been mortified if anyone thought I was big-headed, because around friends and family I'm not at all. But as soon as I crossed the line, I felt like I was performing on the stage, where I belonged. I could rationalize everything that was happening and that's probably why I did so well as a teenager.

'You almost have to live two lives – believing you are superman on the pitch but realizing you can't behave like that off it.

'Because you are a good footballer, everyone expects you to be a role model, everyone expects you to interview well when a camera is shoved in front of your face, everyone expects you to walk on to a stage and speak confidently in front of five hundred people you don't know, even though you are young and still aren't really confident enough to look people in the eye all of the time.

'Everyone expects all of these things just because you can kick a ball in a goal, even though all you've known all your life is how to play football really well. If you can't talk, lots of people say, "He's a typical thick footballer; he's this, he's that." It's a really sad world in that respect; it's pretty harsh. If you even talk about this, the money angle is thrown back at you – as if money somehow solves everyone's problems and makes them superior.

'I learned quickly that I was being myself on the pitch, displaying confidence. Off the pitch, I wasn't so confident; I was quite shy. So I had to develop a confidence that maybe wasn't natural. I had to be different to who I actually was. That doesn't mean I was being disingenuous. What it means is, my progression as a human being was unnatural by the standards of others. I had to come across well all of the time and behave properly. I certainly wasn't a bad lad, because my parents brought me up well. But I wasn't perfect. I wasn't a saint. No footballer is. No person is. We all make mistakes. And I've made many, some big 'uns. I'm sure we'll talk about them.'

When Owen says 'I was born to score goals', he is probably telling the truth. His father, Terry, grew up on the tough Rimrose Valley estate in Thornton near Crosby, seven miles to the north of Liverpool's city centre, and a career at Everton beckoned until Harry Catterick, the legendary manager, decided to release him in 1970 after only two first-team appearances. A nomadic existence as a lower-league centre-forward followed, with professional spells at Bradford City, Chester City, Cambridge United, Rochdale and Port Vale. Son can remember watching father later play for clubs like Oswestry, Colwyn Bay, Caernarfon and Prestatyn, at ancient grounds where 'the smell of Bovril wafted across the pitch and Deep Heat liniment came from the changing rooms'.

For Terry, playing football became a necessity because it provided financial support for the family, which included five children.

'People tend to assume that my dad was one of those dads who makes his kids watch endless tapes of his career but that wasn't the case in our family,' Owen says. 'Playing football and scoring goals was just something he did. He never made a point of sitting us all down and telling stories about his career. There were a few old photos lying about the house but many of them were buried away in a cardboard box in the attic. I've got to be honest, I don't even know what type of striker my dad was. He played. He scored. He came home. He didn't boast about anything. He was very modest.'

Terry Owen's happiest times were at Chester, a detail that explains why the Owen family settled near the town, although football had not created a nest egg. After retiring, Terry and Jeanette ran a clothes shop in Crosby and when that failed, Jeanette worked for the frozen-food company Iceland, in Deeside, while Terry sold policies for Co-op Insurance. He dreaded knocking on doors because of his reserved nature.

Michael was small but grew strong thanks to Terry's subtle guidance. Every Thursday night, steak would be served at the Owen household before weekends where Terry would stand behind whichever goal Michael was attacking, though saying little.

'He wasn't a man of many words, my dad, but I knew he was proud of me just because he was there watching all of the time.'

Michael was the youngest brother of the family by nine years and while the other two (Terry and Andrew) got jobs working for British Aerospace in nearby Broughton, Michael sensed his destiny lay in football.

'I know loads of footballers say the same thing but with me I honestly believed it. It sounds conceited to say I knew I was good but it didn't go to my head and that's probably why I made it.'

Owen's potential was noted at Hawarden Rangers, when he scored 'about 116 goals' in forty games as a twelve year old before deciding to walk out on the club because they did not make him their player of the year, demonstrating the kind of self-assurance that would later propel him to more remarkable feats and perhaps even to Manchester United despite his Liverpool links.

'I joined another team called St David's and although I was training with Liverpool by then, I made sure I was available to play when the game with Hawarden Rangers came around because I was desperate to prove to them what they were missing,' he admits. 'We won 4–3 and I scored all four goals. I felt a bit smug, I guess.'

The desire to constantly prove himself was clear but Owen believes his passion for football was augmented mostly by playing with his dad and brothers in the park rather than by the coaching he received later.

'I just saw it as fun; there was nothing academic about it. I barely kicked the ball with my left foot until I was sixteen but because I was so fast I could chase on to a through pass and have loads of time to select where I was going to place my shot.'

Richard Dunne, the stocky Everton centre-back from Dublin, was the first opponent in youth football that made Owen realize he really needed to toughen up physically and so he joined the Deeside Boxing Club above a pub in Shotton, taking part in two proper fights, in Anglesey one evening (after he'd played a schoolboys' match earlier in the day) and then the Civic Centre in Connah's Quay, winning twice on split decisions.

'I was becoming quite popular at school because of

my football ability but sometimes with popularity you get a lot of jealousy as well. I wouldn't say that boxing made me a more intimidating presence or anything like that, but mentally it helped me look after myself. It taught me that if you get knocked down, you bounce back up straight away.'

Owen supported Everton because of his father's links with the club and his favourite player was Gary Lineker. He contrasts his allegiance to that of Jamie Carragher, the Liverpool legend who grew up as an Evertonian.

'Carra used to go to away games in Europe with his dad. He was a diehard. Listening to him when we both joined Liverpool, I realized that, actually, I wasn't a proper Evertonian at all. Until we were fifteen or sixteen, Carra used to go into a really bad mood if Liverpool ever beat Everton; he was almost physically sick. We'd watch the derbies together and he'd get so nervous he'd leave the room and sit on the toilet. I wanted Everton to win but if they lost, it wouldn't affect me like it did Carra. He was the biggest Evertonian I knew.'

Owen and Carragher's relationship blossomed at Lilleshall, the Football Association's school of excellence in Shropshire, which opened in 1984 but closed in 1999 when many Premier League clubs developed their own youth academies based on the same model. The old system meant young players could not sign professional contracts until they were sixteen and while Carragher had already made his mind up to sign for Liverpool ahead of Everton, Owen took his time deciding what to do because he had more options.

First, he went to Manchester United, where he was

introduced to Alex Ferguson, the first-team manager. Ferguson had rated Owen so highly that he dispatched his assistant Brian Kidd to watch him whenever United didn't have a game and Owen did. After that, he went to Arsenal and at Highbury they provided tickets in the Clock End for a match against Coventry City and taking Owen into the dressing room before the game, where Ian Wright – the club's all-time leading goalscorer at that time – made a fuss of him. From there, he visited Chelsea, where Glenn Hoddle revealed a chart in his office.

'It was a bit surreal because only a few years later Glenn was taking me to the World Cup as England manager, but here he said, "There are a lot of youngsters we want to sign but, look, your name is at the top of the list."'

Owen trained at Everton, where he did not get to meet Joe Royle, then Oldham Athletic, Norwich City, Chester and Wrexham too. With Manchester City, he went to France for a tournament. Yet it was at Liverpool that he felt most confident.

'I decided on Liverpool because of the individuals in charge,' Owen explains. 'Steve Heighway, Hughie McAuley and Dave Shannon were the three youth coaches I'd worked most with and I liked them all. Steve was a particularly big influence. We shared a close bond and my parents liked him too. He was dead straight with all the parents and never led anyone up the garden path, making promises that he couldn't keep.

'I never felt nervous at Liverpool. I felt like I belonged there. I knew all of the lads too. I'd been away at

Lilleshall for a couple of years and I really didn't want to live away from home again. Liverpool were really keen to put me in digs, so I'd be closer to Melwood. But in the end they agreed I could commute from home. I sensed that Liverpool trusted me. And I trusted them. That clinched it.'

Owen's first contract was worth £500 a week plus bonuses. The interest in him was reflected by the commercial deals he signed within a few years of becoming a first-team footballer. First there was Umbro. Then came Tissot, Jaguar, Walkers (who released a 'Cheese and Owen' branded crisp), Lucozade Sport, Yamaha, Persil and Asda.

Although he scored on his Liverpool debut as a seventeen year old, it was his achievements with England that propelled him farthest initially. An entire chapter of his 2004 autobiography was devoted to the 'Wonder Goal' against Argentina at the 1998 World Cup. The manner of the moment represented the bold nature of the person who delivered it.

'When you grow up, your desire to become a footballer isn't related to being famous or having a Ferrari. You just want to be the best. I think that's the case for most motivated people, whatever industry you work in. Yet what comes with it when you're a footballer, there's nothing you can do to prepare for it. You can only prepare to make yourself a better football player: by looking at how early you go to bed, what you eat or how you practise.

'I made my debut for Liverpool [against Wimbledon in 1997] and scored. Straight away, people were talking about me. Within twelve months, I'd become a regular in the Liverpool team, made my debut for England and scored in the World Cup against Argentina, making me well known around the world. That change was a lot to take in – really sudden. If I hadn't had good people around me – a good agent, my family, players I looked up to like Alan Shearer, Dwight Yorke and David Beckham – all of them helping me, taking the pressure away, it would have been easy to lose track of where I was going.

'The trajectory obviously wasn't normal by everyone else's standards but it felt normal to me. I would score goals for Liverpool; I would score goals for England; I'd do well at the World Cup. It wasn't a case of: let's see how I do here. I'd done it all my life – I'd broken records for every team I'd played for. In my mind, it was always going to happen. It might sound arrogant saying it, but if you don't think like that, you won't go anywhere near as far. The way I thought was probably very, very rare.

'When you're young, you don't think anything is impossible. I could probably name [Gabriel] Batistuta of the players in the Argentina team, none of the others. I wasn't worried. But towards the end of my career, I would think about the opponents I would face. I'd know I was in for a game against Rio Ferdinand or John Terry. I'd maybe target the *other* centre-half, maybe play on him instead because he wasn't as quick or as strong. You lose that air of fearlessness.

'When I was eighteen, I feared nothing. I just did it. It didn't matter who I was playing against. I had an unshakable self-belief. Nothing bothered me. The prospect of scoring against Argentina at the World Cup? It felt natural.'

Owen's rise happened at a time when football was changing. Matches were soap operas and the players became celebrities. Owen hired Tony Stephens as his agent, who worked for SFX, the New York-based sports management agency that also controlled the affairs of David Beckham and basketball legend Michael Jordan. For Beckham, Stephens had negotiated sponsorship deals worth £17 million a year, including a £4 million-a-year deal with Adidas.

'Football went boom and David was the first superstar in terms of popularity. He led the way and I followed. I'm naturally shy and I didn't want to go down the route of being in the front pages of the papers all of the time. That in some way contributed towards my image of being clean-cut.

'I have loads of respect for Tony [Stephens]. He helped create a certain image for me. It wasn't necessarily different to how I was or am now but, if I'm being honest, I suppose it wasn't absolutely a reflection of me.

'When I meet new people, one of the most common things they say to me is, "You're nothing like I thought." We spend five minutes together and they say, "I thought you were quite straight, boring and whatever."

'The lads at Liverpool will probably tell you that even when I was nineteen or twenty, inside the dressing room me and Carra were two of the loudest voices – screaming, laughing and instigating pranks. To the outside world, everyone looking in was thinking I was this whiter-than-white angel. Don't get me wrong, I wasn't going out night after night on the lash. But I like a drink and I've been known to enjoy a bet. Some of the values that people associate me with are true but it was dressed up more than the reality.'

Elsewhere in this book, Jamie Carragher says that the football ability that he and Owen shared was aggression – in spite of Owen's widely held reputation as a clean player. Owen reasons this is partly natural but also a by-product of the youth system at Liverpool.

'It was a far cry from what it is now, where everything is done for you,' Owen says. 'It was a tough environment. Everybody wanted it really badly. The standard was really high and the local lads set that standard. You were in touching distance of the first team – you could see the senior players walking into Melwood; you could see them prepare. You could see them train. Every now and then you'd get to have a kickabout with them. It was all very real.

'Inside the youth teams, there would be fights. Every day was life or death – a quest for survival. You had to win your five-a-side. I've stuck my hand through the bedroom door in my mum and dad's house four or five times when I've got home just because I've lost a five-a-side in training or been annoyed at someone for losing us a proper game. You look back and you think, *What was I doing?* I'm as calm as they come; I've got four kids; I've never raised a hand to anyone in my life – I'm not that way inclined at all. But losing in football made me act like a psychopath. When you're in that situation and want something so badly, trying to scramble a way to the top, it can drive you mad.'

Owen recalls getting sent off against Manchester United during his first full season as a Liverpool player for a two-footed lunge at Peter Schmeichel, a goalkeeper almost twice his age and twice his size.

'It was an example of the inner quirk inside me. On the face of it, I'm a nice lad. But put me on a football pitch facing Man United for Liverpool and I change.

'In football, bravery represents going in for a tackle with a 6 ft 5 in. giant with a reputation for being sent off when you're only 5 ft 8. But in my eyes, bravery in football is showing for the ball instead of hiding when you're 1–0 down in front of seventy-five thousand people and most of the crowd are booing. There are different types of bravery. Aggression is the same. In my eyes, I was as aggressive as any player that's ever bloody been. Certainly in the first few years of my career, I'd tackle anyone; I'd kick anyone. This goes back to youth level.

'You look at the best players – they're right on the edge. You see a Luis Suárez bite someone or a Wayne Rooney stamp. It isn't an attempt to condone bad behaviour by explaining why it happens, because you've got to try to curb it, but I've always felt if you take that away from the best players, they're not quite the same.

'When you go on to the pitch, it has to be almost a life-or-death situation. We all feel like grabbing someone, pinching, kicking or even biting, especially when you want to win so much, whether it's in five-a-side during training or during a game. The key is to find a way to stop yourself. If you're not right on that edge – on the precipice of madness – you become normal.'

Many do not realize how injury accelerated Owen's route towards normality. He was only nineteen when, in 1999 at Elland Road against Leeds United, he fell in agony, holding his hamstring – a vital instrument in his body considering his pace.

'Players have surgery on muscles now but they didn't then. So instead of having two sets of fully functioning hamstrings, I ran for the rest of my career on three [tendons] on one and two on the other. The string on my right leg ruptured before reattaching at the wrong place. It meant there was an imbalance in my body, one leg being considerably stronger than the other.

'People are quick to say, "Oh, you weren't as good when you left Liverpool." But if you actually know what happened, you realize that it's impossible for it to have turned out any other way. If you are running on one hamstring that isn't as strong, there is going to be a natural gradual deterioration. You've got power in one leg while the other tries to keep up. That puts more pressure on your groin, your calf and your quads – so you end up pulling muscles elsewhere. And then hernias go. I ended up being prone to muscle injuries because I had one catastrophic injury at the start. It frustrates me because I never had any problems with my bones or ligaments. I didn't realize it then, but the physical foundations of my entire career were built on sand.

'Muscle injuries took their toll on me. You try to kid yourself at the beginning that everything is OK. But there was no doubt my physical ability was on the wane for a long time and my career was slowly being taken away from me. That probably coincided with the period where I stopped being on the absolute edge – when marriage and parenthood came along. Had my mind remained on the edge as my physical capacity declined, I probably would have gone crazy, knowing I couldn't reach the levels I set myself: my brain telling me one thing but my body not being able to do it. It wouldn't have been healthy. I probably came to some realization in the back of my mind that I wasn't as good as I had been. I couldn't sprint as fast as I needed or wanted to. I began to feel less invincible. I realized my powers were slipping.'

It seems remarkable that Owen managed to return to anywhere near the standards he set before 1999, never mind win the European Player of the Year award as he did two years later. That he did underlines what he believes was his strongest quality.

'Mentality,' he says. 'When I was playing, I thought I was really quick and a very good finisher. I realized I had to brush up on dropping deep for the ball sometimes and not just going in behind the defence all of the time. I appreciated that to be a Liverpool player, I had to be able to link others into the game. I couldn't just keep running and chasing after passes. There is no question, though, that my mentality was my greatest asset. There are loads of people who can run quickly; there are loads of people who can finish too. Most of us have a body that is robust and that can do similar things on a football pitch. But there's one thing that separates the great players from the good players – it's what lies between your ears. I had an unwavering dollop of self-belief.

'I remember when Real Madrid came in for me and

I spoke to Carra. He goes, "Mo, you'll never play, will you? They've got Raúl, Ronaldo, [Fernando] Morientes and plenty of others." I think he was taken aback by my confidence. I didn't care. It was almost ignorance. I realized deep down they were great players: Ronaldo was the best in the world for a time and Raúl was the darling of Madrid. But the idea they were better than me never registered. I wasn't bothered about them at all. The attitude was: I'm going there to knock them out of the team.

'Maybe Carra was trying to put me off going. But I think we were big enough mates to have an honest conversation. Of course, I can admit now that other players were better than me. Then, while I was still active – in the first six or seven years – I wouldn't have it that someone else was as good. It's a horrible thing to say out loud because it comes across as egotistical, I realize that. I wouldn't have wanted anyone to think I was a big-headed so-and-so. But deep down that's the way I was even in spite of the injuries. I wasn't worried about anyone.'

The offer from Real Madrid arrived at a time of transition at Anfield. Houllier had left and been replaced by Rafael Benítez. Benítez was determined that he needed to break a British clique that he believed was present in the dressing room. Having already sold Danny Murphy to Charlton Athletic, Owen's position was vulnerable because of his contract, which only had a year left to run.

Owen can understand fan frustration about the issue of Liverpool not receiving as much money as they should have for him but reasons that his agent had gone on a six-month sabbatical, deciding to travel the world, during Houllier's last season in charge, thus delaying negotiations over a contract extension.

'I didn't envisage anyone making a bid for me and everyone agreed that we could wait until Tony [Stephens] returned,' Owen explains. 'It was different then to what it's like now, where clubs are petrified to leave it so late. We were all really relaxed. I was happy; I was scoring goals. I had no reason to want to leave. When Real Madrid made the call, both Liverpool and I had a decision to make.

'I must emphasize, I never dreamed of leaving Liverpool. I always thought that me, Carra and Stevie – we all came through at the same time – would be together until the end of our careers. I never asked for Real Madrid to come in for me and I never touted myself around through my agent. Some players do. I only wanted to play for Liverpool, to be there for ever.

'When Madrid made an offer, my mind began to race. My instinct was to stay at Liverpool. But then I thought that maybe it was a chance to do what Ian Rush did – to go abroad for a year and then return. I wrestled with the decision. I spoke to Rick Parry [the chief executive] and said to him, "What if I just go and come back next summer?" I knew that if I retired having not tried it, I'd regret it. It was Real Madrid – the most successful club in Europe. They had the greatest players: Ronaldo, Raúl, Figo and Zidane.

'I drove to John Lennon airport crying my eyes out, thinking, *What the hell have you done?* I was naive to think I could go there, come back home and pretend it never really happened, because once you make a break from the people and the club you trust, you lose a lot of control. The best-laid plans agreed between Rick Parry and me never came about.'

For Owen, the move to the Spanish capital was similar to Ian Rush's experience in Turin with Juventus two decades earlier. Although on the pitch he was a greater success than Rush, scoring nineteen goals in forty-three starts, he admits he struggled when it was time to leave the training ground.

'In my head, I had this idea of training sessions in the morning followed by afternoons sat in front of a swimming pool in the sun but I made the mistake of not buying somewhere in the first few months. I was married to Louise [Bonsall] by then with a two-year-old daughter. I spoke to Macca [Steve McManaman] before going out there and he loved it but he didn't have kids.

'The club put us in a businessmen's hotel on the edge of the city for five months. Restaurants in Spain do not really open until 10 p.m. and we couldn't have Gemma staying up until midnight every day at the age of two, so we'd put her to sleep at seven, turn the lights off half an hour later and put the only English TV channel on mute.

'I felt guilty leaving Louise alone with Gemma if I ever went out to play golf with Ronaldo or César Sánchez, the back-up goalkeeper. I knew they'd be back in the hotel with little to do. Maybe the club could have done more to help. Certainly, I could have done more to prepare. We never had the support system around us to make it work.'

It was towards the end of his first season when Real Madrid's president, Florentino Pérez, knocked on his hotel room door.

'He said, "Michael, we're happy for you to stay. But also, if you want to go back to the Premier League, we're happy for you to go." I said I agreed that I should go but only if it was to Liverpool. So discreet contact was made with Liverpool. The problem was, Newcastle weren't shy in telling everyone they were in for me too, so it was splashed about the press and everyone knew about it.'

This was in the period when Liverpool won the Champions League in Istanbul.

'Yeah, of course it made me envious,' Owen admits. 'Missing out on a night like that, who wouldn't want to be a part of it? I was a motivated footballer and I cared deeply about Liverpool. I was delighted for lads like Carra, Stevie, Didi Hamann and Sami Hyypiä because they were my mates and I knew how much it meant to them. We'd been in the trenches together before. But it would be dishonest of me to say it didn't make me jealous too. God, winning the European Cup with Liverpool – it would have been the greatest thing . . .'

Owen describes his desperation to return to Liverpool, a return ultimately made impossible by the financial package Newcastle offered to Real Madrid, a package delivered by chairman Freddie Shepherd, who was determined to show Newcastle's frustrated supporters that he still possessed the financial clout to compete with the Premier League's biggest clubs.

'Pérez accepted Newcastle's £16 million offer but I

reminded him that I'd only leave for Liverpool. Pérez said, "Fine, get them to match the deal being offered by Newcastle then." So my agent spoke to Rick Parry and I met with Rafa Benítez, who wanted me back. Rick said that he'd go to £10 million, considering they'd sold me for £8 million twelve months before. I told Rick that Real Madrid would never let me leave for that but maybe they might if he stretched it to £12 million. If everything worked out, I would be going back to Liverpool on less money than I was on before leaving. I was so desperate for it to happen that I told Rick I'd hold fire until the last possible moment in the transfer window and risk staying in Madrid. I knew that Pérez wanted to sign Sergio Ramos from Seville and he was waiting for the funds to come in to complete the deal.'

Owen says he broke down in tears when Parry called him to say Liverpool's budget had been allocated to other areas of the squad and that he could only raise £10 million. It prompted Owen to make sure his agent brokered a deal with Newcastle where the contract stipulated that he could leave for Liverpool.

'So I went to Newcastle for £16 million. Newcastle's determination to get me and to pay such a big fee cost me my dream move. I don't blame Newcastle at all, though. They wanted someone: they made an offer – fair enough.

'Not many people know this but my contract at Newcastle said that if Liverpool made an offer of £12 million at the end of my first season, I could go back to Liverpool. It was £8 million at the end of the second year and £4 million at the end of the third. Everything was geared towards getting me back to Liverpool.'

Owen played at Anfield for the first time in his career as an opponent of Liverpool and returned home that night in December 2005 ashen-faced, with the jeers of those who once idolized him haunting his thoughts, the defeat freezing his soul. Those in the Kop did not realize Owen had tried so hard to become a Liverpool player once more and in the build-up to the match the focus was on the financial rewards he'd reaped by moving to Newcastle instead.

The home fans were merciless, the smattering of boos that accompanied his name when it was delivered over the public address system in the warm-up intensifying to a full-scale explosion when he received possession for the first time. Once Liverpool had eased their way into the lead and the gulf between the two sides had become clear, the insults were roared. 'Where were you in Istanbul?' slipped into 'You should have signed for a big club', though it was the strains of 'What a waste of talent' that cut Owen the deepest.

The reception disappointed Steven Gerrard. 'I played with Michael for several years and he's a world-class player,' Gerrard said. 'He's a legend here but the fans didn't want to see him go in the first place. He deserves a standing ovation here for the goals he scored.'

The memory still clearly pains Owen. He leans forward and his eyes become fixed while describing his feelings.

'Going back for Newcastle, knowing that I'd done absolutely everything – trying to move heaven and earth – to get back, to then be booed, it hurt,' he begins. 'I'm fully aware that it wasn't the whole stadium. If you get a hundred in a crowd of forty-five thousand you still hear it. But for one person to have booed, it broke my heart. I've never felt as low in my life sitting in the players' lounge afterwards, with my family and my mum in tears. People within the club – Carra, the coaches, the staff – everyone was coming to me saying they were so sorry. Some said they were ashamed; it wasn't how the club felt about me.

'I was thinking, *Liverpool fans booing me: how did it come to this?* When I look at other players who have cost fortunes and given nothing back to Liverpool but they return with another club and the Kop sing their name, it's pretty hard to take, especially when I gave my life to the club and scored all those goals, winning trophies. I cost Liverpool nothing and still made them £8 million, although I appreciate why some people think the fee wasn't big enough. Hearing those boos, it represented the worst moment of my career, worse than the injuries.'

In Jamie Carragher's autobiography, the defender reasons that Owen's bond with the Liverpool support had not been as close as someone like Robbie Fowler. While Fowler was Liverpool's player and underappreciated by England, Owen had long seemed like England's player rather than Liverpool's. Even with all the achievements, any player in this position would never be as popular, for Liverpool as a city widely considers itself a separate state from England.

'Listen, I know I'm not alone. I've spoken to home-grown players at other clubs and they have the same gripes. Someone comes from Spain for a lot of money, they score a couple of goals and all of a sudden they're a bigger hero than the person who's been there for years and years, doing it consistently, year in, year out. These players get a song about them and you feel underappreciated.

'Carra and I roomed together for donkey's years. We were best mates. We'd talk about problems: injuries; playing through the pain barrier; the fear of getting dropped; him being moved around by Houllier; the pair of us being caught having a drink. We shared absolutely everything: about women, about money, about football – everything.

'We'd have this conversation all of the time about why I didn't quite have the connection that someone like Robbie Fowler had with the fans. Well, the first thing is, Robbie had already been there and done that; Liverpool already had a prodigal son. He was engrained as a legend before I came along. He was in their heart, the local lad. Maybe if Robbie hadn't been there, I'd have been the chosen one. But Robbie was still at the club and he was the fans' first love. I came along but I was from half an hour down the road. I wasn't a Scouser as such, although I was mentally and at heart because my dad came from Liverpool.

'As Carra rightly says, I scored a goal in a World Cup for a team other than Liverpool, which then threw me to wider prominence. Some Liverpool supporters might have wanted me to rise to prominence by my achievements in a red shirt. I'd have loved that. But I was scoring goals for both club and country. I couldn't have tried harder for Liverpool. I suppose some people forget that sometimes.'

Liverpool's supporters would certainly not forget Owen's next big decision. The first six months at Newcastle had gone reasonably enough. Nowhere else in England does a centre-forward receive more adoration than Tyneside. When Owen arrived at St James' Park, there were some eighteen thousand people in the stadium to see him sign, more than had attended Alan Shearer's homecoming nine years earlier. He seemed to descend in a direct line from Hughie Gallacher, Jackie Milburn, Malcolm Macdonald and Shearer himself.

And yet the supporters never had a song for him and barely ever chanted his name. They objected to his £5 million-plus salary, they objected to his helicopter flights home to Cheshire most days because he did not want to relocate to the north-east. To those on the Gallowgate, Owen was a symbol of expensively bought failure, his tally of thirty goals in seventy-nine appearances unappreciated as he struggled with injuries.

A broken foot did not stop him from going to the World Cup in 2006 but a cruciate knee ligament injury sustained in a match against Sweden ruled him out for the rest of the tournament and beyond. Though there were spikes, from there Owen's career was largely a corkscrew of decline. 'Newcastle ended up being a bit of a disaster if I'm being honest,' he admits.

The desire to return to Liverpool remained, however. 'At every stage – every summer – I was on the phone to Carra telling him to find a way to get me back. "Does Rafa want me?" I'd say. "Does Kenny want me? Does Brendan want me?" It was circumstance that stopped it happening. Whenever I was available, Liverpool had too many strikers. And when Liverpool wanted me, I was injured. By the end, I wasn't the player I had been before and they simply didn't fancy me. I wasn't good enough.'

Owen says his last attempt at a return came after a three-year spell at Manchester United. In choosing to move to Old Trafford after his contract expired at Newcastle, he appreciated the decision would destroy any positive legacy left behind at Anfield.

'I knew Liverpool fans generally weren't going to be happy,' he says. 'But I felt they'd made the first move by booing me in the first game against Newcastle and every game afterwards. I can't emphasize enough how desperate I was to go back. In that summer after choosing to leave Real Madrid, I spoke to Carra every day of the week about it.

'I couldn't have revealed any of this publicly at the time, nobody could have, because I was signing for a club with black and white stripes. Had everyone known the details of my contract – that I could have gone back to Liverpool in a year. If they'd have known how hard I was trying to make it happen – meeting with Parry and Benítez. All of a sudden, it's not great for Newcastle if fifty thousand people are thinking, *Well, we're his second choice*. They probably knew that deep down but didn't need me to rub anyone's nose in it. You have to be professional and respect the people who are paying your wages. That's the way in any walk of life.

'I can only equate people booing me to a situation where your missus leaves you. Do you continue to love her? You probably do deep down and if they ever try it on again, you go back – even if they treat you like crap afterwards. Outwardly, though, you think, *Sod it. If that's how they think about me, then they've shown their true colours.* I kept telling myself, *It's only a handful of people, it's fine, it's fine.* But it wasn't. It hurt me so much and it hurt my family so much.

'It was 2009. I was twenty-nine. I had a few years of my career still ahead of me. There was interest from a few Italian clubs but I wanted to stay in England. I can't even remember who they were because I just didn't want to go abroad. So three clubs here approached me. They were Manchester United, Everton and Hull City. Hull were at the bottom of the Premier League and would probably end up in the Championship. I was left to choose between Everton and United.

'It seemed to me that a lot of Liverpool supporters didn't think very highly of me. But still, I spoke to Carra and tried to get Benítez to do something. I wanted to try to put it right somehow. When it became clear Benítez didn't want to do a deal, I spoke again with [Sir Alex] Ferguson. He was very positive about me. I was twenty-nine years old. Should I have decided to retire there and then?'

Owen believes the decision was easier for him because he'd become immune to the emotions of football by then. This was a cold, hard choice of a careerist.

'When you move club from the one you grew up playing for, you stop viewing football through the eyes of a fan,' he reasons. 'When I was at Liverpool, I had a red mist towards all of Liverpool's rivals.

'Once you move clubs, it changes. I went to Real Madrid from Liverpool. Being honest, how does anyone really expect me to hate Atlético Madrid in the derby? It just doesn't happen. I wanted to win because I wanted to do well and I wanted the atmosphere in training to be good, to enjoy going to work. But I'd be lying if I said I had a deep-rooted passion for Real.

'As soon as you start moving around, you lose all that. You start asking questions about what it's really all about. When I watch football now, I watch it because I love it. I want Liverpool to do well and I like to see Everton do well because I used to support them. But with time, as you move on, you lose that one-club mentality.

'I lost something when I left Liverpool. I lost my fan mentality. If you come through the ranks of a club, you have a professional-footballer mentality but you also have an allegiance. When I got sent off against Man United [in 1998 for two-footing Peter Schmeichel], I was so pumped up. I never wanted to win a game as much as that. Beating United at Old Trafford, what better feeling could there be? I was like a balloon. Once I got into the shower, stood on my own, it was as if something had popped me. All the air came out of me. I fell back down to earth. There was such rage inside me, such anger. I wanted to score a hundred goals and kick every one of their players. It was hatred.

'As soon as you move, you get a wider perspective. You realize that, actually, there are nice people at other clubs and the lads are great. It takes the edge away. You begin to look at clubs because of the people there: the people you are working for. That's why I went to Manchester

United. Because I realized that Sir Alex Ferguson is actually an OK human being. The players were OK human beings as well. I never supported United; I never supported Real Madrid; I never supported Newcastle or Stoke. But I supported Liverpool. It was more than people. Liverpool was a movement, a way of thinking – my entire life. When I stopped representing that, things were not quite the same. My edge wasn't there.'

Owen's story is a reminder that a footballer is not defined just by what he achieves but also by how he is remembered. It proves to be a theme I return to later in the book when I meet Fernando Torres. Owen's career finished at Stoke City in May 2013, after he played nine games that season, scoring one goal. I remind him that twelve years ago to that month, his two strikes won Liverpool the FA Cup final, inspiring the team to an improbable victory – much like Steven Gerrard in Istanbul, when Owen was no longer a Liverpool player.

'I get asked all the time, "What's the best moment of your life? Has to be the Argentina goal, surely?"

'It wasn't, no way, I tell them. That day in Cardiff, being 1–0 down in the heat to a top Arsenal side, plunging to the depths of despair because of the exhaustion, knowing we were being outclassed for long periods. To pull us out of the fire, to be the person that scored the two goals, to do your job and to know your family are watching – it was the best day of my life. No question about it.

'The coach home, seeing supporters line the streets, singing and dancing, knowing we were going to Dortmund a few days later for the UEFA Cup final, having a party with a couple of hundred people sharing an occasion, knowing that everyone in that party was looking me in the eye, thinking, *Fucking 'ell Mo, you've done well today*, it makes me feel emotional. I realize now those occasions are so rare.

'If I could bottle one day and experience it again, that afternoon in Cardiff would be it. It was like poetry. I wish the moment somehow lasted for ever.'

122

CHAPTER FOUR

cultzeros.co.uk

GÉRARD HOULLIER,
The Manager

A NAVY-COLOURED MERCEDES BENZ CRAWLS DOWN THE RUE de Rivoli at rush hour, skirting the edge of the Marais district in Paris. The classy-looking saloon halts suddenly and a person springs out, waving his hands, beckoning me across the busy thoroughfare as fierce midsummer sun beats down on his shaven head.

My lift is Gérard Houllier. The person waving his hands is his chauffeur, Xavier Perez. Xavier is wearing a crisply ironed white shirt from Ralph Lauren, a black tie and black suit trousers. His cufflinks are golden and their reflection glints in the wing mirror of his vehicle.

'Meet Xavier,' Houllier says, after introducing himself. 'He was a goalkeeper not so long ago,' he explains, revealing that Xavier was first choice at Red Star in the 1980s when Red Star were the third team in the capital city behind Paris Saint-Germain and Racing Club. 'I know he has safe hands as a driver.'

Houllier is in his late sixties and, despite not being a football manager for five years, has a work life that remains unrelenting; hence the need for Xavier, who takes the edge off travelling by effortlessly steering him around France with all the smoothness of Alain Prost.

Preparations for this interview afforded me an insight into Houllier's schedule. On Wednesday morning, he was in New York on business, consulting for Red Bull's football teams, and by early evening he had arrived in Rennes, northern France, for a Leaders' in Football conference where he wisely informed attendees that 'athletes of the future need more freedoms – but need to accept greater responsibility'.

It was very generous of Houllier to agree to meet me when he did. It was planned for the Friday at 10 a.m. but when I called him upon landing at Charles de Gaulle the afternoon before to finalize the arrangement, he suggested we convene immediately – despite the arduous journeys he'd undertaken in the previous forty-eight hours.

'I will see you in sixty minutes,' he informed me moments after I emerged from passport control. It was the second hottest day of the year in Paris. The carriages on the Metro were sweaty and the tracks below hideously dry. Services were disrupted. So I arrived at my hotel seventy minutes later in a panic. As Liverpool's manager, Houllier was a stickler for punctuality as well as appearance. I suspected that when he suggests a time – considering how priceless it is to him – he really means it.

Upon opening my suitcase, I realized the reasonably smart checked shirt I'd brought hoping to impress him had creased. The only alternative was a short-sleeved and slightly less creased T-shirt more suited for a day at the seaside . . .

Houllier is sympathetic towards my problems when I hurriedly explain what has happened, flicking his hand to brush away my explanations with marvellous Parisian indifference. Relief washes over me like a cool wave. He is parked in the passenger seat, discussing in French with Xavier the more pressing issue of arranging an appropriate site for our sit-down.

And then Houllier turns slowly to me: 'So you know Carra?' he asks, the expensive leather upholstery creasing as he moves. It is only now I see his face fully. He looks healthy. His forehead is line-free and freckled, his hair swept back and reasonably dark, arms tanned. The sleeves on his spotty Lacoste shirt are rolled up.

I nod in reaction to his question. 'Carra: a fantastic person,' he says emphatically, as though it is a fact rather than an opinion. There is a pause, which suggests that inwardly he might be thinking of the good times at Liverpool. I fill the void by speculating whether Carragher will ever become a manager, like Houllier, reasoning that he seems to enjoy working in the media.

Houllier readjusts himself, sitting forward again, staring into the middle distance, arms folded. There is another long break. 'He should try,' he says, with what sounds like a tinge of hope beneath the words. 'Carra should try.'

It feels appropriate that we are navigating the Rue de Rivoli, a stately boulevard that bears the name of Napoleon's victory over the Austrian army in 1797. France's greatest leader later declared that 'glory is fleeting but obscurity is for ever', and it is a statement that can be applied to Houllier's career, certainly as Liverpool's manager. It is easy to forget just how successful and just how uncompromising Liverpool were under his guidance. So easy, in fact, that on a banner that used to be unfurled across the Kop grandstand, there was one notable absentee. The flag read 'Success has many fathers' and contained images of managers who have won trophies in the last fifty-five years. There was Bill Shankly. There was Bob Paisley. There was Joe Fagan. There was Kenny Dalglish. There was also Rafael Benítez. But there was no Gérard Houllier – despite the fact he added more silverware to Liverpool's trophy cabinet than any manager in the previous two and a half decades.

Houllier's status amongst Liverpool supporters is, indeed, a peculiar one. He led Liverpool to the League Cup, FA Cup and UEFA Cup in 2001, as well as to the quarter-finals of the Champions League and second place in the Premier League the following year despite the season being disrupted for him personally by ill health. Suffering from chest pains at half-time of a crucial league fixture with Leeds United, Houllier was rushed to Broadgreen Hospital before undergoing an emergency eleven-hour heart bypass operation. Signed off work by doctors for a year, he returned to management in five months but things would never be the same again. In the next two seasons, he bought badly and, together with what were perceived to be overly cautious tactics, the adoration towards him steadily eroded. When Rafael Benítez was appointed as Houllier's replacement in June 2004, the change was welcomed.

Returning to the present, we are approaching La Louvre, probably the most famous museum in the world. Xavier turns sharply to the right and drops us off on the Rue de L'Échelle, a street of high-end fashion shops and hair salons. Houllier knows one of the proprietors and after a brief conversation with the middle-aged man dressed solely in linen and possessing majestic silver hair, we arrive at the Hotel Normandy through its bar entrance. The venue is brilliantly raffish and brilliantly French.

Before leaving us, Houllier's friend whips out a Sunday newspaper magazine supplement. The weekend before, it had featured an interview with Michel Platini, which took place at the same venue. Houllier seems proud to tell me this. 'Michel . . .' he says, whispering as if it were a secret that he was here, '. . . is still God.'

The Normandy is the type of hotel that could feature in an espionage movie where members of the French Resistance design the downfall of their captors. Or maybe it could be used for a gangster epic about the rise and fall of Jacques Mesrine. I imagine Gérard Depardieu as the criminal overlord peering between the blinds of this quiet setting, wondering who might come for him next.

In this instance, a shard of daylight cuts across the otherwise dim room, which is furnished with oxblood-stained leather couches and mahogany tables, and has a burgundy-painted ceiling. Huge oak doors are left open, so a velvet curtain separates inside from out, and a faintly stale smell of tobacco from a different era hangs in the air.

Next to an unplayed piano, a hostess trolley has today's issues of *L'Équipe* and *Le Figaro*, while from behind a small horseshoe-shaped bar a Moroccan waiter named Farid serves healthy measures of Pernod-Ricard and Campari to a couple of portly local men. Anticipating Houllier might like some wine, I ask for a glass of Sauvignon but instead he has a bottle of Evian in a schooner with lime, explaining that he is entertaining his wife Isabelle this evening, having not seen her in eight days.

When speaking of the moment he resigned from Liverpool, allowing Houllier to manage the club alone following five difficult months in a joint role, Roy Evans described his counterpart as 'far cuter than me', nevertheless admitting that maybe Houllier had the tools to advance Liverpool whereas he, ultimately, did not. The next few hours are proof that Houllier is an incredibly intelligent person. He is multilingual, able to switch between languages seamlessly – never to be found searching for the right words and consistently appreciating nuances. He is also passionate, emotional and brooding. To term him as knowledgeable feels like an understatement. His obsession with football – he calls it a 'virus' – irradiates the fug of the Normandy. He speaks with the authority of a lecturer in a university hall.

Rather than waiting for a question to be asked, Houllier moves quickly to remind me about the achievements of the team that he built.

'You see, many people appreciate entertainment but they do not understand pleasure,' he says thoughtfully. 'Life is not just about aesthetics, the arts. It is about foundations and creating something that can last a lifetime. In football, a lifetime is only very short. You have a cycle of three years, then you change, develop and grow again.

'The most important compliment I had was from David Moores after we won the UEFA Cup in 2001,' he continues. 'David said, "Gérard, you have put Liverpool back on the European map. You have also hauled the club into the twenty-first century." When I look back, that's exactly what happened. I think winning the UEFA Cup helped the players believe they could win the Champions League in 2005. They were able to draw on experiences from before. It gave them the appetite and the confidence to compete with the best teams in the world. Before, Liverpool would lose to Strasbourg.'

He moves on to a story from the player he appointed as Liverpool's captain, a platform that enabled him to become a legend.

'Steven Gerrard told me that he believed the experience

of winning the UEFA Cup four years earlier helped Liverpool win the Champions League in 2005. And this is the point. The word help is important. In football, there are always claims that person A or person B was solely responsible for achieving something. Football regularly becomes about the individual. But success is not achieved without a team. It is not achieved without help.

'I would say we changed a lot of things towards the end of the nineties that were very important to the long-term future of Liverpool. David came to see me in Paris, along with Rick Parry and Peter Robinson. They wanted me to join Liverpool for one particular reason. They told me that the club needed to change but it also needed to rediscover the culture of winning trophies – silverware. Rick, particularly, was very clear about that.

'We changed the habits in terms of the way the team prepared and practised. We brought a different attitude to training, demanding that the players looked after themselves in terms of diet. I personally think we also signed a group of players that went on to play together for a long time: players from different countries, different leagues and different attitudes – probably more in tune with what was happening elsewhere in football. This is not a criticism of what happened previously. But sometimes you need to change to evolve.'

Before Houllier, time stood still at Liverpool for nearly forty years. Players would come and go but the methodology remained fundamentally the same as the baton was passed on to different managers. Success meant there was no desire for adjustment. When Graeme Souness, a former European Cup-winning captain with Liverpool, was appointed as Kenny Dalglish's successor in 1991 following unparalleled success at Glasgow Rangers, where he oversaw the modernization of Ibrox, the training ground, diets and squad routines, he met fierce resistance amongst the Liverpool players when he tried to introduce the same ideas at Melwood.

Houllier believes had it not been for Souness's reign, considered disastrous by most supporters, he would not have been in a position to 'help' Liverpool towards the end of the decade.

'As a player, I loved Graeme Souness; he was one of my idols,' Houllier says. 'In France, he was viewed as the ultimate British footballer: physically, technically and tactically very talented. I was aware of his problems as manager at Liverpool because I read books about him when I was appointed. He admitted trying to change things too much, too soon. So I made the decision to change things gradually. Maybe that helped a little bit when I replaced Roy in the middle of the season. As a manager, you learn that it is very important not to break the habits of the players at this time.'

In replacing Souness with Evans, Liverpool returned to tradition. All-time leading goalscorer Ian Rush was allowed to eat his pre-match meal of beans and sausage on toast again (banned by Souness), the players were afforded a greater level of social freedom, while, like before, injuries were treated by Ronnie Moran, who made running repair jobs (Souness had wanted to develop a clinic at Melwood where conditions would be treated properly, but this request was refused by the board).

Meanwhile, at other clubs, nutritionists and conditioning coaches were being employed, squads were becoming fitter and more professional, and young British players were benefiting tactically and technically as well as socially (by not drinking so much) from sage advice delivered by a host of experienced imports. Liverpool were trapped within a Celtic insularity and Evans spoke of not wanting to sign a 'sexy foreigner just for the sake of it'.

Rather than signing one, Evans ended up sharing his job with a foreigner after three successive seasons where Liverpool threatened to engage in a championship race only to puzzlingly fall away in the final months. A perception existed that Evans was too lenient with players and a desire developed to appoint a disciplinarian capable of instilling the organization and forward thought that Souness had dabbled with years earlier.

Few in Britain had heard of Arsène Wenger before he was recruited as Arsenal's manager in 1996. In two seasons, he not only inspired the club to the title, after they had been mid table at his point of arrival, but also transformed the way Arsenal were viewed: from defensive dullards to attacking sensations. Wenger came from France. Liverpool's board began to ask if they could discover someone similar.

Houllier's association with Liverpool began decades before, when he moved to the city in 1969 to work as a teaching assistant at Alsop Comprehensive, a one-time grammar school no more than a mile and a half away from Anfield on the Queens Drive ring road, where Walton becomes Bootle. He also studied, completing a thesis entitled 'Growing Up in a Deprived Area'. It focused on social issues in Toxteth, an area he still refers to as 'Liverpool 8'.

'Liverpool was a port and *the* major trading post in the north of England,' Houllier remembers. 'The port goes into decline and Manchester builds an international airport. A lot of harbour masters and immigrants from the Commonwealth lived in Liverpool 8. There is a struggle and the poverty starts. The identity of the area changes completely and gradually it becomes tougher to live in Liverpool than it was before. By 1970, I think more than 20 per cent of people in Liverpool were unemployed and levels had not been that bad since the 1930s.'

Despite the struggles, Liverpool still had its football. In the 1960s, the teams of Bill Shankly were immortalized, while Harry Catterick's Everton were known as the 'Merseyside Millionaires' because of their spending power. Houllier stood on the terraces of the Kop when Liverpool beat Dundalk 10–0 in a UEFA Cup tie and there with him that night was Patrice Bergues, visiting from France, a friend whom he would eventually lean on as Liverpool's assistant manager. Houllier submersed himself locally by playing centre-forward for one of Alsop's old boys' sides on a Saturday morning in the Zingari League, a competition where only the toughest survived.

After a year, Houllier returned to the farming village of Thérouanne in north-eastern France, where he had grown up as the only son of a farmer who turned to butchery. Houllier saw a future in academia and taught at different primary, secondary and grammar schools before becoming a lecturer in a school of commerce by his mid twenties. He continued to play amateur football with Hucqueliers and then Le Touquet, and enjoyed it so much that when a job as a coach at nearby local club Noeux-les-Mines was advertised in the paper, he decided to abandon the educational path and go for it. 'The virus,' he says, 'was with me. I could not resist.'

Noeux-les-Mines's history was in coal mining. He arrived there in 1976, initially as head coach, and was later appointed manager. In his six years at the club, Houllier – with Bergues playing in midfield – took them from the lower reaches of France's third division to the verge of promotion from the second. It was an astonishing rise and enough to convince first-division Lens that Houllier was capable of taking charge of a bigger club.

There were other coaches around with long careers as professional footballers behind them but Houllier used his inexperience as motivation, compensating for his shortcomings by allowing his raw obsession to take him further. His studious manner meant days were long. For six days a week, he would leave home at 6 a.m. and not return until 11 p.m. at the earliest. Houllier believes the levels of commitment as well as his innovations were the only way to make it possible for a small club like Noeux-les-Mines to compete against those with greater resources, and they also gained him respect amongst his peers.

'There were more opportunities for people like myself and Arsène Wenger to become coaches – why? Because the French FA were very serious about coaching education. This attitude was there in France, Italy, Holland and Germany thirty or even forty years ago but it is a relatively recent phenomenon in England.

'With my background, if I was English, I would not have had a chance at that time. As a player, you have to learn your trade, so why should it be different for coaching and management? Listen, to be a doctor you need seven years. To be an engineer, you need five or six years. To be a teacher, you need time as well. To be a coach, it should be the same. I do not think you need to have been a top player to become a top coach. To be a top jockey, do you need to have been a horse? Of course not.'

In Lens, Houllier took charge of a small-town club that represented another coal-mining community, one that demanded its team match the diehard commitment of the fans. Cries of '*à la mine*' would be screamed at players who did not give 100 per cent and, like Liverpool, Lens was a place not without its social problems, with many of the mines long closed for business.

Under Houllier, though, Lens qualified for the UEFA Cup and recorded two top-seven finishes in three seasons. The success led to an approach from Paris Saint-Germain – the richest club in France – and a year later PSG achieved the first league title in their history. The arrival of Houllier was celebrated as the catalyst and on judgement day he was held aloft by the players inside the Parc des Princes.

Argentine striker Omar da Fonseca, who played under Houllier in Paris before later clinching two titles at Monaco with Wenger in charge, recognizes similarities between the two coaches. He speaks of previous experiences where coaches tended to be former players 'who lived and breathed the game but nothing else'. He describes Houllier and Wenger as having a more 'futuristic approach' than the others. Houllier was good with psychology and particularly impressive when dealing with the media. 'Because of his background and his language ability, he was able to deal with a cross section of players.'

Houllier's time in Paris came to a mutually agreed end after a disappointing 1987–88 campaign, and he joined the French Football Federation, first as a coach before becoming technical director and then Michel Platini's assistant for the 1992 European Championships. When Platini stepped aside following a group-stage exit, the reins passed on to the next man in line. At the age of forty-four, Houllier had taken twenty-two years to propel himself from parks footballer in Liverpool to the most important managerial role in France.

Houllier describes how he made it his 'mission' to see his country qualify for the 1994 World Cup in the United States, and with two games to go all they required was one point each from favourable home fixtures with Israel and Bulgaria. Despite being bottom of the group, Israel sneaked an astonishing 3–2 victory in the Parc des Princes before David Ginola carelessly surrendered possession in the final minute against Bulgaria, enabling Emil Kostadinov to secure an improbable win for the visitors. France were out of the World Cup and in the aftermath Houllier infamously berated Ginola as a 'criminal'. A feud has existed between the pair ever since.

After being replaced by Aimé Jacquet, Houllier returned to the FA and was tasked with the responsibility of reorganizing France's football structure at youth level. In 1996, his side, which included Thierry Henry, David Trezeguet and Nicolas Anelka, beat Spain in the final of the under-18 European Championship. Two years later, the presence of Henry and Trezeguet was crucial as France's senior team lifted the World Cup on home soil.

Liverpool first made informal contact with Houllier about the possibility of taking on a role at Anfield in 1997 – a full twelve months before he was unveiled as joint manager with Roy Evans. Liverpool had gone as close to the title as they would under Evans in the 1996–97 season, eventually finishing in fourth place by virtue of goal difference, having gained the same number of points as Newcastle United in second. Poor defeats towards the end of the campaign undermined Evans' position.

'There was a phone call from Peter Robinson early that summer,' Houllier explains. 'But I was very much involved in the preparation for the World Cup. I couldn't leave. It would have been treason for anyone to walk away from their country at that moment. I would have appeared in France as a traitor.'

Twelve months later, Houllier's contract was up and he decided to try something different. Celtic, having won the Scottish title for the first time in a decade, had spoken to Houllier about replacing Wim Jansen. Sheffield Wednesday had sacked Ron Atkinson and they were even more persuasive. Houllier was tempted by England. 'I loved English football.' He was very close to moving to Hillsborough.

And then Robinson called again, wishing him luck. The pair had kept in regular contact ever since Houllier, like many coaches from the Continent, had visited Anfield to study methods during France's winter break. Arsène Wenger had made the same trip in the mid 1980s when he was at Nancy.

'Peter said to me, "I would like to congratulate you on your move to Sheffield." I was silent. "What, you haven't agreed terms yet?" Peter made his point very quickly. "If you haven't agreed to go to Sheffield, then I would like to speak to you." There were a few issues with my contract in Sheffield, which delayed the appointment. So I said, "Peter, of course I will speak to you." The following day, Peter arrived in Paris with Rick Parry and David Moores. Within ten minutes, we had reached an agreement.'

It was unclear which role Houllier would take at Anfield. Robinson's approach and the hastily arranged meeting in Paris had not been ratified by Liverpool's board. Houllier would potentially become the club's first foreign manager and the first outside appointment since Bill Shankly forty years earlier.

Initially, the board favoured keeping Roy Evans in charge. It was suggested that Houllier should take Ronnie Moran's job as first-team coach. But Robinson felt it would have demeaned Houllier's pedigree. A position as director of football was also put forward but again Robinson believed that Houllier needed to have access to players and be able to instil discipline. In the end, the board agreed to make them joint managers and Houllier says he agreed it was vital that Evans should remain. 'I thought he'd done a good job in the years before. His experience was essential.'

It did not concern Houllier that he had not managed at club level for more than a decade, although he admits it was a different challenge compared to the national team.

'Club [football] is day-to-day involvement – it never stops,' he says. 'With the national team, you have time to form a wider perspective but in that sense building momentum is more difficult. You have less time to prepare your team, so you have to be incisive with every decision. Personally, I prefer being with a club, because there you can build up, develop. I took great enjoyment in seeing players develop both as footballers and as people. With a club, this is possible; you know you are having a serious impact. You can prepare on a short-term and medium-term basis as well as having a long-term vision. With the national team, you prepare for the next game, always.

'When I went to Liverpool, I felt very prepared because I had experienced management at every level, from amateur to international. My time as technical director was very important because it taught me how to step back and look at everything from above. You could not be a coach on the field all of the time. With

France, I prepared a game in a ten-day window. As technical director, I learned how to prepare for the next ten years. I realized I had to win trophies very quickly at Liverpool, because that is the demand. But I realized too it was a long-term job. I realized Liverpool needed somebody to oversee everything.'

Four months after arriving at Anfield, results were not good and the squad was confused by the arrangement in the dugout. While the old players turned to Evans, the new deferred to Houllier. The relationship was dysfunctional and Houllier suggested at a board meeting he would agree to Evans finishing the campaign in sole charge before handing over the reins to Houllier, providing the desire was there.

'It did not work because we had different opinions on how the team should prepare and maybe how players conducted themselves,' Houllier explains. 'I was the hard one and Roy was the easier one. We'd put a session on and some players would say, "Roy, I'm staying in the gym . . ." It didn't work, anyway. It worked at the beginning. But soon it did not. Picking the team was not the main problem.

'I went to speak to the people. I said, "It's Roy's team." If Liverpool still wanted me in the summer, I would come back. But Rick Parry stepped forward and made a point about how the players would feel like they were the rulers if that happened.'

At this point, the influence of Tom Saunders, the conduit between the boardroom and Melwood, was significant.

'He was fantastic,' Houllier says. 'If you ask Phil

Thompson, he will tell you. Tom was always supportive, always there having a nice word – a lot of wisdom. During one board meeting, he stood up and said, "Mr Houllier, we recognize we are not yet the best team in the world. But we have trust in you. We are patient people. Do what you have to do – do what is good for the club. We will support you." I left that meeting knowing I could now do what was necessary to change Liverpool – and with the confidence to see it through.'

Houllier takes his time to outline the task he faced.

'The role of the Liverpool manager was threefold. The number-one mission: get results, get trophies. Rick Parry, I asked him, "What do you want me to achieve?" He told me Liverpool had a silverware tradition and that must be upheld.

'The second thing, I would say, was to leave a legacy. When I left, I don't think anyone could argue [that he'd not achieved that]. Some managers don't think like this. Sam Allardyce, for instance, he buys, he buys, he buys. You have [Youri] Djorkaeff and so on. Players are [aged] 34–35. Then he leaves and what happens? Nothing is left. We signed players for the long term: Hyypiä, Henchoz, Hamann. We used young British players. I think the best way is to leave behind a way of thinking and put the club one step forward, where everybody contributes. Because of your style, your management and your personality, you can leave an imprint on the club. We improved Anfield, we built a different Melwood and, as David Moores said, we took Liverpool into the twenty-first century. The players we had were not all old at the same time.

'Then the last mission is to make your players progress. I would say Carragher progressed. I would say Murphy became a better player. I had to put him on loan at Crewe to learn a different way and come back with different values. Michael [Owen] became Ballon d'Or. Hyypiä – nobody knew him before. And Heskey, nobody believed in him but I did. If he had had more belief in himself, he could have achieved more. Sometimes you do not succeed absolutely with everybody. Robbie [Fowler] had some good times and bad times. When I look back, I think we did OK. Six trophies in five years is pretty healthy.'

When Houllier arrived at Liverpool as joint manager with Roy Evans in the summer of 1998, he describes the squad as 'talented but underachieving', with a defence that was 'a bit too weak'.

'We had a good striking force with Robbie, Michael Owen and Steve McManaman, although I knew quickly that Steve was going to leave us for Real Madrid,' he says.

The problems at Liverpool were deeper than anyone on the outside really appreciated. This was a dressing room led by Paul Ince, who called himself the 'Guv'nor'. When Houllier quickly arrived at the conclusion that Ince should be sold, he received a call from Alex Ferguson – who had made the same decision at Manchester United three years earlier. Ferguson told Houllier it would prove to be one of his best judgements as Liverpool manager.

'It is a very difficult decision to get rid of the captain,' Houllier insists. 'In the long term, it proved to be an important call. Why? When I got rid of Paul Ince, then

142

Steven Gerrard, Michael Owen, Jamie Carragher, Danny Murphy and David Thompson, they all blossomed. Paul was a huge player and a fantastic player. I liked him a lot. He was captain of the national team and captain of Liverpool. Why did I get rid of him? Because I felt the other younger players needed to be able to breathe. Paul was the organizer of the social occasions. There were parties, not just ones arranged by him. I wanted this to stop and for the players to focus.'

It was clear that Ince's time at Liverpool was at an end a few days after a defeat to Manchester United in the FA Cup following two late goals. Liverpool had led from the third minute when Michael Owen scored. It was two months into Houllier's reign as sole manager and Liverpool had defended as well as they had done in an away game in the years before to hold on to the lead. In the seventy-first minute, Ince signalled that he needed to be substituted.

'We were close to knocking United out,' Houllier remembers. 'It would have been a huge result for us. They eventually went on to win the treble, so historically we know how important these moments are. Paul said he had a strain. He walked off the pitch. I thought, *Wait – you're captain of Liverpool. You are 1–0 up at Old Trafford against your former club*. If the captain of Liverpool leaves in that sort of game, he only goes straight to hospital. A few days later, Paul was training again.'

At a team meeting, Ince told Houllier in front of the rest of the group that training needed to be more focused on attacking. Houllier saw this as a challenge to his authority. It was true that Liverpool had struggled for goals in the months since he became manager but defensively the team were conceding fewer. Houllier considered this more important.

'I implemented training sessions aimed at helping the tactical relationships between defence, midfield and attack. That was my coaching. But in the five-a-sides, I'd stand back and watch what was happening. I kept all of the results from the five-a-side matches, knowing which players had won and which players had not. Paul enjoyed the five-a-side matches. But he was not winning. So when Paul was unhappy about the amount of attacking work, I reminded him in front of the group that in the sixty or so five-a-side matches that had taken place in the months before, he'd only been on the winning team something like five times. And that was the end of the discussion.'

Houllier liked the characteristics of English players, however. 'First, they fight harder,' he says. 'They really have a great desire for their team, their club. They are very competitive.

'Second, they are loyal: loyal to their manager, loyal to their teammates. They are straightforward. They tell you the truth and they don't cheat. They have a huge respect for the hierarchy: the boss is the boss.'

Yet at Liverpool, the players had too much power and when the power is with the players, Houllier believes there is also unrealistic expectation.

'The pressure comes from the discrepancy between the team's potential and what they can really do. When I came to the club, I had Babb, Harkness, McAteer . . .

you name them. We bought Hamann, Henchoz, Hyypiä. For the cohesion of the team and the club, you need to stay together for a minimum of three years. I was given that opportunity. I arrived in 1998 and in 2001 we won five trophies.'

Jamie Carragher says Houllier possessed an English attitude when it came to the way he wanted Liverpool to play. Houllier stresses, though, that he did not want to change too much, too soon.

'I am not a great believer in revolution despite the fact I am French! I prefer slight reforms, convincing people to change. I did this with Carra and Danny Murphy particularly. They had a wild side. They listened. Both of them took the right turn, learning from the senior international foreign players like Hyypiä, who was very important. Jamie Redknapp was also a good player but was injured. There were a few problems with Robbie Fowler and I wish I'd known him two or three years before, when he was at his peak.'

Houllier says he 'reached' for the young local players he thought had the mentality to deal with the pressures of being a footballer in the twenty-first century. He explains, for example, that he gave Fowler and David Thompson 'many chances to get it right'. Eventually, though, both were sold.

He speaks about Jamie Carragher like an adopted son.

'Jamie was clever in reading the game and learning from his experiences, both good and bad. He played in several positions: central-midfield then left-back and right-back. Maybe he wanted to play in one position but

he never let that desire get in the way of his performances. He was patient with himself and patient with me.
We had Henchoz and Hyypiä in central-defence and that
is, of course, the position where Carra ended up. But I
explained to him from the beginning that I saw him as a
player who would evolve and find himself. In France, we
had [Patrick] Battiston and [Maxime] Bossis, and Carra
was like them. They started their careers at full-back and
eventually became the main centre-back. The experience
in the early years gave them a different perspective of the
game. They were faced with different situations. I would
say that to be a full-back you need to be a better player
than a centre-back in possession of the ball. Carra never
got the credit he deserved for his football ability. He was
an excellent passer of the ball and rarely gave it away.
I remember many games and many goals where he was
there at the start of the build-up.

'Carra is a highly competitive person. In terms of
wanting to win, he was Luis Fernández. Sometimes you
get players with talent but they do not get as far in their
careers because of a lackadaisical attitude. Carra probably had less talent than some. But it was his attitude
that determined his life. Talent is nothing without
professionalism: doing things the right way and managing details.

'That was a big challenge for me generally. Convincing
players that talent is one thing, but the way they work
and practise will help them blossom. I personally believe
Carra is the best example of this: maybe not so talented
but so determined, so engaged, so competitive, so hard
working and team-thinking.

'His fear drove him on. Some players have a fear of not being up to the task but they are able to turn it into a positive. Don't get me wrong, Carra was very confident and I liked that. Michael Owen was the same. Stevie – he was a bit afraid at the beginning but quickly became confident. In fact, the manager can often be the confidence builder and breaker for the player. But only the player can internalize the balance. It's very difficult to find someone who can mix fear and confidence as well as humility and ambition. Above everything, if you fail to prepare – well, you know the Scout saying. It is one of life's truths.'

He had not even heard of Steven Gerrard when he arrived at Liverpool but within a few weeks of Roy Evans' departure, Houllier rewarded his 'aggressive' perform- ances in the youth sides with a first-team debut.

'Every manager has his own philosophy. I liked to use wide players but those with experience of playing in-field. I realized the team needed to be more solid. Central-midfielders understand the demands of each position because they are in the middle of everything that happens. They receive the ball from the goalkeeper, the central-defender or the full-back and then release it wide, forwards or backwards again. So they have a better tactical appreciation of each position.

'I was looking for somebody to play on the right. Steve Heighway said to me, "Maybe I have an answer to your problems." He said I should go to the academy to watch a youth game. The game was against Blackburn, I think. I had seen the player in a practice match at Melwood but you can only tell in the real games when the competition is fierce. After five minutes, I knew that the player would not fit. His name was Richie Partridge. But in the middle of the park there was this guy shouting at others, tackling hard and passing the ball fiercely long and short. He was quick and he could read the game. He was really making an impact. So I asked who he was and they told me he was an under-18. He was just helping out because there had been injuries. So I said, "Maybe I'll stay." In the second half it was the same. He was ruling the place, controlling the pace of the game, you know? He had not long turned eighteen and was nearly two years behind most players. At the end of the game, I spoke to him. "What is your name?" I asked. He told me he was Steven Gerrard. I said, "Tomorrow you train with the professionals at Melwood." He was a bit nervous and told me a programme had already been set up for him at the academy the following day. "No, Steven, you are with us now."

'The next morning, there was a challenge to be won in midfield during a training session. Steven Gerrard beat Paul Ince. I said to Patrice, "This boy is ready."'

Gerrard's body was not yet accustomed to the demands of professionalism, however.

'Mentally, he was one of the strongest boys I have ever known. But he wasn't able to train because he was injured a lot. They couldn't find the cause and this frustrated me. If you can't train, you cannot prepare for the job. You have to be able to respond to seventy games a season. I had this in mind for Steven because his potential was massive. But the injuries, the strains – they would not stop.'

Houllier organized for Gerrard to be treated by a team of external physiotherapists in France.

'The biggest problem was, some people did not believe in him because of the injuries. This is the truth. There was a feeling at Liverpool before that if you suffered from injuries, you would not become a player. But I realized his potential. He excited me. Stevie's body was growing, growing and growing. He needed time. And I gave him time.'

Before Houllier settled on the cheaper option of Sami Hyypiä and Stéphane Henchoz, he wanted to install a young British pairing at centre-back.

'Sol Campbell was one idea and Rio Ferdinand was outstanding too. I liked Ferdinand a lot. He was a very modern defender, able to build possession from his touch. He was a defender too and sometimes people forget that. But I had £12 million to spend and I needed to reconstruct the defence with that money. Ferdinand was the first one I thought of. He was eighteen years old. And the price was £12.5 million. I needed two [centre-halves], not one.

'It is thanks to Peter Robinson that I found Hyypiä at Willem II. He had a friend who worked for a TV crew covering European football. A lot of times, he was in Holland. He told Peter there was a good centre-back. My initial reaction was to tell Peter that if there was a good centre-back, Ajax, PSV Eindhoven or Feyenoord would have taken him. I was reluctant. It was only because I could not find what I wanted that I went to see this player. After fifteen minutes, I knew I would take him. I could see that he could defend and play; he passed the ball very confidently. I could not believe that nobody else had signed Hyypiä.

'Henchoz was at Blackburn. Roy Hodgson is a friend of mine and he was their manager. I went to Blackburn and every time I liked him [Henchoz]. He was stubborn and always seemed to be in the right place. In the end, Hyypiä cost around £2 million and Henchoz was £3.5 million. We had money left to buy Hamann. And this was the base of the team for the next few years.'

Houllier used the history of Liverpool as a bargaining tool with higher-profile targets.

'Liverpool is known for two reasons: the Beatles and the football club. It has a special resonance in peoples' minds. It represents magic. Liverpool remains a big hit in terms of its culture, its history and personality, as well as the warmth of the town. We managed to sign Markus Babbel and lots of clubs wanted to sign him. The competition was fierce. I convinced Babbel that in a short period of time, we would win trophies. I convinced him that winning trophies at Liverpool would mean more than it might at other clubs because when you win something for Liverpool, the people, they remember you for ever.'

Financially, he felt backed by the club's board 'up to a certain level'.

'We were not as rich as the others,' he says. 'But I realized Liverpool never had been. The idea always was to buy young players and develop them. I think John Arne Riise was a good example of this. We bought him for a small fee, had his best years – under Benítez as well – then the club sold him to Roma for a higher fee. This was our game. Other clubs could afford mistakes and it would not matter too much. When we made a mistake – and there were some – it mattered more.'

Liverpool were widely considered to be a flaky team under Roy Evans. Two years into Houllier's reign, the reputation shifted. Liverpool became obdurate and horrible to play against.

'When you are a manager, you should always ask yourself: what is going to hurt your opponents?' Houllier says. 'I knew Roma, for example, could hurt us because they were a very good team. You try to stop that. But you also know they have weaknesses in areas where we are strong. I thought about the weaknesses and flaws of every team we played against and sometimes our team selection would reflect that. This idea was new to Liverpool, because previously it had been the same team week in, week out. It took people time to understand that rotation was needed. We achieved some great results this way: a 0–0 in Barcelona, for example, where Emile played on the left and Michael up front on his own. We were criticized for being defensive after the game and I could not believe it. It made me even more determined to win the second leg, which we did 1–0 [thanks to a Gary McAllister penalty]. People remember the second leg because of the atmosphere inside Anfield. But for me, the impact of the first leg was more important. It said to Barcelona, "This Liverpool team will not concede goals, even in the Nou Camp." Psychologically, it was damaging for them and brilliant for us.'

Houllier uses five words to describe the 2000–01 squad that achieved an unprecedented cup treble and qualified for the Champions League for the first time since its inception by finishing third in the league. He also reminds me that by winning the UEFA Cup, he is one of only two Frenchmen to lift a European trophy as manager – the other being Luis Fernández in 1996 when he led Paris Saint-Germain to the Cup Winners' Cup. (Though Zinedine Zidane became the third in 2016 through his Champions League success with Real Madrid.)

'My players were generous, talented, believing, ambitious and resilient,' he says. 'They used to enjoy themselves. In training, you could feel the camaraderie. A good atmosphere developed very quickly. There was pleasure and performance.'

When he became Liverpool's manager, the club could afford to appoint different coaches who specialized in fitness, goalkeeping, defending and attacking.

'Before training, I would hold a meeting and tell all of my coaches what I wanted,' Houllier adds. 'I would then watch what was happening and only get involved when there needed to be an intervention tactically.'

Yet, the responsibility of leading the club took over his life. It was part of the job description to be obsessed, to treat it as a 'mission'.

'Yes, you have to be 150 per cent focused,' he continues. 'It's not a job; in fact, it's a mission. There are times when you lose and you have to try to show you are not affected. You have lost? OK, next game. Don't waste your time and your energy on what went wrong. It sends out the wrong message. Some managers watch videos. But I had faith in my players. I liked to use video more to show what the players had done right rather than what they had done wrong. You cannot do anything about the past.

'There are times when you need to recharge the battery and do something different, whether that's going for a meal with some friends or going to the cinema. But you can't have much of that. On the outside, people see the end of the season as a time when football shuts down. Managers do not.

'I remember a quote from Bill Shankly about the most important day in a manager's year being the day after a season has finished. Everybody else at the club goes on a break. But you don't. You are preparing again for the next challenge. You have to put the season in the past, learn lessons from what went wrong and get on to the next stage. I'd always done that. This is the most important time. You have to change the team. And success – to a large degree – is determined by the players you sign and the players you sell. So there is no time to relax.'

Houllier is adamant that it was genetics – thin arteries run in his family – rather than stress that caused him to suffer from high blood pressure, contributing towards him being rushed to hospital at half-time of the game between Liverpool and Leeds at Anfield in October 2001 with chest pains.

During a busy summer, where he was again active in the transfer market, Houllier had not taken a rest before the start of a season where Liverpool won the Charity Shield and the European Super Cup, before starting well in the league. Normally, he'd take a short break in the first week of September when most of the players were on international duty. Instead, he went scouting, back to France, where he watched Anthony Le Tallec and Florent Sinama Pongolle: players he would later sign from Le Havre.

He did not know what was happening when the chest pains began during the game against Leeds.

'It happened at half-time. If it had happened at the end of the game, I would not be here now talking to you,' he says starkly. 'At full time there was unbelievable traffic around Anfield and the ambulance would not have got through. At half-time, this was not the case. I was very lucky.

'I thought I had the flu. I wanted to have some vitamins and return to the game. But Dr Waller, the club doctor, stopped me. He was very insistent. He knew me. He wanted to take my blood pressure and quickly decided we should go to the hospital. After that, it was a matter of luck. There are only three cardio specialist hospitals in England and one of them is in Broadgreen, just a few miles away. The traffic meant we were there in less than ten minutes.

'Again there was more luck. The surgeon who usually operates on such illnesses was meant to be spending the weekend taking his daughter to Leeds. Instead, because he was tired, he stayed in Liverpool. So he was close by – a succession of lucky moments.'

Houllier immediately underwent an operation to repair his aorta. It was a procedure that was expected to last nine hours but stretched to eleven and a half. It was uncertain whether he would live.

'Again, the next day the team was flying out to Kiev for

a Champions League match. Imagine if it had happened on the plane. I would have died.'

During his three-week stay in hospital, he was up on his feet and walking around, and he had a television installed in his room so he could keep up to date with the latest football news.

Phil Thompson soon started advising him on team selection and other issues. He insisted Rick Parry keep him abreast of important football-related developments. In December and January, Houllier was involved in the signings of Abel Xavier and Nicolas Anelka. While Houllier was convalescing, Anelka flew to Corsica to meet him.

David O'Leary, the Leeds manager, regularly received calls from Houllier, often at curious hours. O'Leary described him as a 'night owl, working away at night'. O'Leary later publicly suggested Houllier should quit football management. 'I've told him,' he said, 'this job isn't conducive to coming back after an operation he's had.' At the Liverpool Echo Sports Personality of the Year dinner, Houllier told the audience there were people who thought he should forget about football entirely. He then added, pertinently, 'Maybe I should forget about breathing.'

Doctors had told Houllier that he should take eleven to twelve months off work. Instead he officially returned in less than five. He was fifty-four years old.

'We needed to beat Roma 2–0 at home. In my place, Phil [Thompson] had done a fantastic job. I asked him whether he thought my presence for this game would help – maybe bring something that people did not expect.

155

So I told nobody. I did not want the press to focus on me before; I did not want the players to be distracted.'

When a frail-looking Houllier appeared in the dugout moments before kick-off, the roar seemed to emerge from the guts of each Anfield stand.

'We won 2–0,' he smiles. 'I have spoken to Fabio Capello [the Roma manager] since and he told me that when he saw me, he realized Liverpool would win. The reaction from the players was spectacular.'

In the short term, Houllier had chosen his moment well. And yet history suggests he came back too soon. The first sign of his judgement not being quite what it was came in the Champions League quarter-final when Liverpool were defending an aggregate lead in the second leg against Bayer Leverkusen, only to decide to replace the defensive-minded Didi Hamann for Vladimir Šmicer, an attacking midfielder. The result was a 4–2 defeat.

'I tried something different to try to upset the opponent,' Houllier reasons. 'We'd have played Manchester United in the semi-final. It would have been more of a problem for them than it would for us.'

He mentions again that success in football is often determined by recruitment and sales, and it is particularly important to get the timing right. Before Houllier's illness, his record was strong in this field. Afterwards, it was not. Houllier reasons that his judgement had not abandoned him but flexibility had. He was on strict instructions to rest more frequently and rather than flying somewhere in Europe to watch a target immediately after a Liverpool match, he would go home to Sefton Park and spend the evening with his wife Isabelle instead.

'The initial decision was mine: which type of player we needed and in which position. The scout would provide a list, maybe with some new names. We saw the player several times and then sent different scouts. We'd enquire discreetly about personality. "Is he a team-thinking player or too individualistic? Does he work hard in training?" You have to be careful. We were misled with two or three players. You buy a player and learn when he arrives that he likes to go to nightclubs. You have to take advice from the right people, of course, but ultimately as the manager you are accountable. If the player fails, it should be your responsibility. It's your call. I always made the last call.'

Towards the end of the 2001–02 season and into that summer, Houllier was told he must rest rather than devote the amount of time that he had to recruitment in the years before his illness. He is talking about record signing El Hadji Diouf, Senegalese compatriot Salif Diao and French midfielder Bruno Cheyrou when he mentions players that later 'did not lift the team to expected levels'. Houllier admits relying on the opinion of Patrice Bergues, who had been Diouf's manager at Lens, when he recommended the forward. 'We could have done better,' he admits.

Houllier had taken Nicolas Anelka on loan from Paris Saint-Germain in December 2001. In spite of Anelka's chequered past, when he had supposedly struggled to fit in to the social structures at Arsenal and Real Madrid, there were no reports of problems in relation to Anelka's behaviour at Melwood before Houllier decided a permanent deal was not going to happen, choosing to sign Diouf instead.

'First of all, it was a good idea to sign Anelka – to help us finish the season before,' he begins to explain. 'I didn't keep him because his representatives were very unfair to Liverpool as a club. We'd resurrected his career.'

Houllier's friendship with Laurent Perpère, the Paris Saint-Germain president, had led to a compromise between the clubs over a transfer fee. That prompted Liverpool to deal with Anelka's financial adviser and the meetings, though intense, went reasonably well. Liverpool soon suspected, though, that someone, somewhere was negotiating with other clubs on Anelka's behalf.

Houllier explains what happened next: 'They wanted so much money it would have raised a problem within the changing room in terms of the wages he was earning. So we told them we couldn't go that far. We managed to reach a compromise. But then I heard there was a chance he would go back to Arsenal. At the same time, he was negotiating with Manchester City and this, I believe, was an attempt to drive up interest, create a competition and increase his earnings. I felt that I was not going to win. I feared that if I kept him and he did well, there would be another round of negotiations soon after to try to increase the value of his contract. If he was unhappy, he might try to leave for another club. The process had taken too long and, ultimately, it did not deserve the energy.

'I was right about Anelka because he's had half a dozen clubs after leaving Liverpool. He's moved around too much. Other managers had the same problems. At least I had the courage to withstand the pressure of those representing him. From a football point of view, it would have been interesting to keep him. He was gifted. But from the club's point of view, it was a danger. As a manager, I thought about the club and the stability of the dressing room.'

Diouf struggled for goals, was shunted out on the right wing and was banned for spitting at a Celtic supporter during his first season as a Liverpool player, with Houllier warning him at the time that 'the stigma of what you did will follow you around for the rest of your career'.

Jamie Carragher said that in Diouf's first week training at Melwood, he realized the player did not possess the speed to be a success in the Premier League. Houllier cites a different issue.

'Diouf should have worked but did not,' he insists. 'The top of the roof is mental. You build the house: physically, technically and tactically; Diouf, he understood tactics. But you are half the player without the right mentality. Stevie and Carra – they had the roof.'

During his last two seasons in charge, the tide of opinion turned against Houllier. It became public knowledge that criticism from former players at this time cut him deeply, though he also mentions several names who had condemned his team long before – even when results were good. Ian St John, who had been one of Bill Shankly's players, was one of them, snappily referring to Houllier as 'the Frenchman' when working as a radio commentator.

'There are things you can control in life and things

you cannot control. If asked now, maybe I will say that I paid too much attention to things I could not control. Sometimes I was hurt because it was coming from former players. Even Carra said to me, "Why are they always having a go at us?" We were doing our best for the club and I felt they should have been more supportive. You cannot control the wind, the rain or the state of the pitch when you play away. You cannot control the referee – there is no point trying to change his decisions. You cannot control what is in the press. Everybody is entitled to have an opinion, even if it is not the right opinion and it hurts. You need to live with a thick skin sometimes. But what you can control is the way you are going to react – the way you take it; the way you hold your composure rather than being impulsive.

'We were labelled a defensive team and when you have a label, it is difficult to shake. In 2000–01 we scored 127 goals. I think only two Liverpool teams have scored more goals in one season. And you don't win anything without a good goalkeeper, a good defence and a good striker. On the pitch, at least, it is as easy as that.

'The next year we finished ahead of Manchester United and with eighty points. In the previous decade, Liverpool had not finished ahead of Manchester United, so when that happens you'd expect to win the title. Unfortunately, that year Arsenal went on an incredible run. Still the criticism came from the same people. They were waiting when the results were not quite as good.'

The player Houllier really wishes he'd signed was goalkeeper Edwin van der Sar, who was given a tour of Melwood only to agree to join Fulham. Jens Lehmann was his second choice that summer and was close to being bought from Borussia Dortmund along with Tomáš Rosický. Both would later sign for Arsenal.

As we finished our initial summit at the Normandy, Houllier invited me to meet him the next day in his office. When I arrive, he is thinking about the changes that have happened in management and football.

'The game is younger: the players are younger, the coaches are younger, the people in key administrative roles are younger,' he says. 'With youth, you have energy. People will commit their lives to the quest to become greater. From my own experience, I know it is good sometimes to step back and watch. When you do that, you see details: the attitude of the players, the way they react when they lose the ball. By stepping back, you see their form. When you stand in the middle telling everybody what to do all of the time, you gain control but you lose perspective.

'Players need tough love,' he continues. 'It is important to be accessible. Players should feel like you are approachable at all times. I remember taking calls at 7 a.m. Their problems became mine. As a manager, you make decisions but you also need to appreciate the human impact of those decisions. You should explain them. For that, you receive the respect.'

Houllier stops to consider the number of trophies Liverpool have won since his departure in 2004. There have been three in eleven years, a Champions League and FA Cup being delivered by his successor, Rafael Benítez. Houllier won six in five years. 'So we didn't do too badly.'

History, indeed, should reflect better on his reign. Bill Shankly took charge of Liverpool in 1959 – twelve years after Liverpool's last league title, a period where nothing was won in between. When Houllier was appointed, eight years had passed since the last championship. Although he achieved more silverware than Shankly in a shorter period of time, Liverpool were further away from the title at the point of his departure than they were when he arrived. I ask Houllier what might have happened had it not been for his illness. He seems reluctant to think about it. It seems to frustrate him. He prefers to reflect on the legacy he left behind. He takes me back to the day he arrived at Anfield as manager.

'Look at Shankly; Shankly goes, who comes? Paisley. Paisley goes, then it's his assistant, Fagan. Fagan goes; Dalglish. Dalglish goes; Souness. Then Roy Evans. I could understand the headlines "GÉRARD WHO?" But the most important thing in any managerial reign is to consider how you leave a club, what shape it is in then. That is more important than what it is like when you arrive. I thought about this a lot at the beginning. They [the supporters] will always remember you if you leave a legacy. I can confidently say I left a legacy for Benítez.

'Number one: me being there before broke from the tradition of the Boot Room. It proved there was another way.

'Number two: Benítez had a team, one that won the Champions League. Twelve of those players were with me the year before.

'Number three: I also left with the team in the Champions League. If we had not finished in the top four in 2003–04, Benítez would not have featured in the Champions League the following year. Also, he had new facilities and a set-up that was Continental in its standard compared to the way it was before I went there.

'All of this, it makes me happy. Had it not been for my illness, would Liverpool have won the league? I wish I knew for certain.'

CHAPTER FIVE

cultzeros.co.uk

NEIL MELLOR,
Kirkby Graduate

NEIL MELLOR WAS TWENTY-NINE YEARS OLD WHEN HIS football career was terminated while playing for Preston North End down in the third tier of English football. He fell unchallenged, his knee buckling, never to recover.

Mellor's manager at Preston was Graham Westley, who infamously once delivered bad news to his players via text message at nearly two in the morning: who was dropped, who was training away from the main squad. Westley was the only manager, indeed, that Mellor encountered who had never operated at the very top level of the game.

'It was a very different regime to what I had seen or experienced before,' Mellor recalls. 'Let's just say I wasn't enjoying it. It was the harsh reality of where I ended up.'

However, Mellor also describes Preston as his 'happiest time', when Alan Irvine was in charge and the spirit amongst the squad reminded him of the early days at Liverpool's academy.

'Loved Alan – loved him,' Mellor says, admitting that most players will speak well of the managers they thrived under. 'On that basis, what would I say about Gérard Houllier?' he asks, pausing. 'Nice enough man, never really made me feel wanted.' And Rafael Benítez? 'Very straightforward, maybe too straightforward for some. I knew where I stood.'

Mellor scored goals in a League Cup semi-final, a last-minute winner against the Premier League champions, Arsenal, and then tipped a crucial Champions League tie in Liverpool's favour when all hope had previously seemed lost. He delivered on big occasions. When he closes his eyes and thinks about it, he can still hear the noise of the Kop when his shot raced past Arsenal's Jens Lehmann from thirty yards; he can see the blur of colour in the celebrations seconds later as he stood with his arms wide open as if he belonged there, with masses of joyous people jumping around and cheering in front of him.

And yet he became a player known for moments rather than matches, featuring in just twenty-two games for Liverpool, many of them in a period when he tried to ignore agonizing knee pain in an attempt to prove himself to Benítez because, aged twenty-two, he felt it was his last chance to become a regular feature in Liverpool's team.

Mellor does not want to make what happened thereafter sound like a hard-luck story. Yet misfortune is at the core of his journey. There is also a prevailing sense that his emergence came at the wrong time: when Liverpool were flush with strikers, when more and more money was being spent on young foreign talent, when the lines of communication between Melwood and the club's academy were not as open as they had been in the past.

'I was a goalscorer and some would say I was little else,' he reasons. 'Fair enough – there were some days where I'd be quiet, where I wouldn't be involved in the game at all. Of course there were areas that needed improving. Goalscoring, though, you can't teach it. You either have that killer instinct or you don't. I was a bit old-fashioned like that. I sometimes wonder whether I was the right player, at the right club, in the wrong decade. Managers at the top level wanted more than goalscoring from their strikers. Thierry Henry transformed the way football was viewed and played.'

If the Mellor family had a business, it was football. Father Ian's professional career was almost at an end when Neil was born in 1982.

'I never got to see him play but my dad was a huge influence. He'd experienced professional football. He kept my feet on the ground. Throughout my youth, I was the standout player, playing two years above my age group and always scoring goals, hitting great figures. His message to me was consistent: "Listen, until you play a hundred games for the first team, wherever that may be, you're not a footballer." Fair enough, I was doing well, but until that happened there was a lot to do. It made me more determined and kept me hungry. I was desperate to reach that figure of one hundred games and hear my dad say, "You've made it, son."'

Ian Mellor scored for Sheffield Wednesday in a 4–0 thrashing of city rivals, United.

'I grew up being reminded of that most days in my childhood by Wednesday supporters: "Your dad – what he did in the Boxing Day Massacre . . ." as the game became known. "Can I just shake your hand?"

'That happened in 1979 and people still talk about it now. I suppose there are similarities between me and my dad in that we are remembered for particular moments: mine came against Arsenal and his in the Sheffield derby. When I spent a season on loan at Wednesday, people still wanted to talk about it. The fans have never forgotten.'

There are other parallels between the careers of father and son.

'Perhaps neither of us really fulfilled our potential,' Neil admits. 'We were both let go by Manchester City when we didn't want to leave. He got moved on against the wishes of the manager, Malcolm Allison, who resigned off the back of the decision by the board, so my dad says. Allison was a big manager for City. He was in hospital and when he came out my dad had been sold. Allison was furious.

'My dad scored goals for City. He tells me about one at Highbury against Arsenal which flew into the top corner. He made his debut in '69 and played with some of the greats: Franny Lee, Colin Bell and Rodney Marsh. City were a good side then. He scored for City against Valencia in Europe too.'

Ian Mellor moved around all the leagues, from City to Norwich to Brighton, Chester City, Sheffield Wednesday and Bradford. Financially, a career in football did not set him up for life.

'When he finished playing, he had to sign on. He stood in the dole queue in Sheffield, where we lived in the early days, and someone goes, "Why are you here?"

'"Cos I've got no money!"

'Fans couldn't believe this was the reality for a professional footballer. There was no money back then. It was a struggle bringing up four kids. Holidays? I didn't go abroad until I was nine or ten. It was tough for my mum and dad. He eventually got a job with Puma and kept himself ticking over that way. My parents would take turns: my dad would come back from work and then my mum would go out and do part-time stuff wherever she could find it.

'I have an older brother, Simon, and I think being around older kids made me develop as a footballer a lot quicker,' Mellor continues. 'Simon is eight years my senior. I was best man for his wedding and he was best man for mine. We're best mates now but back at the beginning he must have seen me as a pest – asking to play footy with his mates all of the time. Even though I was so much younger, I was scoring goals, putting them in the top bin on the park. Being in that environment toughened me up.

'I think my dad learned some lessons raising Simon before me too. Simon will admit that he didn't have the football talent I had but my dad pushed him. Later, he laid off on me, took a back seat. The other dads, they'd go mad at their kids if they played badly. I think mine learned to be quiet and let me make my own mistakes.

'I loved football so much from a young age. I got an indescribable buzz whether it was scoring goals for my local team, Priory, or my school. I just loved sticking the ball in the back of the net. I used to say that I didn't care where I played, as long as I became a professional footballer. If it wasn't as a forward, full-back or midfield would do. I feel fortunate that I was good enough to always play in the position I enjoyed the most.'

The Mellors moved to the Cheshire town of Sale near Manchester when Neil was five years old.

'Around the house, we had lots of photographs from my dad's playing career. I had the bug of wanting to be a professional footballer. I was desperate to follow in his footsteps. People would say, "What happens if you don't become a footballer?" I couldn't tell them. It was the only passion I had. Academically, I was bright. I never finished bottom of the class. I had a reasonable focus. But I only wanted to be a footballer.'

Manchester City became Neil's club.

'Simon supports Sheffield Wednesday because he saw my dad play there. But it was always about City for me, even though they were awful. It was around the period in the mid to late 1990s when they dropped into the Third Division – utterly depressing times.

'Shaun Goater was my hero because of how he scored goals. Technically, he wasn't a great player. But he was always in the right place. That was a gift. I admired Alan Shearer from a distance. Going to watch City, though, I expected to see Goater score. I loved the feeling of me potentially being that player, imagining someone else coming to a game and expecting me to score. Everyone would walk away and go, "Goater – he didn't play well but he scored." I was similar.

'I was a ball boy at Maine Road for a couple of seasons. I was there the day City got relegated from the Premier League, believing a draw with Liverpool was enough to stay up. It was bizarre because the rumour went round we were safe. It was my job to go and get one of the corner flags by the away end and run into the tunnel. The despair was terrible. How could City get relegated? There were lots of tears, not just me – from players as well. It was a surreal day.'

Mellor was integrated into City's youth system aged ten.

'The training centre was at Platt Lane in Moss Side and the standard was really high,' Mellor remembers. 'Phil Jagielka [who became Everton's captain] was there. So was Joey Barton, who was on a month-to-month contract. If I'm being honest, I didn't think Joey would have a long career in football. He wasn't very good compared to the others. But he had a desire to make it, which pushed him further. He's had a really good career towards the high end of the game.'

Mellor was the top scorer for six successive seasons in

his age group at City. He explains his release at sixteen as a consequence of internal politics.

'I was never given a proper explanation by the two fellas in charge, Alex Gibson and Jim Cassell. I was devastated; my entire life felt over. Six new lads had started training with us: three from Everton and another three from Ireland. I got the impression their presence had to be justified in some way. Why would any club reject their leading scorer? I still can't work it out. I went through the gates for the last time at Platt Lane crying my eyes out. I thought my dream was over.'

Five goals in a game for England schoolboys against an academy side from Bolton Wanderers alerted Liverpool scout John Rock.

'In my first trial game at the academy in Kirkby, I scored the winner for the under-16s against United and that helped a lot. Rick Parry was Liverpool's chief executive and I came on as a sub for his son, Jamie. Then in my second game, I got a hat-trick against Newcastle.'

Steve Heighway, Liverpool's academy director, invited Mellor into his office.

'He said to me, "Neil, you're raw, but we'll give you a three-year contract." Over the next week, United, Blackburn and City – bizarrely – got back in touch, all of them offering me deals. I think City realized it would look bad for them if they released their leading scorer and he went on to score goals at Liverpool – a bigger club. As far as I was concerned, Liverpool were the first to have some faith in me when I was down. I wanted to show a bit of loyalty because of that, so even though I still loved City, I went to Liverpool.

'I was put in digs on Anfield Road behind the away end. Eight of us were in there, Irish lads like Richie Partridge, Michael Foley, Paul O'Mara, Kevin Doherty. We had a great laugh. All of us were on one side of the house and Stephen Wright's parents lived on the other side. Stevie was a player at Liverpool too and he played a few times for the first team as well. Sandra, his mum, was great and looked after us all, making sure we always had our food prepared, clothes cleaned and the house maintained.'

Mellor considers himself fortunate that his emergence came at a time when young footballers could breathe socially.

'Now, it's impossible,' he says. 'If you do something a bit daft, there's always someone waiting with a camera phone. We were lucky. At the beginning, I had a girlfriend and I'd spend a lot of my weekends in Manchester with her, travelling back after matches. It wasn't until the under-19s that the proper nights out started: playing Youth Cup games, winning and going out afterwards, buzzing with our £50 bonus, which was almost as much as our weekly wage. They were good nights but I wouldn't say they were wild. Just a group of average teenagers having a laugh. It'd usually involve a pint in the Merton Pub in Bootle, which was the biggest pub in the area. One of the lads was Steve McNulty – a tank of a defender who plays for Tranmere now. His dad worked the doors at the Merton, so he let us all in and took care of us. Then we'd head over the road to a nightclub called Sullivans, known locally as Sullys.'

Mellor spearheaded the attack of Liverpool's youth

teams with Brian McIlroy. It proved to be a prolific partnership despite the lack of a relationship off the pitch. While Mellor progressed into Liverpool's first team, McIlroy ended up playing for the Holy Ghost Sunday team in the Crosby and District League.

'Yeah, we both scored lots of goals but he didn't beat me once. I think Brian was an Evertonian. Maybe he disliked the fact I wasn't a local lad. He was a talented player, quick. But he was the one person in the team I wasn't close with. We complemented each other well yet the friendship just wasn't there. My closest mates were Neil Prince, Michael Foley and Matty Parry, the goalie, and Steve McNulty.'

The coaches at Liverpool would turn a blind eye to partying. The club's strength had grown from the 1960s until the 1980s through the fast and powerful teams that bonded on Sunday afternoons in the public houses of West Derby, where drinking sessions lasted until the next morning. At the start of the new millennium, it wasn't quite the same, as the weight of expectations on footballers grew, but Heighway was wise enough to realize that young players needed to live normal lives in order to ensure egos remained level.

'I remember getting beaten 3–0 by Barnsley. Heighway was fuming. He had a proper go at everyone. Quite a few of the lads had signed long-term contracts the week before, going from £75 a week to £400 a week. Heighway told us that none of us deserved it. He singled me out and called me a coward because I didn't win many headers.

'On the bus on the way home, the lads were down

but we all agreed that we needed to sort it out by going out and having a few drinks. So that's what we did. We had a big old discussion, things got said and then we agreed to move on from it all. That's the way it should be in football: being able to air your opinion and then get on with things. If socializing helps that process, then so be it.

'Hughie McAuley ran the bollocks out of us the next day in training, where I spoke to Heighway. I said to him, "I'm not having you call me a coward in front of my teammates, no way." He told me to prove him wrong. So I worked harder on my heading and I did. We went the rest of the season undefeated.'

Heighway is described like a godfather, the all-seeing eye of Liverpool's academy. He had studied economics and politics at Warwick University before being signed by Liverpool from amateur club Skelmersdale United. He played more than four hundred games for Liverpool, then emigrated to America, playing in Minnesota and Philadelphia, before returning to Merseyside in early 1989, helping progress the careers of Steve McManaman, Robbie Fowler, Jamie Carragher, Steven Gerrard and Michael Owen.

'One of the first things Steve told me was, "If you want to succeed at this football club, you have to support it." That stuck with me and I educated myself. I went to countless cup finals and huge games at Anfield, seeing the passion of the supporters. Former clubs will always mean a lot to players but Liverpool completely changed me and I haven't looked back once at Manchester City – the club that rejected me as a boy, my dad's team. Now

I'm a man and a dad myself, I'm a Liverpool fan. That won't change.'

The mere mention of the name 'Heighway' commanded respect.

'Some players were scared of Steve. Everyone had ultimate respect for him because he was a great player for Liverpool and a great coach as well. Liverpool had standards and Steve set them. He'd join us in training sessions and be one of the best players. He never asked us to do anything that he couldn't do.

'From the training pitches in Kirkby, you could see cars arriving and leaving. When Steve's Mercedes rolled up, everyone would go, "Fuck, here he comes", and suddenly the level of training rose considerably. Players would start passing with a bit more authority rather than trying to look cool about it; they'd run more – close the opponent down. You had to be on your toes with Steve around. You'd think you'd been doing well and suddenly he'd stop sessions and tell you where you were going wrong. Some young players would drop a level because of his criticism but I was the opposite. He would drive me on. It was like, *Right, the main man's here now – let's have a bit of this.*

'You look at some of the coaches today who have all the badges but they haven't played at the top level. As a player, the ones you admire most are those who've been there and got the T-shirt. Steve Heighway had won everything there was to win at Liverpool. The parents idolized him. The players responded to that. I trusted him 100 per cent. There are some great coaches currently in the game who have never played at the highest level but for me it helped to have at least one who had.'

Dave Shannon and Hughie McAuley were also vital: people that had been involved at Liverpool since the 1980s.

'Brilliant coaches,' Mellor says. 'They were just as important as Steve in terms of drilling the message home about what it meant to represent Liverpool. They didn't allow you to become blasé about it and take Liverpool for granted. They made you feel like you were doing the most important job in the world and that we were privileged to be where we were in life. Dave and Hughie worked tirelessly to improve us as players, setting such high standards to maintain.'

In Mellor's eyes, the Liverpool way – an undefined set of rules by which every club employee should work and live – was actually Heighway's way, or at least he was the messenger, the person who linked the past to the present.

'Steve developed players and people,' Mellor says. 'He reminded us regularly that only one thing was certain in our football careers: that eventually we'd leave the football club. Nobody got to stay for ever. So we should enjoy – cherish, even – every day we had.

'Heighway was always on the job. He never stopped. Everything he did was geared towards the development of players. He'd grab me in the canteen at lunchtime and say, "Mells, I need you sharper – let's play table tennis." He'd pull a pristine bat from the drawer in his office and give me the one that had been used for years. We had some great battles. I was the top table-tennis player at the academy and the pair of us would be sweating our tits off by the end but that's what he wanted: a competitive environment.'

Five miles separated the Kirkby academy from Melwood, the first team's training base in West Derby. The separation was not only measured geographically. Though Houllier had used graduates like Jamie Carragher and Steven Gerrard at the beginning of his reign, the pressure to maintain success saw him use the transfer market for new players as the years progressed. Later, when Rafael Benítez took over, he did the same thing. Initially, opportunities were given to midfielders like Darren Potter but soon his approach shifted, causing an impasse between himself and Heighway, who chose to retire in 2007 because of his frustrations. It is damning that since the academy became active in 1999, no youth player who made his debut for the first team after that year has made more than seventy appearances for the club.

When asked to describe his impression of the relationship between the two sites by 2002, Mellor uses one word.

'Distant,' he says. 'Very distant indeed. I think Houllier changed the mood. Before that, Steve's relationship with Roy Evans was close. Roy went and, although Houllier initially gave some players an opportunity, something soon changed. Maybe it was the pressures of the job, I don't know. I'm not sure what it was. It was very rare that any of us got the opportunity to train at Melwood. And when we were invited there, it wasn't really to train; it was a case of getting chucked into a game for the reserves. I played with players like Jamie

Redknapp and Gary McAllister before I'd even trained with them or knew anything about them as people. It was hardly ideal, because any team needs a bit of trust to be successful.

'For a period, it was like two clubs existed within Liverpool: the first team and the reserves, then the under-19s and everything below that. I was scoring a ton of goals for the under-19s but players like John Miles, Ian Armstrong and Chris Thompson were getting in ahead of me at reserve level. I couldn't figure out the selection policy. It was very frustrating because I felt I was better than them.'

If a teenager plundered the number of goals Mellor scored for Liverpool's youth teams now, there would be a clamour for first-team selection.

The other young academy players to get chances under Houllier were John Welsh and Jon Otsemobor. Welsh was widely known in the city as the best player of his age and compared to Steven Gerrard. At the age of twenty, Otsemobor made headlines when, as a bystander, he was shot in the buttocks by an armed gang-member in a Liverpool nightclub called the Wonderbar.

'What held some of us back was that Liverpool were starting to go down the Continental route with Houllier. At the very beginning, he promoted the English boys but by the time I was ready for the first team, the foreign lads were getting more of a chance. He bought Daniel Sjölund in my position. Then later he went and signed Florent Sinama Pongolle and Anthony Le Tallec. None of them were hitting the same figures as me but I never got the opportunities like they did. That's the way it was – the politics of football.

179

'I think Houllier saw what was happening at other clubs like Arsenal, who were recruiting the best young French and Spanish players. Houllier didn't want to appear out of touch – not doing what the other leading clubs were doing – so he followed the trend.

'I liked Pongolle – he was a good lad, I got on with him. But was he really that much better than me? Was he worth all that money? The same can be said for Le Tallec, although he didn't mix as much. He was a bit different to Pongolle. Whether it's right or not, you always felt a French lad under Houllier would get a better chance.'

Liverpool signed El Hadji Diouf in the summer of 2002 from Lens for the second highest fee in the club's history. The Senegalese international played in Mellor's position. His arrival meant more competition.

In a later interview, Jamie Carragher recalled his state of despair when he quickly realized Diouf was not up to the standard required.

'Do you remember being at school and picking teams for a game of five-a-side?' Carragher asked me. 'We did this at Liverpool and Diouf was "last pick" within a few weeks.' Carragher said he never met a player 'who seemed to care less about winning or losing', while Mellor recalled his early tangles with a teammate who 'only wanted the glory for himself'.

'When we signed him, I was excited. I thought, *Wow, this guy's going to be amazing*. He was a star of the World Cup and had a bit of edge about him; he was a bit spiky. In the first week of training, there was a sense of disappointment, an *Is that it?* sort of thing. He was nothing special. It hit me then that a club can spend a huge amount of money and it doesn't always work out. Michael Owen and Emile Heskey were miles better than him.

'My first game for Liverpool was against Ipswich Town in the League Cup. In the changing room beforehand, Gérard Houllier asked who wanted to take the penalties. I put my hand up straight away because I saw it as an opportunity to make a mark. I wasn't great at pens but I viewed it as a free shot at the goal. If you score on your debut, it gets remembered. Houllier looked me in the eye and agreed.

'In the first half, I wasn't great – a bit nervy. In the second half, I got better. I won a pen – the old trick of waiting for the defender to clatter into me from behind. By the time I got up, Diouf had the ball under his arm in front of the Kop. We were 1–0 down. I looked at him and said, "Give me the ball, Dioufy." But he was a senior player who hadn't hit the heights, especially in terms of goals. I realized if I kicked up a fuss – especially in front of the Kop – the fans would have been thinking, *Who's this mouthy young kid?* They didn't know who Houllier had said was on pens.'

Mellor looked towards Steven Gerrard, who was Liverpool's captain for only the second time that night. He looked towards the bench. 'I realized I was on my own. Inwardly I said to myself, *Fine, let him take it.*'

Diouf equalized and Mellor was substituted by the time the penalty shoot-out came around, which Liverpool won. 'OK, the team got through and Liverpool ended up winning the cup that year but it was a bit of a sliding-doors moment for me. Imagine scoring an important penalty in front of the Kop on your debut. The opportunity was taken away from me. Diouf was a selfish man. I realize players have to be single-minded. Selfishness is different.'

Mellor's next start came a month later at Maine Road against Manchester City in an FA Cup match. Again, Diouf was involved in the narrative of his afternoon.

'I would have scored had Diouf squared it to me when I had an open goal. Instead he tried to beat Peter Schmeichel at the near post from a daft angle. I was thinking, *What are you doing, mate . . . what are you doing?*'

Three days later, Mellor scored his first Liverpool goal during a 2–1 defeat at Sheffield United in the League Cup semi-final first leg, the first moment that suggested he could deliver in important games and, soon after, he was offered a new contract. Mellor, though, only played another six minutes of first-team football that season and, under pressure because of bad results, he believes Houllier lost the courage to persist with young players.

'At the end of the day, Houllier gave me my debut for Liverpool, so I have to be grateful and respectful,' he says. 'When we won the League Cup final by beating Manchester United, he included me in the match-day squad of seventeen but only sixteen needed to get changed. I travelled with the squad and trained the night before, when he told me I'd only be needed on the bench if someone else got ill. Nobody gets ill in the hours before a final, do they? Fair play to Houllier, though. He recognized my contribution in the semi and made sure I received a winners' medal. It was a kind gesture.

'But there's always that thing nagging at the back of my mind – did I get given the best platform to show what I could do? I'll always remember going to Thailand in the pre-season with the first-team squad the following summer. I was flying – doing really well. Then he turns around and asks me whether I want to go to West Ham or Sunderland on loan. I knew I wasn't at the level of Owen or Heskey; I didn't expect to start games. But I always believed that if I felt out of my depth then I'd know. And in no way did I feel out of my depth.'

At West Ham, pertinent lessons were learned.

'I grew up a lot. I had to ring up the Sunderland manager Mick McCarthy and explain to him why I didn't want to go on loan to him because I'd chosen West Ham instead. How many players do that? Do they get their agents to do it? My dad, being an ex-player, told me to pick up the phone and tell him straight. I was shitting it because Mick is a very strong character. I wrote everything down on a piece of paper and read it out. It was tough but he accepted my reasoning. I wanted to play for Glenn Roeder because he had a clear plan of how he wanted to develop me as a player.'

Roeder was sacked before August was over, however.

'The club had big players: David James in goal, Tomáš Repka, the mad Czech full-back, Stevie Lomas, [Don] Hutchison, Michael Carrick and Jermain Defoe. I remember getting picked up by the team bus for the first game of the season at the service station after signing from Liverpool the day before and Defoe scribbled out the name West Ham United on his headrest and replaced it with Manchester United because he wanted to go there. The mood wasn't great at the beginning.'

Mellor was placed in lodgings in Chigwell with Matt Kilgallon and then David Noble.

'I didn't score the goals that I hoped I might. It was tough. I was away from my family and my friends for the first time at a place where I hoped I'd be able to show that I was capable of playing for Liverpool. But I wasn't showing I was capable of playing for Liverpool.'

The demand for promotion meant frustration was lurking on the terraces at the Boleyn Ground.

'I began to realize what three points meant to people, that's for certain. I remember playing Bradford City and getting booed off at half-time because it was only 1–0. I was thinking, *'Kin 'ell, we've played well there – we just haven't scored enough*. Experienced players like Christian Dailly stepped forward offering encouragement. He said that if we won – even if it was 1–0 – everyone would go home happy. That was an eye-opener about the demands of senior football. You can play well but it's not enough. You have to win. And we won 1–0.'

Roeder was replaced by Trevor Brooking, a West Ham legend and former England international.

'I loved it under Brooking; I played more or less every game. Three up front: me, Defoe and David Connolly. Life was great for a brief period. But Trevor reminded everyone that he wasn't there for the long term, just temporarily. And then Alan Pardew came in . . .'

Mellor did not start again.

'Pardew told me that he'd inherited me and that he wanted to sign other players because he knew I wasn't there for the long term. That was perfectly under-standable, because he'd come from Reading and was guaranteed that he'd be given the time to rebuild. I ended up in the reserves at West Ham. There was no point in me being there, so I asked to go back to Liverpool.'

Things were changing at Anfield as well.

'Gérard Houllier left as manager and when I heard Rafa Benítez was coming in as his replacement I thought, *Great, the new guy might give me an opportunity.* I felt as though Houllier had given me games but not the trust. The rumour went round that Benítez had watched videos of all the reserve games from the end of the season before. He liked the look of Stephen Warnock, the left-back. I hoped he might have seen something in me too, because after coming back from West Ham I'd scored ten goals in four games for the reserves. Surely he'd want to get me involved?'

In the first week of pre-season training, Mellor broke down with a knee injury.

'Rafa sat everyone down. "I've got twenty-five players here and you are my squad, you'll all be needed." For the first time, I felt part of the group as opposed to filling in like before. But suddenly the chance to really impress the new manager was gone almost straight away.'

Mellor says he made shortcuts in his return to fitness. He appreciated that his twenty-second birthday was looming and time was slipping away to prove himself.

'I wasn't fit and I played at Millwall in the League Cup. Rafa dragged me off after an hour and he was right to do so because I was rubbish. I was sitting in the dress-ing room afterwards thinking, *Oh my god – how bad am I?* My dad told me, "Son, that's not good enough if you want to play for Liverpool."'

Mellor made the decision to carry on despite the discomfort in his right knee, using painkillers and injections instead of an operation that would have ruled him out for the season.

'There were a few injuries in the team. The club had broken its transfer record again to sign Djibril Cissé and he was out. I saw that as an opportunity for me. I was managing the injury and taking risks to stay in the manager's plans, to get ahead.'

Mellor began to think back to the nine-month period as a teenager when a back injury curtailed his progression at a vital time and he had to watch other young players filling the vacuum he'd left behind.

'They were horrible times,' he says. 'Getting the bus at half seven in the morning, walking through Stanley Park in the pissing rain because I didn't have a car. I didn't have enough money for a taxi either because the wage was low. I'd get on the bus and think, *Fuck, there are some weirdos on here at this time.* So I'd sit alone.

'Nothing was laid on a plate for me to get back to fitness. I was injured and it was a case of the club asking a serious question: *Do you want to be a footballer or not?* The physios told me I had to be there for nine. So I'd get there for twenty to nine. Timekeeping was a big issue at Liverpool. It was disrespectful to be late. They didn't make it easy. You had to do whatever was necessary to be there at nine o'clock. It was character building.

'When you're out at that age, it eats away at you. You

think about the other players getting in ahead of you, making more progress. You wake up in the morning and fall asleep late at night thinking about it.'

Physical concerns were parked to one side and two late goals against Middlesbrough in the next round of the League Cup saw Mellor's confidence soar.

'Emlyn Hughes had passed away a few days before and it was quite an emotional occasion at Anfield. When I scored, the noise was deafening. I thought to myself, *You know what, I can do this.* At the same time, I couldn't manage to get in and out of my car without my knee aching. I couldn't even walk up and down the stairs.'

For his perseverance, Mellor earned a run in the side. For two months, his routine followed the pattern of training, tablets, injections and games. 'It was agony,' he says.

And yet, if he thinks hard, Mellor can still see the ball from his shot swelling the net against Arsenal, who arrived at Anfield as the Premier League champions: a side that had not long lost its record of forty-nine games undefeated. After Xabi Alonso's opening goal, Patrick Vieira had equalized.

'I went up to Sol Campbell in injury time and asked if he'd swap his shirt with mine. "All right," he said. A few seconds later, Kaiser [Didi Hamann] got fouled and from the free kick I challenged Vieira somewhere near the halfway line, I don't know why I dropped that deep. There was another collision between Harry Kewell and one of the Arsenal defenders and suddenly it dropped nicely for me . . .'

The half volley followed a strange trajectory, rising

initially before sinking, taking a low path towards the Kop.

'And then it went in,' Mellor says, smiling. 'It was my instinct. People say I was shattered, deciding to have a go from so far out. But I could sense the chance of a goal.'

Mellor calls it a 'Roy of the Rovers moment'.

'To score the winner against the best side in the country in the last minute in front of the Kop – how many people dream of that? It was amazing. I wanted to stand there for ever, to capture the feeling in a bottle. I've never taken drugs but I think it was the closest thing to a natural high.'

That Sunday, Liverpool's players went to the Living Room nightclub in the city centre. Mellor was too tired.

'I was emotionally shattered. I went home with my mum and dad and watched *Match of the Day* 2 on TV. Gordon Strachan was complimentary about my performance. I was made up. Then I went to bed.'

Had Liverpool not beaten Arsenal in the last minute, maybe they would not have had the faith to rescue themselves from an impossible position two weeks later when Olympiacos visited in the Champions League group stages. Liverpool were behind at half-time and needed to score three without reply to have a chance of progressing. Mellor recalls a flat mood in the dressing room before Jamie Carragher stepped forward.

'There was no doubt in his mind we could turn it around. He jumped up and goes, "Right, lads, we can fucking do this." Benítez went through his tactics but

Carra was the one instilling belief. "We can fucking do this."

'Rafa needed goals. I was only a substitute. Surely he'd bring me on. Then he turned to Pongolle and gave him the nod. I was fuming inside. *We need goals here and I'm kicking my heels.*'

Pongolle took two minutes to equalize for Liverpool. For half an hour, little happened. Then Mellor was introduced for Milan Baroš and two minutes later he prodded Liverpool into a lead and within touching distance of progression.

'I didn't celebrate. I grabbed the ball and took it back to the halfway line as quickly as possible.'

Wave after wave of attack followed.

'It was like a kids' game,' Mellor continues. 'For all Rafa's tactics – which were important – some of his best results were achieved in chaos.'

When Steven Gerrard thumped a shot past Greek goalkeeper Antonios Nikopolidis with injury time approaching, the roar seemed to rise from Anfield's bowels like thunder. Liverpool were through. Mellor was riding with the story. He was becoming an important part of Liverpool's short-term history and he hoped that, soon enough, he would be regarded an important player. Yet within a month, he'd played his last game for the club.

The following Saturday, he was selected as Liverpool's centre-forward in the Merseyside derby at Goodison Park, an occasion he describes as 'scarring'.

'We met at the Suites Hotel in Kirkby beforehand and one of the staff said he had a bet on me as first goalscorer. I went into the game thinking, *I fancy myself today*. Steven Gerrard had a free kick on the right-hand side and he whipped it in. I had a diving header from six yards in front of the Gwladys Street End. Somehow, I've ended up in the back of the net and Nigel Martyn has saved it. I couldn't believe it. Imagine scoring in front of the Gwladys Street End, seeing the faces of all the disappointed Evertonians.

'I stood in the showers for ages afterwards wondering what might have been. The atmosphere was different to anything I'd experienced before. You could sense the real dislike for Liverpool. You could sense we really weren't welcome. Scoring against Everton would have eclipsed Arsenal and Olympiacos. But I didn't. And we lost 1–0.'

The next Sunday, Mellor scored against Newcastle United during a 3–1 win. It was the weekend before Christmas.

'I went out celebrating at the club's party and probably drank too much,' he says. 'I got tonsillitis. We played West Brom on Boxing Day and beat them 5–0, and I couldn't play. Another missed opportunity.'

Mellor never recovered. He played once in the January, a League Cup semi-final victory over Watford.

'I got dragged off at half-time and Rafa said, "That's not good enough." I said, "Rafa, I can't move because of my legs; I'm in bits." My knee was swollen. But Rafa told me to play for the reserves the following day. I said, "If I can't play for the first team, how am I going to play for the ressies?" In the end, I lasted forty-five minutes. That was me: done. I was having an operation. Season over.'

The surgeon told Mellor his knee was so damaged that he had only a 50 per cent chance of playing professionally again. The Champions League final in Istanbul came and went, and so did the start of the new season. He went to Wigan Athletic on loan, where he scored the winner on his debut against Middlesbrough. Yet the knee problem had not disappeared and after two more games he was ruled out for the rest of that campaign as well. Mellor signed for Preston North End but did not make his debut until February 2007 due to further complications. By then, twenty-six months had passed since he last completed a competitive game of football.

In Alan Irvine he found a manager who believed in him and when the Scot was appointed at Sheffield Wednesday, Mellor followed him on loan, a move that set him on the same path as his father thirty years before.

'I wanted to feel trusted by the managers I worked for and I felt the trust from Alan. Why? He was making me a better player. I would drive into training every day looking forward to what he had in store for us. I knew I would enjoy it and there would always be a variation. He created an atmosphere that everyone wanted to be part of whether you were in the team or not.'

Mellor retired in 2012 and now lives with his wife, Rebecca, their two kids and dog near the affluent western coastline of Wirral, where the views stretch across the River Dee into Wales. He encourages his seven-year-old son to play football in the back garden but struggles to join in because the pain in his knee remains. At weekends, he covers matches for Sky Sports, having taken a media course at the University of Staffordshire. It satisfies him that his name will remain in stone for the goalscoring contributions against Arsenal and Olympiacos. Then comes the 'but'.

'I did the maximum I could with the body in the condition it was,' he says. 'I'm fortunate that I experienced moments in my career that are unique and historical. Some players, they make four or five hundred games and people say, "Good player, but, er, what is he remembered for?"'

'I feel I didn't fulfil my potential, which is frustrating for me. Whether it was lack of opportunity, injury or lack of ability, I'm not sure. Deep down, I think I had more to give. It's something I have to deal with and accept. Otherwise, I know I'd probably go crazy. So many footballers do in retirement because there's a long time to think about the way your career has gone, good or bad.

'That's why you've got to keep busy.'

192

CHAPTER SIX

cultzeros.co.uk

DIETMAR HAMANN,
Kaiser

THE MUSCLES IN DIETMAR HAMANN'S BODY EASED AND SLOWLY
his brain began to relax. Pulling hard on a cigarette, he
stared past the person who'd supplied it and into a place
beyond the walls in front as he contemplated the magnitude of what had happened.

Liverpool were Champions League winners on
penalties, having been 3–0 down to AC Milan at half-
time – a moment when Hamann's introduction to the
game was deemed necessary. It later transpired that
Hamann had scored Liverpool's first penalty in the

shoot-out with a broken foot. The occasion had taken him to a platform where there was no pain. He had not felt a thing.

Now, in the early hours of the Turkish morning, when all was somehow settled in Liverpool's favour, the winning team's dressing room was strangely quiet. Hamann's teammates lay around in disbelief. Some drank bottles of beer. Others blew into their bottle tops, creating a nervous whistling sound.

'We'd left the dressing room two hours before, dead and buried,' Hamann remembers. 'Yet we'd come back and the cup was in our dressing room and not theirs, shining brightly on a treatment table, all alone. For a short period of time, everyone seemed too scared to touch it. It hadn't sunk in that it was ours.'

Hamann had smoked since he was a teenager, usually Marlboro Lights. He approached David Moores, the chairman, and the only other smoker at the club.

Moores' entire body was trembling, his clothes drenched in indeterminate liquid. His face was reddened and tears were falling uncontrollably from his eyes. Moores had been in control of the club for fourteen seasons and had already decided to sell it to someone else. He must have appreciated this would never happen again. It had never happened before.

'David liked Marlboro Red cigarettes and they are a bit stronger than Lights, let me tell you,' Hamann continues, amused. 'I thought to myself, *This is the perfect time to sit back, take it all in and kick back.* So I said to the chairman, "David, come into my office," and led him by the hand to the showers, which hadn't been turned on yet. "David, can I have a cigarette?" I asked him.

'He always called me Kaiser: "Kaiser, what if the manager finds out?" he said, the strain showing even more. "Just tell him you own the fucking club," I told him.

'Rafa had asked me on his first day in charge about the rumours, whether I smoked. It was best to be honest. "Yes I do, boss." He showed no expression and walked away.

'David took ages to open the packet because his hands were shaking so much. I think both of us needed that drag to settle us down. We stood there for five minutes in the dry shower saying nothing to each other, me in my full kit and David in his suit. Ash had fallen all over the floor. It felt like that cigarette you have after sex.'

Hamann's Liverpool career seemed to be over after six years. Rafael Benítez had offered him a new contract at the start of 2005, before unceremoniously withdrawing it. Hamann decided that the next few days should be spent partying. He partied in the hotel in Istanbul. He partied on the flight back to Liverpool. He partied in the Sir Thomas Hotel after the parade around the city was completed, singing 'You'll Never Walk Alone' with John Aldridge on a stage. And then he partied with his family and friends. He did not expect to be summoned by Benítez to Melwood for what seemed to be a debrief. Hamann was unshaven and very tired indeed when the call came.

'Rafa had a reputation for being quite strict but I saw him differently,' Hamann says. 'Rafa was straightforward rather than strict. As a German, I appreciated that approach because I'd grown up around it. I don't think any player could claim he did not know what was expected of him under Rafa when they went out to play. He was very organized and very clear. He was not a control freak. He did not insert himself into your private affairs. But when you were at Melwood on football duty, you were his property.

'Of course, he could change his mind too. And that shows you, perhaps, that he isn't quite so stubborn as some people make out. When I walked into that office after Istanbul, I thought he might want to thank me for my efforts and say goodbye, although I figured that would be an unusual thing to do, because he wasn't one for goodbyes. Instead, he offered me a new contract for another year. I didn't expect him to perform the U-turn. But that was Rafa: he made big decisions and didn't care too much about what people thought about them.'

Hamann was an unusual breed of footballer in the twenty-first century – perhaps unique to his working environment. He expressed himself socially and did not make much of an effort to hide it, potentially risking the scalding of his manager or his club. He did not train particularly well either. Yet all his managers, including Benítez, trusted him to perform with extreme tactical discipline on the pitch.

Hamann's recruitment by Gérard Houllier for £8 million in 1999, along with six other foreign signings during the same summer, was supposed to herald a new dawn of professionalism at Anfield. The Spice Boys era was over, yet in Hamann, Liverpool were getting a midfielder who knew how to enjoy life away from the stresses of his occupation. Jamie Carragher recalls, with surprise, how Hamann marked the end of a night out with his new teammates by hailing a taxi early one morning in Liverpool's city centre. His unusual method was to lie on the tarmac of Castle Street and wait hopefully for a car to spot him and brake.

'This is absolutely true, of course,' Hamann admits. 'The English dressing room is very different to the German dressing room. You go in and you hear the music. It's like a nightclub sometimes. In Germany, there is peace. We control the rage. Yet in England . . .

'I have always enjoyed a beer with the lads,' he continues. 'In Germany, my big buddy was Mario Basler. We had some great times together. I understand why clubs – Bayern particularly – try their best to control players. Sometimes you need control but not always. I am convinced that if you share a common bond socially, it will show itself on the pitch too. But you mustn't go too far. As a footballer, it would be easy to take advantage of your position and wealth. So I guess you have to find a balance. I drank mainly in the Everton pubs around Liverpool. I could relax there. The Evertonians didn't want to have anything to do with you.'

Hamann is already eating a late breakfast of bacon and eggs, using heavily buttered toast to mop up the runny yolk when I arrive at a greasy-spoon café in Alderley Edge, the prosperous Cheshire town where he lives. The skies are oily and sunken but the rain cannot be seen due to the heavy condensation on the windows.

'Today is football weather,' he announces, shaking

my hand and grinning earnestly. 'I loved playing in these conditions. It was faster – more unpredictable.'

Hamann is an Anglophile. As he slurps through two mugs of steaming hot coffee, he speaks in an accent that can drift wantonly from Liverpudlian to native Bavarian in the course of a single sentence. He uses slang terms like 'different gravy', when analysing the abilities of Benítez, and 'fannying around', when describing the pedestrian football he loathes. Hamann recognizes he is neither a typical German nor a typical footballer, considering the acceleration towards vanilla professionalism that he witnessed in the later stages of his career. He misses little about the mundane routine of a footballer's life in the modern age.

'I finished playing nearly five years ago and there have only been a couple of occasions where I've wished I was active again,' he says. 'I had the best time. Nothing could have worked out better than it did. If you gave me the chance to be twenty-five, I wouldn't take it because my memories are happy.

'I had a spell [as manager] with Stockport County but I can't really see myself as a manager or a coach in the future,' he reveals. 'I found it hard to be on time for training as a player. I paid my fair share of fines. As a coach or a manager, you have to be there even earlier. To get in the car at seven in the morning and spend the next ten hours every day for at least six days a week over the course of eleven months a year in the same intense routine doesn't really appeal to me.

'As a manager, you have to sacrifice a lot. You have no private life and a limited social life. Someone else is always waiting to take your place. You've got to be focused and 100 per cent prepared to give every second of your life to it. If you are not, you shouldn't do it. You'll fail.'

Hamann's favourite pastime involves lying on the couch in front of his television and watching cricket. During an important Test series, he stays up late into the night and through into the morning. He did not even know what cricket was when he first arrived in England. He admits to blowing vast sums on spread betting, especially early in his retirement, when he was removed from that word he uses again and again, the 'routine'. An Australian batting collapse against South Africa once cost him nearly £300,000.

'Cricket is a sport I could talk all day and all night about,' he says. 'I sat in the Long Room at Lords last year. What a place that is: the history. Some great cricketers have had lunch there. I could name a lot of them if you wanted me to. When I came here, I did not know who Beefy Botham was.'

Hamann insists Jamie Carragher, his former teammate, likes cricket too, joking he might not talk about it too much because of his working-class roots.

'Carra is like me: he enjoys strategy sports, where you have to use your brain,' Hamann continues. 'Especially in Test matches, there is so much to think about. It's a game over five days, so you have to consider the quality of the pitch and the predictability of the weather: how many spin bowlers to play, whether you play a spinner at all; the batting line-up, who should bat in what order, who opens the batting with Alastair Cook [the England captain], who I think is one of the great modern leaders of sport.'

It is possible to imagine Hamann as a number 3 batsman standing wearily at the crease, repelling the fiercest bowling attacks for days on end, though not registering a necessarily impressive amount of runs. He played football that way: a subtle but reliable presence in the middle of midfield, missed when he was not there.

'There is a solitude at number 3,' he says. 'You have more to think about than an opening bat. Staying in for as long as possible has to be the aim usually. Although I'm not sure whether I'd like to face the new ball.

'I know Freddie Flintoff pretty well and I've had a knockabout with him in the nets,' Hamann carries on. 'Some of my friends turn out for Alderley Edge Cricket Club and when they're one short I play for the third team. It's hard to pick up a new sport the older you get. If I could make a 50 or a century for the over-forties, it would rank as high as winning the Champions League for me. I really mean that.'

He reasons that both his upbringing in conservatively minded Bavaria and his emergence from Munich's most illustrious football club explains why he can simultaneously respect authority and be rebellious. There are also his strong opinions.

Hamann was four weeks old when his family moved from the quiet town of Waldsassen to a middle-class suburb called Solln in the gravel plain to the south of Munich. Yet Solln, Hamann says, is not a beery place of leather-clad, thigh-slapping bonhomie, where men sit in Oktoberfest tents singing songs while wiping foam from their moustaches. 'Some nice houses and some grey tower blocks, with enough sports facilities to keep the kids busy,' is his memory of childhood. 'Unremarkable, basically.'

Further out from Munich and into the countryside, the mood changes and a patently wealthy region opens up. There is a famous German movie telling the story of a group of Bavarians that win the Olympic bobsledding medal in the 1950s. Asked where they are from, they reply, 'We are from Bavaria. That's near Germany.'

Bavaria might have the money of Hertfordshire but it also has the attitude of Yorkshire. And like Texas, it is one of the areas in the world where rural rather urban life defines the way things are.

A poll in 2013 showed that 25 per cent of Bavarians would be in favour of leaving the Federal Republic. That is only 5 per cent less than the number of people in Scotland who, before the No Campaign set about its business, said they wanted independence from the United Kingdom.

'The Bavarians are a bit like the Scousers,' Hamann says. 'You either love them or you hate them. Both have had a big influence on the cultures of the countries they exist in but don't really feel a part of the country necessarily. Within the country they polarize opinion. Bavaria is the biggest region in Germany. I wouldn't say we claim to be better than the rest of Germany. But we certainly claim to be different.'

It becomes apparent there is more to Hamann than funny stories and eccentricities. There is a pleasant direct-ness about him, an occasional abruptness, which might explain why he relates to Rafael Benítez the straight-talker, though Hamann can recognize he did not play for Benítez as long as others who are not so positive in their recollections, nor was he at Liverpool when off-the-field issues with ownership began to influence what happened on the pitch.

There is nevertheless a confidence in Hamann's analysis, which is delivered in a matter-of-fact way. He begins this interview by speaking about how his first professional club, FC Bayern Munich, lead as Germany's most successful team both in sporting terms and financially, relating his thoughts to experiences in England. The day before, Bayern had flattened Wolfsburg, from northern Germany, 5–1.

'Bayern's evolution has been natural and the club cannot ever be accused of being in the middle of a revolution,' Hamann says. 'The discipline is clear and consistent, and it is administered by people you respect because of their standing in the game. In England, it has always been very different. Where are the former players on the FA board? Where are the former players involved at the biggest clubs – clubs like Liverpool?

'I was friends with Mario [Basler] and we'd enjoy a few shandies now and then. The club would know because they have a rein on what is happening. Even if it were five days before the next game, they would not be happy. [Uli] Hoeness found out and we'd be in his office explaining ourselves. Does that happen in England, where the ownership groups are based in America or the Middle East?

'The loyalty of players is questioned all of the time in

football now, whereas the loyalty of the club is never an issue. A player might sign for a manager who is sacked within a few months or the owner might change. It happened to me at Newcastle, two games into the season. Suddenly the person that signed me was gone, and in a new environment – no matter how much you are paid – you feel vulnerable. You think, *Why did Newcastle allow Kenny [Dalglish] to buy me for so much money when he was clearly under pressure? Where does this leave me?* It gives you an excuse not to perform. There are fewer people to be loyal to.

'In Germany, Spain, Italy and France, there isn't a desire at academy level to recruit the best young players from all over the world. They largely focus on the talent in the region of the club. It means clubs like Bayern can implement a pay structure, which is one third basic pay, one third on appearances and one third on bonuses. In effect, more than 50 per cent of wages is based on performance.

'Here, in England, that isn't the case. Young players get paid a lot of money no matter what their performance; they don't know any different, so they grow up with a sense of entitlement. It results in a mentality issue – that it is OK to lose.'

He continues, 'In England, the attitude is: if you lose and something bad happens to you, we have sympathy for you. In Germany, the attitude is less sympathetic. For example, in the 1990 World Cup final, Lothar Matthäus could not take a penalty because the stud in his boot had broken off. It was 0–0 with five minutes to go against Argentina, so he asked his best mate of twenty years,

Andy Brehme, to take the kick instead. Brehme tucked it away, Germany won the World Cup, but people still have a go at Matthäus for supposedly bottling it – even though the goal was scored.

'In England, there is a message that it's OK to fail. You can see Paul Gascoigne as another example – again at the 1990 World Cup. He was booked in the semi-final and, knowing he would miss the final, was too upset to take a penalty in the shoot-out that followed. If that happened in Germany, he would not have been allowed back in the country. Gascoigne would have been accused of letting the team down and the whole nation.

'Compare Gascoigne's response to the reaction of Michael Ballack, who received a second booking in the 2002 World Cup semi-final, meaning he would miss the final. Michael was arguing with Carsten Ramelow, who'd given the ball away leading to the foul. I know because I was standing next to Carsten!

'Michael said, "Come on, lads, we've still got twenty-five minutes left to play." Rather than feeling sorry for himself, Ballack's reaction was to go and score the goal that got Germany to the final. He celebrated too. Like Gascoigne, Ballack cried but he did it in the changing room once he'd completed his job. In my view, Ballack was a hero for this but in Germany nobody talks about it because we see what he did as normal. The attitude is, *You miss a final – so what? It's a team game . . .'*

Hamann describes himself as an individual with the capacity to express his personality without disturbing the balance of the collective.

'I liked to do things my way but without harming the

performance of the team. If you knew how to handle me, which I don't think was particularly challenging, then you would have a performance on a Saturday.'

His father was a policeman, so the rules at home were clearly defined and he understood boundaries. Having excelled at science and mathematics in school, he completed national service, where he learned to shoot a gun. He refers to his emergence as a professional footballer as a 'drift'. It helped that his school was next door to the Wacker München football club.

'Wacker had some decent kids: Turks, Serbs, Croats,' Hamann remembers. 'My father was the coach and he wanted us to play quick and direct, using only two touches. If you went one on one with the goalkeeper and there was another guy next to you and you didn't square it so he has an open goal, even if you scored yourself you would get substituted. The idea was: always pass the ball to the person better placed. I think in the long term it made me more of a team player. And in Germany, if you are not a team player at heart, you do not get very far.'

Aged sixteen, Hamann received proposals from 1860 Munich and Bayern Munich. The decision was swayed in Bayern's favour because the training ground was fifteen minutes away by bus. He was placed in a team two years above his own age group and his goals as an attacking midfielder pushed him towards the first team. For the first time as a footballer, he smashed into a wall of unhappiness, admitting that he was too young and naive to deal with the forceful personalities he encountered inside Germany's most successful football club.

'There was no togetherness whatsoever,' he says flatly. 'I came through with Christian Nerlinger, and Markus Babbel, who later played for Liverpool, and that helped to some extent because we suffered from similar anxieties. It was impossible to fit in when there was no common bond. The dressing room was divided between the young German players, the older superstars – many of whom didn't like each other – and then the Italian- and French-speakers. The biggest problem was Matthäus and [Jürgen] Klinsmann – the biggest personalities – never got on. It wasn't a nice environment to play in.'

Matthäus believed that Klinsmann had plotted to replace him as captain of the German national team and the enmity was cemented when Klinsmann won the European Championships of 1996 without Matthäus being part of the line-up. Back at Bayern, Matthäus apparently had a bet with Bayern's general manager against his teammate scoring a certain number of goals in his second season, and, although he lost the bet, the season culminated with Klinsmann being vilified in a tabloid when he refused to grant the paper exclusive interviews, and then his sexuality was questioned by a television host.

When Bayern coach Giovanni Trapattoni substituted Klinsmann with a debutant amateur player for what would prove to be his only appearance for the club, Klinsmann reacted by kicking an advertising board on the side of the pitch and the moment was played again and again on German television.

In the dressing room, Hamann can remember how the

bad mood between the pair was magnified by a culture already present where each person was looking after himself – a culture far removed from the team ethos pressed upon him from an early age.

'Everybody made it difficult for each other,' he says. 'The old players were suspicious of the young players. Nobody gave you a helping hand or made you feel comfortable, enabling you to express yourself fully. They made their feelings clear: that you were a kid who did not belong in first-team training. They recognized too that if you did well, there was a chance that they might get removed from the side. I wouldn't say it was bullying. But it was borderline. For a while I wasn't able to show my ability because I was too nervous and too insecure about myself.

'It reached the point where I was playing for the second team and scoring goals but as soon as I became involved with the first team my form disappeared. I thought that my future might be away from Bayern: in the second division at another club. Maybe success elsewhere would earn me the necessary respect to go back to Bayern and prove all of them wrong.'

Gradually, Hamann grew in confidence. He began to appreciate that players need not have the same outlook on life but fundamentally must be motivated by the same things.

'At Bayern, it was drilled into you from an early age that first is first and second is last,' Hamann says. 'German players are pragmatic. There are some who purposely tackle certain teammates harder in a training match because their presence is a threat. These aren't deliberate attempts to injure but if they get injured, then so be it. We had training sessions where the coach had to stop the game because it was getting too feisty. But at least the intensity was the same on a Saturday. I liked this because it is better than playing eleven versus eleven and fannying around at half pace in a training session. It gives the players in the B team a chance to show the manager that they should really be playing on the other side by tackling really hard.

'In England, the attitude was completely different. You aren't allowed to tackle your teammates in training. This surprised me because in England the game was supposed to be more physical. It made me wonder whether it is all for show; beneath the anger maybe the players are too nice.

'You need a balance, of course. At Bayern, a lot of the players didn't like each other and at times it took something away from our performances. Other times, it possibly added to our performances because some players were desperate to prove others wrong. I would say there were a lot of alpha males with their own agendas but fundamentally we wanted the same thing in a sporting sense when it came to the match. The results and the trophies proved that.'

Hamann recognizes that learning to deal with the politics of the dressing room helped to build his self-confidence. He chose to move clubs at the age of twenty-four because he felt he wasn't getting the recognition he deserved at Bayern.

'That showed I had overcome my confidence issues,' he says. 'As I got older, I found it harder to score goals.

I did not have the necessary acceleration to move away from opponents and get a shot off. I'd love to have been an attacking midfielder but an attacking midfielder who doesn't score goals is not going to be selected very often. The progression was to go further back, because it suited me. At Bayern, I was asked by Trapattoni to fill in the space behind Mario Basler. Mario was one of the most gifted players but he wouldn't run backwards. We played with a unique 3–3–3–1 formation and it meant that I, quite often, was a wing-back. Although it wasn't natural for me, it improved my understanding.

'I'm not a precious person. But Bayern supplied six players for the 1998 World Cup squad and I was one of them. Even though I was playing for Bayern every week and a German international, I knew I could do an awful lot more and take on greater responsibility, become regarded as a senior player.'

Hamann explored options abroad because he considered any other German club to be a step down.

'The first team to make an offer was Real Betis in Seville. They were really ambitious and had just signed the Brazilian player Denilson for a world-record fee. Seville is a beautiful city. I liked the sound of it. But Newcastle came in and they were keener. I was 50/50 and had Betis been as keen as Newcastle, I'd probably have gone there. Kenny [Dalglish] met with my agent and had a really persuasive argument. He made me realize that my game would suit the Premier League more. I saw Newcastle's players too – legends. They had John Barnes; Ian Rush had been there the year before. Then there was [Alan] Shearer, Shay Given and Gary Speed. I saw the heartbeat of a successful side.'

After Dalglish was sacked, Hamann was pushed again into a more attacking role by his successor, Ruud Gullit. Gérard Houllier was bold in spending £8 million to take him to Liverpool the following summer.

'I met Gérard and liked him straight away. He told me that he wanted to build the midfield around my experience. He had sold Paul Ince and needed another leader in there. Nobody had really spoken about me as a leader before and, considering I'd left Germany to find more responsibility, this was music to my ears. I really felt wanted and the fact he used so much money to sign me gave me huge confidence.'

Hamann was less keen on Phil Thompson, however. He responds swiftly when asked whether he'd previously encountered someone like the assistant manager with a notorious temper.

'Er, no . . .' he says, pausing. 'There is no doubt, on occasion, it helped get results. But maybe Thommo got angry too often. Gérard was always quick to intervene if he was going too far. "Leave it, Phil. We'll speak Monday." The number of times he said that in the changing rooms . . .'

Hamann's mind wanders to a match at Southampton in 2000 when Liverpool let a three-goal lead slip in the final twenty minutes.

'Thommo went so mad at Markus Babbel that Markus reacted and threw a boot at him, and it all kicked off big time. Is this approach healthy? Probably not. Having said that, hard feelings were not held for too long. A lot of the boys didn't take Thommo's rants so seriously. You realized it was best to take your medicine and laugh about it later. It became another part of the routine in that period.'

Hamann found the enthusiastic personality of Sammy Lee, the first-team coach, even more annoying to deal with than Thompson's rage.

'Sammy was relentless with his enthusiasm with every other player but me,' Hamann explains. 'I have to admit I couldn't be assed training at 100 per cent all of the time. That wasn't my style. Sometimes I had to say, "Sammy, do me a favour and leave me alone." I knew my own body. I was twenty-five when I joined Liverpool and I appreciated what I had to do to perform on a Saturday.

'In pre-season, I'd never miss a session. I did everything I was told. I was a good runner and I'd be towards the front. During the season, I would know when to get a sweat on and when not to. Other players are different, of course. Carra and Paddy Berger – they needed to be on it all of the time to have the confidence to execute their competitive game.

'Me? I'd try to find a space on the pitch to hide during full-scale training matches because I learned that going crazy in training did not improve my levels on a Saturday. If I tried like Carra or Paddy, I would have been fucked, too tired.

'You have to trust the players. I'm not sure Sammy trusted me all of the time and it got on my nerves. He wanted everyone to make sure they were warmed up, for example. "Sammy, I've warmed up in the car with the heaters on and I've never pulled a muscle in my life." These conversations happened all the time. He would encourage everyone else and if someone gave the ball away five times in a possession game, he'd encourage them, being positive. If I did it once, I'd get a bollocking.'

There were other people inside Liverpool's dressing room whom Hamann took to straight away. Jamie Carragher was one of them.

'At the beginning, it is fair to say that Carra was a bit of a lad. He liked a joke. He liked a night out. But when he played, he played hard. He wasn't someone who cracked jokes and then disappeared on a Saturday. He backed everything up.'

Carragher came from Bootle, a modest area a few miles north of Liverpool's city centre. A few weeks after Hamann signed, Carragher invited the German to join him in Bootle for a night out. They entered a bar known locally as Cornelius's Place, a dive with a jukebox and a small selection of draft lagers.

'It was so dark in there, I remember walking out a few hours later and my eyes beginning to hurt because of the light,' Hamann says. On another occasion in the early days, Carragher remedied a bad defeat by suggesting a few drinks in Liverpool city centre. 'We ended up in Flares and the lads got down to "Super Trouper" from Abba. It wasn't the type of thing Houllier liked us to do. But Carra knew better. The night out helped us recover from our disappointment. Everything went wrong against Leicester. There was no point in dwelling.'

Hamann cannot stop laughing when he recalls a scene

outside the team bus before a European away game in Valencia.

'Michael Owen spotted Carra's dad, Philly, in the crowd. He was dancing in the street, singing – shouting – Liverpool songs. Everyone leaned to one side of the bus to see what was going on. If it was my dad, I'd have probably hidden in the toilets but Carra reacted by banging on the window, encouraging him. "Go 'ed, lad," he shouted.'

Hamann says the spirit under Gérard Houllier was the best he's experienced at club level.

'Any successful team has the right blend. If you want to win, you firstly need players you can rely on. That's the bottom line. In that group, you need young and old – a mix of stamina and pace – and players who can put their foot on the ball. I played in twelve finals for Liverpool and we only lost three. I think that shows Gérard chose the right players, players who could respond when the chips were down, players who did not get too hyped up or nervous. Markus [Babbel] was one of them, and Stéphane [Henchoz] was the same, Sami too. They were all defensive players and each one of them had a good temperament. In attack, we had players who could make a difference. In 2001, Michael Owen won a lot of games for us.'

Houllier transformed Liverpool in less than two years from a team with a reputation for throwing everything away to one skilled in methods of recovery. Hamann credits the manager's perception for judging moods as the main reason why Liverpool won three cup competitions in less than four months.

'I remember driving to Melwood and thinking, *I can't be assed training today*. I walked in and Patrice Bergues, Gérard's right-hand man, was waiting for us. "Don't get changed yet, lads. We're going to the David Lloyd gymnasium for a swim and a sauna." He read my mind and, probably, a lot of the boys' minds. Nearly everything Gérard did in that period was right.'

For Hamann, though, one decision stands above the rest as a sign that Houllier's time as Liverpool's manager was somewhere near an end. In 2002, soon after Houllier's return from his heart scare, Liverpool were 2–1 up on aggregate against Bayer Leverkusen with half an hour or so of the Champions League quarter-final remaining. Liverpool were protecting a lead but by replacing Hamann with Vladimir Šmicer, an attack-minded player, Liverpool's midfield was left wide open.

'There was so much confidence amongst the players that we genuinely believed we'd beat Man United in the semi and Real Madrid in the final,' Hamann says. 'Real Madrid didn't scare us one bit. We were bouncing, really bouncing.'

After Hamann's substitution, though, Leverkusen scored three goals and knocked Liverpool out.

'Earlier that month, Houllier had told me that in all his time as manager, we'd never conceded more than three goals when I was on the pitch. We were in command before Houllier took me off. I couldn't understand the decision. I was fuming and totally gutted.'

Hamann's phone rang at the team hotel later that night.

'It was Gérard. "Didi, I want to speak to you, will

214

you come downstairs?" I wasn't the only one there. He told the whole squad that nobody should speak to the press about his substitutions.

'Although I agreed to go along with his idea, it said to me that, deep down, he knew he'd got it wrong. Houllier had never chosen to hold a team meeting so soon after a game before. Usually, he'd take a day to collect his thoughts then run through things.'

Back at Melwood, Hamann was summoned to Houllier's office.

'I was planning to really have a go at him but as soon as I entered the room he looked up at me in the same way a headmaster does to a pupil and asked me straight why I underperformed in Leverkusen. That threw me off course. He explained that he was disappointed in my role in Leverkusen's first goal but I tried to reason with him that I'd got caught out of position because Steven Gerrard had dived in on Michael Ballack and that I had to try to recover the situation.

'When I look back now, I can think of Thommo sitting there beside Houllier and saying nothing. That just wasn't his way. If I was responsible for a mistake, he'd have laid in to me. His silence said a thousand words.'

Houllier kept his job for another two seasons. It proved to be a long farewell and by the time of his departure the groundswell of opinion was against him amongst Liverpool's febrile supporter base. Hamann, though, is defensive of his former manager when reflecting on the legacy he left behind.

'He [Houllier] is definitely underrated in this country,' Hamann says. 'Critics talk about the players he bought who didn't perform at Liverpool but he also bought Sami Hyypiä for £2.5 million and built a team inside twelve months that was capable of winning trophies.

'He used to be a teacher, so he was very good at communicating with people and creating team spirit. You saw that in how many finals we played and won even when we were under pressure for a lot of the time. We won the Champions League after he left and so many of the players were his signings. He deserves credit for the team he left behind.'

When Liverpool won the Champions League twelve months later, Houllier appeared in Liverpool's dressing room, much – supposedly – to the annoyance of Rafael Benítez, the winning manager.

Like Houllier, Benítez's modest career as a player did not warn of his rise as a coach. His high point had been at Parla, a fourth-division club from the Madrid suburbs, where he first showed signs of the path he wanted to follow by making notes of everything that happened during the course of a season: scores, scorers, injuries, cards and details about set pieces.

Benítez began as a player at Real Madrid and went back there, aged twenty-nine, as a coach, serving a four-year apprenticeship in the youth set-up. Raúl would become an icon at the club and a week before his debut he'd been under Benítez's wing with the second team, missing a couple of easy chances in a game at Palamós.

Like Houllier, Benítez had a reputation for building teams with strong defensive units while recognizing the importance of match-winners within the block. Unlike Houllier, Benítez suffered the whiplash of a

216

few failures early on in his career, which are likely to have had a significant effect on the way he approached management.

Benítez was sacked from his first senior position at Valladolid after clashing with Aljoša Asanović, the creative midfielder, over his tendency to break from position. From the moment Asanović carelessly gave away a penalty, the Croatian became a part of the problem rather than the solution. Such was Benítez's determination to instil tactical discipline that when he was involved in a car accident where he skidded on a sheet of ice, the Valladolid forward joked, 'Boss, we're glad you're all right and that nothing happened to you,' he said. 'We were worried that the video recorder would miss you.'

Benítez then lasted just seven matches in charge of Osasuna, which scarred his morale. Knowing his reputation was under threat, the next job had to be the right one and eighteen months later he was carried around the pitch shoulder-high at Extremadura after sealing promotion into La Liga.

Like Houllier at Lens, Benítez made up for the things he didn't have by going to the extreme in the basics to achieve impressive results. The players at Extremadura trained until they were physically exhausted and Pako Ayestarán, the assistant whom he met at Osasuna, was nicknamed 'the pain in the neck'.

Benítez banned chewing gum because he wanted his squad to appear more professional. He tried to instil instinct through repetition in training patterns, and in his team talk before matches he would ask players for details about their opponents, checking whether they'd been listening. On away trips, teammates were paired off in rooms according to their positions on the field.

His relationship with the Extremadura chairman, however, gradually eroded because of disagreements over the facilities at the club, which Benítez deemed unsuitable. The chairman did not see them as a priority considering the small resources at Extremadura, and though Benítez eventually got his way, he left after suffering relegation back to the second division in spite of a good fight against the odds.

From there Benítez went to Tenerife, where upon his arrival he overcame a division between old and young players in the squad to seal promotion again. In the Canary Islands, he learned to deal with a more inquisitive media, giving time to those who'd been critical of him and a bit less to his supporters.

When Valencia needed someone to replace Argentine Héctor Cúper, three other coaches were approached first before chairman Pedro Cortés thought of Benítez, asking him, 'Have you got the guts to manage Valencia?'

The appointment was viewed as a gamble considering Valencia had lost the Champions League final twice in the seasons before, while Benítez, at best, was knocking about in the lower reaches of La Liga. And yet Benítez displayed courage immediately by replacing the popular Santiago Cañizares as captain and offering shared duties to midfield duo David Albelda and Rubén Baraja.

What followed was Valencia's first La Liga title in thirty-one years, toppling the Barcelona and Real Madrid monopoly by creating a wonderful team based around his hallmarks: an organized defensive base, aggressive full-backs, ball-playing midfielders, fast wingers and a hard-working centre-forward. Two years later, when he achieved the same feat, Benítez also won the UEFA Cup, easily beating a Marseille team in the final that had earlier knocked out Liverpool.

Benítez became restless, though, and wanted more control in order to make his position safer. He wanted to sign Samuel Eto'o from Mallorca when the Cameroonian centre-forward was approaching his peak. When he ended up with Mohamed Sissoko, a young midfielder from Auxerre, he commented publicly, 'I've asked for a table and they've bought me a lamp.' In the summer of 2004, there were offers to join Roma, Tottenham Hotspur and Besiktas.

At Liverpool, Hamann liked Benítez from day one. Others were less impressed.

'Rafa reminded me of Trapattoni at Bayern,' Hamann says. 'His English wasn't very good at the beginning and sometimes the players would have to fill in the gaps. But I knew the Italians and Spanish put a greater emphasis on tactical strategy than coaches from other nations. I knew straight away Rafa was class. Trapattoni made training sessions incredibly long and Rafa did the same, so I was used to this. He would go over and over what he wanted for two to two and a half hours. It did not impress some of the lads who were used to training off the cuff a bit more. We were in the States for the pre-season and on the bus some of them were complaining, saying, "This is shit." But I thought the opposite. *Just you wait. This fella's a different gravy.*

'I was in a later stage of my career by then and I thought I knew everything there was to know. But Rafa introduced new methods and made me think differently about the way the game was played. He also had a way of letting the players know where they stood while keeping them guessing at the same time.

'This, for me, is very important because it keeps egos in check. His message was clear from the very beginning: the player who plays two or three games a season is as important as the one that plays forty or fifty. What happened in 2005 proved that, because Florent Sinama Pongolle and Neil Mellor scored two of the most important goals in the season yet didn't play as much as some of the others.'

Hamann cannot remember a conversation with Benítez about anything other than football.

'He would say, "This is what I'm like, this is what we are going to do; if you are not on board, then do one, go somewhere else." He didn't care about individuals; all he cares about is the team. In my eyes, that's the way it should be and I also think this is why he has a track record of success.'

In his second autobiography, Steven Gerrard revealed that his relationship with Benítez was cooler than it had been with any of his other managers. Hamann is not being critical of Gerrard when he explains how a relationship between manager and player usually works on the Continent. Hamann says as long as a manager helped him achieve success, he didn't care what his style was like, or, indeed, how he appeared to be as a person.

'Do you want a manager you can call when your missus has the flu or do you want a manager who wins the Champions League?' Hamann asks. 'I don't care whether I can phone the manager; I want him to get the best out of me and the team. I think some players expect managers to be like Alcoholics Anonymous: there on stand-by for twenty-four hours a day. But this is a professional game. Rafa's honest and doesn't bullshit. Maybe that's too much for some people.

'He treats the players like adults. You see now, some managers like to say they are strong man-managers when the reality is very different. I thought that Rafa's man-management was very strong, because you knew exactly what he expected of you on the football pitch. And, usually, he stuck to his convictions. When you are Liverpool manager, so many people are looking to knock you down. If you start listening, you fall. That's probably what happened to Gérard Houllier.'

Hamann is confident enough to say publicly what he has said privately to both Gerrard and Jamie Carragher – two people he considers friends.

'Before Rafa's arrival, Carra was a utility player. Gérard always found a place for him but it was never at centre-back. Rafa put him in the middle and made him one of the best English centre-backs. If it wasn't for Ferdinand and Terry, Carra would have eighty England caps. It was the same with Stevie: Stevie was a very good player before but Rafa took him to the next level.

'OK, some things happened between both of them after I left, things I should probably not tell you because it is their story and not mine. But I think what he did do is improve players. He brought an even tougher mentality to the club. Nobody really believed Liverpool could go and win the Champions League. Rafa believed it could happen and that helped the players.'

Whenever Benítez revealed Liverpool's team to the squad one hour and ten minutes before kick-off, Gerrard's name would reliably appear last.

'Rafa would refer to the rest of the players by their first name or nickname. So, it would go: "Jerzy, Steve, Carra, Sami, John; Vladi, Didi, Xabi, Harry; Milan and finally Gerrard."'

Hamann can understand why that might have annoyed Gerrard.

'OK, Rafa did things a certain way. He was very particular. But history only judges managers by what happens on a Saturday and a Wednesday night. And Stevie played his best football in his career by a mile under Rafa. He doesn't need to love him. But he must acknowledge this surely.'

Hamann defends Benítez even though he was not selected to start the Champions League final. Benítez, in fact, went through the team with Gerrard and Carragher the night before.

'So it wasn't as if they never spoke, not at the beginning anyway,' Hamann says. 'Carra only told me this information a few days later and I'm glad he didn't tell me before because my head would have been scrambled. There was nothing to be gained by saying I was dropped. In those first two years, Rafa would pull Stevie to one side almost every day and run through things with him. It wasn't as if he thought Xabi or Sami were more important to him, he was interacting with Stevie more than anyone else.'

Hamann says he cannot remember being 3–0 down at half-time in any other game during his career other than in Istanbul.

'I'd always played for good teams,' he explains. 'Yes, maybe Rafa made a mistake in not selecting me from the start. But a big part of success is rectifying your mistakes and making decisions that change the course of events.'

In the dressing room, Hamann's only specific instruction was to try to stop Kaka and Clarence Seedorf, Milan's attacking midfield pair, from running the game. Benítez reminded Hamann of his responsibilities at set pieces.

'The general idea was to give Stevie more space to play in, because the midfield was very crowded. Rafa, even though he was only forty-five at the time, was a successful, experienced manager. I would have felt slightly insulted if he told me what I needed to do, because it was pretty obvious what the plan should be from a defensive point of view: stop Milan's attacking players.'

Somehow, Liverpool won on penalties.

'I would put any trophy I won abroad above the best trophy I won with Bayern Munich,' Hamann says. 'You have so many obstacles to overcome in England: the language, the culture, making sure the wife and kids are settled; then there's the football, the pace and the massive expectations.

'With Liverpool, you have to ride the emotion of the club and the city. You have to use that emotion to your advantage and not let it undermine your game. Gérard

Houllier always said, "Warm heart, cool head." I never had a problem with delivering that, because I didn't think about playing until two minutes before the kick-off.'

Though Benítez relented after the Champions League final and gave Hamann a new contract, his Liverpool career was over twelve months later and he joined Manchester City. His playing days finished at Milton Keynes Dons before a few months in charge of Stockport County. Though he does not wish to take on the role again, the art of management fascinates Hamann. He considers himself fortunate to have played under a few of the greats. There was Franz Beckenbauer, then Otto Rehhagel, Giovanni Trapattoni, Kenny Dalglish, Gérard Houllier, Rafa Benítez and Sven-Göran Eriksson.

'I liked Trapattoni a lot,' Hamann says, before offering a story. 'At Bayern, we'd lost a home game two days before and in the next training session he was trying to tell us that it wasn't possible to apologize to the fans by showing up at the stadium and saying sorry. His German was OK but it wasn't the best. He told us that we had to show some balls. He was searching for the word *cojones* in German, so one of our South American players told him the word for fanny instead, *mushi*. "Yes, yes, we've got to go out there and show the fans that we have a fanny," he kept saying over and over again. The lads tried not to laugh because it was a serious situation. Eventually, the whole room erupted. Thankfully Trapp joined in when he realized the mistake.'

Hamann lived near Rafael Benítez on the Wirral peninsula. The pair keep in touch.

'I remember going round to his house and Barcelona were on the TV. The whole world was going crazy about their style of football, so Rafa grabbed hold of salt and pepper shakers and began to try to explain to me how to beat them. The guy never stops. That's why he's one of the best in the business.'

On a social level, Hamann details why he could relate to Sven-Göran Eriksson the easiest.

'City were taken over by Thaksin Shinawatra, who was the [former] prime minister of Thailand. The season had finished and Mr Shinawatra decided that the squad should travel to Bangkok for a trip. Sven knew that he was being replaced as manager. All of the players did too. I was relaxing on a sun lounger out by the pool when Sven appeared holding two champagne glasses. He handed me one, so I asked, "What are we celebrating for, boss?"

'Sven just turned to me and said, "Life, Kaiser, we're celebrating life."

'That was Sven for you. He was my kind of guy.'

CHAPTER SEVEN

cultzeros.co.uk

XABI ALONSO,
Maestro

IT IS WINTERTIME AND SNOW GENTLY BEGINS TO FALL ON Säbener Strasse, the affluent tree-lined residential boulevard that runs south from Munich's centre. On one side, the low-rise chalet homes of middle-class families sit quietly, as elegantly dressed men stroll by during their morning walks accompanied by their elegantly dressed partners. Over the road is the training complex of the city's most famous football club. Above a glass-plated front of clinical German design, a sign reads with awesome confidence: 'FC Bayern'.

Space is used sensibly here. I wait at one entrance sponsored by Audi, which leads underneath the training pitches and into an intensely lit car park. At 9.30 a.m. on the dot, the automobiles of that particular manufacturer begin to arrive, their engines smoothly purring. Each Bayern player gets issued with the same car when he signs and while on club duties the player is contractually expected to be seen driving it.

The companies Bayern work with are obvious, because the logos of Adidas, T-Mobile and, indeed, Audi are plastered everywhere. Bayern thrives because of these alliances but also because of success on the pitch. The smell of freshly cut grass slices through the freezing air, reminding me that Bayern exists because it is a football club first.

'I'm over here, mate,' Xabi Alonso calls, poking his head out from behind the wall of an alternative access point, the use of the word 'mate' a reminder that five years living on Merseyside can have a long-lasting influence on a foreign player's vocabulary.

The training session on this specific Thursday does not start for another hour and a half, yet a group of workmen in their luminous jackets are waiting expectantly at the highest point above the facility. Alonso is already in full training kit, his flip-flops belying the weather. It is easy to believe that at Bayern, while Pep Guardiola is manager before his next move to Manchester City, most things begin on time, that the Bayern machine waits for no person.

'You'd be surprised, not always,' Alonso informs me, stroking his gingery-bearded face as we pass the pitch-side cameras of the club's in-house television station. I realize he is joking when he clarifies his comment. 'On one occasion we started five minutes late,' he says, delivering it deadpan. 'You have heard of *mañana* haven't you? Not in Germany they haven't.'

The Säbener Strasse site offers Bayern's entire roster of teams, from the Bundesliga seniors down to the under-8s, elite training and playing conditions. The stars of today and tomorrow hone their skills on five grass bowling-green standard pitches, two of which boast undersoil heating. Across eighty thousand square metres there are two third-generation artificial turf pitches, a beach volleyball court, a multi-purpose sports hall, a service centre for supporters, a performance centre for players, a head office for directors and a youth academy apart-ment block that accommodates up to fourteen players aged from fifteen to eighteen whose home towns are too far away from Munich for the daily commute to train-ing. There are also Bavarian beer cabins for the fans on the days they are invited in to watch.

'This is a club that really takes care of everybody,' Alonso continues, sinking into one of the leather couches next to Bayern's canteen with the smell of strong coffee wafting between us. 'The organization is perfect, the best I have experienced in my career. A lot of people ask me why Bayern get it so right, why the club is so successful. I always say it is the attention to small details and the fact this place feels like a community. It is run by ex-players who understand the game. Financial decisions are taken but they are always determined according to football sensibilities. In the modern game, when players and managers come and go, it is very difficult to achieve this atmosphere. But Bayern have got it because they are always planning for the future while focusing on the present at the same time. The organization means there is no excuse not to be successful.'

Alonso left Liverpool in 2009, when the running of the club could not have offered more of a contrast to the situation at Bayern now. A league finish of second the season before represented Liverpool's best performance since 1990 and yet the club was lobotomized – run by a pair of feuding owners who were separated from Merseyside by an entire ocean and several time zones – eighteen months away from the edge of financial administration and potentially, had it not been for the supporters, complete collapse.

Watching Alonso train makes you question why Rafael Benítez deemed it appropriate to try to sell him in the first place. Alonso was close to leaving in 2008 when the manager made it clear that he wanted his sale to fund the signing of Gareth Barry from Aston Villa, and although Alonso remained for another twelve months, he concedes 'something changed' in their relationship at that moment.

Alonso was twenty-six years old then and he is thirty-four now. He remains the player his teammates look for, the one who never hides, the manager's coach on the pitch: a description once used by Benítez, in fact.

He starts in almost every game for one of Europe's greatest teams, believing this is only possible because of the levels he meets in training sessions, where 'the quest to prove myself remains day after day after day'.

He emphasizes the point by punching his right fist into the left palm, an action repeated several times during the course of an interview where he speaks eloquently, wisely and frequently with passion. Unlike some footballers, he loves everything about the game, displaying his intelligence by challenging popular misconceptions.

'Without that love,' he says, pausing, 'I'm not really sure whether I'd still be playing.'

After the team warms up, I later watch him take part in a simple drill known in England as 'strings', where one player stands in the middle of a circle, being fed passes. At Bayern, the central figure's control is expected to be in the release, because he is afforded only one touch. Alonso is nourished by Philipp Lahm and Thomas Müller: multiple title holders with Bayern and World Cup winners with the German national team, feats Alonso has also achieved in his post-Liverpool years.

Alonso is the only player in football history to have experienced the management of those considered as the great four modern European coaches: Benítez, José Mourinho, Carlo Ancelotti and Pep Guardiola. Each one of them has admitted that success follows them because they find a way to govern the midfield, the area where Alonso plays. He is far too modest to acknowledge that his presence and brain have been a crucial influence in all of the teams he has performed in.

'If you win the midfield, you probably win the game,' he confesses. 'But that doesn't mean the players in the midfield are the ones alone who determine that, because now we have strikers who drop into midfield and defenders who move up into the midfield. It is the area you must dominate. If you have control of the midfield, you have control of the game and you have more chances to win.'

Though reliably tasked with influencing the deepest midfield position, Alonso explains that his brief at each club has been slightly different. At Liverpool, Benítez wanted him to feed Steven Gerrard; at Real Madrid the target – Cristiano Ronaldo – was slightly further away, meaning longer passes. At Bayern, where the game is shorter, Guardiola has called Alonso a 'funnel'.

'In my position, wherever I have been, I have needed to be responsible,' Alonso says. 'You are in the middle of everything. You don't have to take many risks. It is not like a striker, who tries different things to define the outcome of a result. For me, the midfielder is about security, balance and collective play. My first thought is to appreciate my teammate and his needs. I think about every other player on the pitch, because I will receive passes from every position: the goalkeeper, the centre-back, the full-backs, the attacking midfielders, the wingers and the striker. If there is a player like Luis García, who was great in between the lines of the opponent's defence and midfield, you know you can give them more balls into a little space. If there is a player who does not have the quality in those small spaces, you have to ask them to run, to expand the game.

'I am the link between the defence and the attack, so I have to be a solution for my teammates as well, to help move the ball from one side of the pitch to the other. At every club, this has been my job: Sociedad, Liverpool,

Real Madrid and here at Bayern. As I get older, I think I become stronger mentally and this makes me a better player because in this position you need to be streetwise and to use common sense. It is frustrating that physically you lose something with age. I guess that is life: you gain wisdom while other faculties fail.'

Alonso, however, has not just acted as a comfort blanket for others throughout his career. He has scored some outrageous goals. At Liverpool, two were delivered from the halfway line: at Luton Town's Kenilworth Road, then against Newcastle United at Anfield. These were not his only attempts.

'Yes, yes, yes, but where is the risk in that?' he asks quickly. 'There is no risk. If the shot does not result in a goal, it does not matter, because nobody expects me to score. In these situations, only the goalkeeper looks stupid. I don't try to do things that might make me look stupid, because the risk is there. How many times have you seen me run into the box with the ball, dribbling past players? It's uncommon because it's not my game; it's not my thing.

'For my game to be better, I need to be surrounded by better players than me. My game is not to have one great action. My game is to be consistent throughout: to bring the ball in the best and quickest possible way for the best players to make the last action. I know what my strengths and weaknesses are on the pitch. My duty is to be risk averse.'

It seems strange for Alonso – or any other footballer – to speak of vulnerability, especially in this age when many project a persona of being able to take on the world. He begins to slap the side of his thighs, illustrating where his problems lie.

'Well, it's not a weakness; it's a fact,' he corrects himself to some extent. 'I know I am not the quickest player on the pitch. I will not change, because it is not in my legs. I know how to work around it. I have to be quick in my mind and not my legs. Whether you are a football player, a writer, an actor or a singer, you need to appreciate how you are, what you can do well and what you cannot do. Only then do you become stronger. The word in English is "perception", I think.'

There was a time in English football when 'midfield' and 'battle' equated to hard tackling and, more often than not, outright intimidation. Alonso arrived at Liverpool as a floppy-haired twenty-three year old with a different idea of what aggression really constitutes.

'I have always said there are different types of aggression,' he explains. 'You can tackle aggressively but you can also pass aggressively, although I prefer to use the word "authority" here. Of course I was aware of the previous Liverpool midfielders. I had seen videos of Graeme Souness. Wow – what a player, what a player. I loved him. My father was a midfielder and he loved him too. Souness commanded an entire pitch. By the time I started playing, football was moving, though. You couldn't get away with rough tackling. But you could still pass with aggression, with "authority", do everything convincingly, as Souness did.

'A small fraction is the difference between a good pass and a bad pass,' he continues, before he uses the flesh of his thigh as a prop again, clouting it with some conviction. 'This is always on my mind. *Pace on the pass*, *pace on the pass*. Soft passes are not good. They are risky. You have to trust that your teammate has the technical ability to deal with the pace, to deal with the aggression and take on the mantle of authority.'

Alonso views passing as a creative art – proactive – compared to tackling as destructive and therefore reactive. He does not see tackling as a quality at all and when he has spoken about this in the past, his view has been met by criticism, particularly from English defenders.

'I stick with my opinion. I know it is viewed differently in Britain. It's not the action [of tackling]. It's the idea: the cause and the consequence. I love to tackle. But if I could avoid it, I think I have done better in my job. If I tackle, sliding across the floor, it means that I – or someone else – have been caught out of position at the start of the move and that drives me crazy because team shape and balance is crucial. At Bayern, this is what we practise all of the time: "shape, shape, shape". If you spend too much time on the ground, it means your positioning is not so good. I would say I pride my game on positioning, being in the right areas – that's why I get chosen.

'It's a different view. I remember reading the programme in the dressing room at Anfield before a game. There were interviews with young players. There were questions like, "What are your qualities?" Many of them would say tackling. This shocked me. OK, some days you need to tackle. But I'd never aspire to have my main quality as tackling.

'Stevie's [Gerrard] tackling? OK, of course, I love it. They are spectacular and the crowd gets so excited. But for me, I get excited when he receives the ball and plays the last pass before a goal. That makes me smile the most. This is his greatest strength. Seeing the pass, seeing what other players do not see.'

Alonso thinks similarly about courage: the quintessential British quality that supporters of most clubs look for in their footballers.

'Again, courage can be defined differently,' he says. 'Some fans want to see players up for a fight and when they lose they ask where the characters are. But there is a lot to be said about players who will take possession of the ball when the atmosphere is bad and attempt to take responsibility for the team. When I was very young, I used to think to myself, even if the team I was playing for was losing heavily, that I must keep showing for possession, show my belief. Of course you need passion. You can lose with passion and you can lose because of passion. There is a right way of winning. There is a right way to lose as well. Striking the balance is key.'

Alonso thinks differently but that does not make him an extremist. He does not believe in the 'death by football concept' that infested football management for a while, where many teams tried to play like Barcelona.

'There is a middle ground for everything,' he says. 'We think of Spanish football as "pass, pass, pass". We also think of English football as running and tackling: "run, run, run, run". Spain has been very successful with their idea in recent years but it could change and every other nation might try to be like England. English clubs dominated European football in the 1970s and 1980s. How many times did English clubs win the European Cup? All of them played 4–4–2. It was only when AC Milan switched to 4–4–2 in the late 1980s under Arrigo Sacchi that football changed and Italy began to dominate European competitions. Football goes in cycles – there are trends.

'What I think is, you must protect your identity and believe in it even after bad results. When I started playing in San Sebastián as a twelve year old, it was all about playing good football and using technique. It was also about a tactical understanding of the game: learning a position and the responsibilities you have to your teammates. I was never encouraged to run after the ball, to run with the ball or to make great sliding tackles. I was taught to control and release, then show for the next pass. It was a very simple strategy. When I played for the national team and won the World Cup all those years later, the strategy was the same. The process carried across decades.'

Alonso's father, Periko, won successive La Liga championships with San Sebastián's Real Sociedad at the start of the 1980s before moving to Barcelona, where he played alongside Diego Maradona and Bernd Schuster, achieving another title in 1985. It is difficult to explain what it meant to the supporters of Sociedad to win the league so soon after the Franco years, considering the hardships suffered in the Basque country.

In many of the bars in San Sebastián's cobbled old quarter hangs a black and white photograph showing

Jesús Zamora, Periko's moustachioed midfield partner, scoring the goal away at Sporting de Gijón in 1981. The goal secured the point needed by Sociedad to win the title that Real Madrid players had thought was theirs. While celebrating after a 3–1 away win against Real Valladolid, they heard of Zamora's intervention over the radio. The year before, Sociedad had surrendered the title in similar circumstances to their enemy from the capital by losing unexpectedly in Seville, having gone the entire campaign undefeated up to that point.

Alonso spent the first six years of his life in Barcelona but as soon as Periko moved the family back to San Sebastián, he started playing football on the city's La Concha beach. Despite the broad sweep of golden sand fringed by the clear waters of the Cantabrian Sea, as well as the handsome grid of alluring Art Nouveau architecture behind, there was an obvious challenge to playing football in such a setting.

'I learned to adapt to circumstances very quickly. If the sea was too high, it was impossible to play and you would have to wait until the next weekend,' Alonso clarifies, enjoying the memory. 'It meant waking up at seven in the morning to set up the goals and mark the lines of the pitch before the tide came in. It was a tradition for the young to do this. It made you appreciate the game a lot more because you could never take it for granted. I'd be angry all weekend if we couldn't play.

'Not being on a super-perfect pitch helped my technique also. I learned to adapt. The ball would not always run the way you wanted it to run, so you had to be alive all of the time. If you risked taking your eye off the ball, you'd look silly. No kid wants to look silly.

'Mikel Arteta [the future Everton and Arsenal midfielder] was involved in these games too. We lived in the same neighbourhood but went to different schools. When it came to the selection of the teams, we'd get picked on opposing sides because I guess the rest saw us as the most talented footballers.'

Alonso cannot remember seeing his father play and, despite his background as a professional, Periko did not attempt to impart knowledge or put pressure on any of his sons, including Mikel Alonso, who would also later feature professionally for Real Sociedad before a couple of unsuccessful spells in England with Bolton Wanderers and Charlton Athletic.

'I remember reading in England about the parents getting too involved, all the shouting and screaming, telling their kids what to do all the time; it was as if the disease was exclusively English. Let me tell you, this happens in Spain as well. The parents, they have so much passion. They try to translate that passion to their kids. It does not matter where you come from. I see it here in Germany too. It is a part of the wider society we live in now.

'My father left me to learn and do my own thing. Of course, he'd always try to be supportive. But he never tried to push me, "You have to do this, you have to do that." There was advice but it was always very gentle. I only saw videos of him playing. Like me, he was a defensive midfielder. He was very physical and could mix it with powerful opponents. He also knew how to pass and move into the right areas.'

Alonso considers himself fortunate in being able to witness professional footballers at work with his own eyes from a very young age. After retiring from playing, Periko moved into management, first with Tolosa.

'I was a very lucky boy. When I was five or six years old, I would go with my father to the training ground on Saturday mornings. The first team would train on one pitch and I would warm the goalkeepers up on the next pitch with my brother by shooting at them. You grow up with an impression of a goalkeeper being good or not so good. It is only in these moments you realize how high their level is. Their professionalism stood out. They were fit and agile. They seemed to be the size of buildings compared to me. Through these experiences you begin to appreciate how good you have to be to beat them. And I did a few times.

'When you are young, your mind is very receptive to what it sees,' Alonso continues. 'My father was a professional footballer, so it was normal for me to witness how a professional footballer acts in a professional environment. He did not have to tell me anything, because I saw. He was a player and then he was a manager. I would hear him tell other players that it is not about making a debut. It's about maintaining a high level for a decade. Only then are you a real professional. That has always been in my mind. If you are not at your top level, no matter what you have done before, someone else will come and kick you out of the team.'

Alonso's favourite players played in the same position that he would later make his own. There was Real

Madrid's Argentine, Fernando Redondo, Pep Guardiola from Barcelona, as well as the Portuguese midfield duo at Real Sociedad, Carlos Xavier and Oceano. His own dreams began and ended at his hometown club, though he did not join them until he was seventeen.

'I did not think I would become a footballer,' he says. 'I led a normal life until I was sixteen. Normal school. Normal upbringing. People talk now about the distractions when you are a young footballer. I was fortunate that I did not have any distractions from being a young person, because football can take over everything. In the long term, I think this has helped my outlook on life. Maybe it is more balanced than someone who has been at an academy from the age of five or six, as happens in England now. I was able to enjoy other things and maintain a raw passion for football.'

Other clubs had asked him to enrol at their youth academies. At sixteen, he rejected an opportunity to sign for Athletic Bilbao.

'They had two teams at each age group and for the under-16s they wanted me to play for the second team. Bilbao is one hour away by bus. I said, "No, I prefer to stay at home instead with Antiguoko." My dad knew football. He did not get directly involved too much. But from the back he was pulling the strings. "Don't try to rush it," he'd tell me all of the time.

'Within a year, I had made my debut for the first team at Sociedad. Everything happened so fast. The second year, I went on loan to Eibar and then came back. John Toshack helped make me an important player. I had no time to think, *What if this happens? What if that happens?* My football career just happened. Living without the anxieties of wondering about the future all the time helped me.'

Toshack could not recall a youth-team player having such an impact at any of his previous clubs. 'Everyone seemed to play better when he was on the pitch,' Toshack said after Alonso had told his manager that he 'was not afraid of responsibility', a moment which led to him being awarded the captaincy in a final attempt to change the atmosphere and avoid relegation. Sociedad were bottom of the league when Toshack made the decision in January 2001, and when the season was over, they had survived. Toshack was feted as a hero, but without Alonso's direction on the field it would not have happened. 'We knew we had a special player on our hands,' Toshack said.

Alonso displays his humility by crediting Toshack, the former Liverpool striker, as 'the great saviour of football in our city' and the only one with the faith 'to treat a kid as an adult in an adult's world'. Yet by the time Alonso was ready to leave in the summer of 2004 for a new challenge, he had emerged as a new leader of the club. In the two seasons before he moved to England, the public address system at the Anoeta Stadium would make the same announcement whenever his substitution was deemed necessary: 'And coming off is number four, Don Xabi Alonso.'

Alonso had been close to joining Real Madrid, where he would have replaced David Beckham in the centre of midfield, but Madrid had doubts about his pace and mobility.

'It dragged on and on and on and on with Madrid. It was exasperating. Then Liverpool approached with a very serious interest. Madrid had taken a couple of months to reach the same point in negotiation that Liverpool reached in a couple of days. I was like, "Come on, it's either going to happen or it is not – decision time." I decided that if Liverpool wanted me so much, I preferred to go there. I saw Liverpool as a great chance, a top club.'

He describes how he formed his childhood impressions of English football 'through the keyhole of the television camera, following only the ball'. Even from afar, however, he could spot differences from what he knew in Spain.

'I can remember the 1995–96 Premier League season very clearly. In Spain, they started to show Premier League games and Serie A. Until that moment, I had only seen Spanish football. The English? It caught my eye. It was different because of the atmosphere. It was sometimes difficult to hear the commentator because of the noise inside the stadium. I liked watching Paul Ince, Gary McAllister, Roy Keane and Peter Beardsley. They were all similar: aggressive. You might not think Beardsley was aggressive, because he was creative. But in creating opportunities he was very aggressive: he passed with conviction. The intensity of the game – wow – it was end to end, no breaks. I liked that football. It is fresh in my mind. Shearer went to Newcastle. The Liverpool players wore white suits for the FA Cup final – they had some courage, no?'

Alonso made his Liverpool debut against Bolton Wanderers in a game where Sami Hyypiä broke his nose and Rafael Benítez called Sam Allardyce's side a 'basketball team'.

'We lost and I walked off the pitch, thinking, *I'm going to have to learn really quickly about English football*. It was wild: long ball, second ball, big physical players – Kevin Nolan, Kevin Davies up front; Allardyce chewing gum and shouting orders from his technical area. The crowd was noisy but I could still hear Allardyce. When Bolton won a free kick, the army from the defence moved forward and the ground began to shake.'

Some footballers claim they do not notice what happens on the terraces when they play.

'I notice . . .' Alonso says '. . . both the good and the bad things that are said. I loved England from the first minute. It's about the sound of the stadium. When there is silence, it is not because they don't care about the game, it's because they are paying attention to what is going on. But when they show emotion – admiration or anger – the noise is like lightning hitting a tree. I sometimes wonder whether a crack will open up across the pitch. For me, the sound of the stadium in England is the best. When a goal is scored in Spain, people shout "*Gol!*" but only once. In England, it's "Yeah!" a million times. I love this. In England, the passion of the football is the best. Of course, you need more than just passion to be successful. You need ideas and the strength to stay with those ideas through bad times.'

Alonso felt at home almost straight away. Rather than live outside the city as many do, or even in a prosperous suburb such as Woolton or Formby, he bought an apartment in a Grade I listed building in the Albert Dock, an area surrounded by bars, galleries and with broad views of the Mersey. His girlfriend, Nagore, now his wife, moved with him and worked at the prestigious Hope Street Hotel over in the Georgian quarter, where the Liverpool squad would gather before home games.

'I could smell the marine air and it reminded me of San Sebastián,' he says, smiling, though the smiles do not extend to the memories of the wind blasting in from the Irish Sea: 'The most difficult thing to get used to, not the temperature.

'A lot of players came to Liverpool from Latin American countries while I was there and many of them did not adapt quickly enough,' he continues. 'It resulted in them being left out of the team and from there the future collapses. In many cases you have seen players not being able to adapt and therefore not being able to show their levels [of skill].

'In my case, it did not happen. I was determined to absorb and learn as much as possible. In England, people eat a lot earlier than in Spain, for example. In Spain, I could arrive at a restaurant at midnight and the place would be busy. In England, even at weekends, most places are closed by 11 p.m. For me this was not a problem, though. It is a matter of intelligence. You cannot change the culture. You have to accept it and adapt and live with it. It's not really a drama. Come on – get over it!'

In successive summers when Alonso was thirteen and fourteen, he'd spent a month in Kells, Ireland, having enrolled on a school exchange programme.

'This was important for me and maybe a bit of luck.

From the first moment in Liverpool, I was able to communicate with my teammates and to be involved. I could not talk perfect English but at least I could express myself. In the first press conference, I spoke in dodgy English but at least I tried it.'

The family Alonso lived with in Kells supported Manchester United. Along with the Merseyside derby, this was the game he looked forward to the most.

'The Merseyside derby is for the city. During the week, Everton fans, they will tell you what they think. There is banter. It is semi-serious. It still acts as motivation to beat them, because when you fill up at the petrol station and you see the same people every couple of days, and you know they are Evertonians behind the counter, the idea of seeing them after losing in the derby is not very appealing.

'The taxi drivers in Liverpool, they speak a lot. Many of them seem to be Evertonians as well. They like to talk about Liverpool, to tell you where as a player you are going wrong. I loved this. I would argue back with them and they appreciated it. The humour in Liverpool is very different to any other place I have been. They give it, but they take it back.

'There is a community spirit in Liverpool that I believe does not exist anywhere else in the world in a city of its size. I used to walk around the city from my apartment and go shopping. The people, they would be very respectful. It might not be the same for a local player, because there is so much focus on them, but as a foreign player, you can live a normal life. I travel a lot around the world and sometimes I will see a face and without hearing that person's voice I will know they are from Liverpool. It's something to do with the way they look. Liverpool people have a mark.'

Alonso is not one to exaggerate. He describes games against United as 'like war'.

'The supporters do not see each other every day, so when the teams come together it is not so normal. There is a clash. These games, there is no friendliness whatsoever. I would compare it to Madrid and Barça: there is a geographical distance between the clubs, as well as many other things. There is less of an understanding. So when they meet, it is like a collision. I played against Roy Keane. It was his last full season at United. I could see his eyes. He really wanted to win those games. But I looked at Carra and Stevie too. It was always going to be hostile.'

Alonso says the spine of Liverpool's 2005 Champions League-winning side was already there by the time he arrived. He equalized to make it 3–3 in the final against AC Milan by scoring the rebound, having seen his initial penalty saved.

'Carra, Stevie, Sami and Didi were all huge influences on everyone else. All different characters, strong personalities. When each one of them spoke, I listened. They helped me improve as a player and as a person, and when I went back to Spain to play for the national team I felt a lot stronger through the experiences shared with them. English football has had a profound effect on the improvement of Spanish players. Pepe [Reina], Cesc [Fàbregas] and David Silva might say the same. [Gerard] Piqué did not play many games for United's first team but the experience helped him when he returned to Barcelona.

'I liked Carra the most,' he continues. 'He is the biggest Scouser in the world. We got on well from day one. I think he realized that I loved football and he loves football too. We would watch games together and talk about it every day. I think he respected that I would enter arguments with him. He was always very loud; you could hear his voice above everyone else's. I would say, "Carra, shut the fuck up, you have no idea!" He liked all of that: the confrontation. He had ability of course and his reading of the game was fantastic. But I think he, maybe more than anyone else, was driven by the confrontation, the challenge of proving yourself every single day.'

Alonso believes winning the title in 2009 would have been more satisfying than the Champions League, because 'to win the league you need to have everything.

'These were my happiest times at Liverpool: Pep to [Daniel] Agger, Agger to me, me to Stevie and Stevie to Torres. Sometimes it would take less than ten seconds. The spine in that team was the best I've played in. You also have Carra and Mascherano in the side – top-class players. There was skill, steel and speed; it was very competitive, very intense. Very, very determined and committed.

'This side did not win anything together but we felt we could win everything. We had a few stupid draws at home and in the end that's why we did not win the league. We always had that feeling, that belief and confidence. Nobody scared us. We went to the Bernabéu and won. We went to Old Trafford and won. We went to Stamford Bridge and won: big games, big occasions that define seasons. It frustrates me so, so much. In 2005, we won the Champions League with a not-so-good team. In 2007, we lost the Champions League final with a better team and a more convincing performance. In 2009, we played the best football and lost the least amount of games but still did not win the league. That is the beauty of football, I guess. It is not a straight line.'

The highs, indeed, may have been exhilarating but the lows were equally excruciating. While Alonso was helping Spain win the European Championship in 2008, he was also coming to terms with the fact that Rafael Benítez was trying to sell him against his wishes. As Spain's open-top bus crept through the centre of Madrid amidst the celebrations, there was a niggling thought at the back of his mind that his time on Merseyside could possibly arrive at a sudden and disappointing end.

Benítez had believed that Alonso could be as influential to his Liverpool side as Kenny Dalglish was to Bob Paisley's and as Dennis Bergkamp had been at Arsenal.

Yet by March 2008, the cracks in the relationship between Alonso and Benítez started to show. Alonso had missed the second leg of a Champions League last-sixteen tie against Internazionale at the San Siro to be with his wife as she gave birth to their son. 'Which I'd have done a thousand times.' Benítez, though, had missed his own father's funeral because of Liverpool's commitments at the 2005 Club World Championship in Japan and Alonso's decision came at a time when his form had dipped. At the end of the season, Benítez made a controversial decision.

'Rafa came to me and was very clear. He said, "Xabi, we need the money to sign other players that I want." In order to make that money, my name was the first on the list to be sold. I said, "OK, Rafa, no problem. I am a professional. I understand that." There was interest from Juventus. There was interest from Arsenal. But the clubs could not agree terms. I was ready to leave, because the manager wanted me to leave. It did not happen, though. So the next year, the situation was different. I went to Rafa: "OK, a year ago you wanted me to leave and I accepted it. Now I want to leave . . ." In the end, there was an agreement but it was not easy because he wanted me to stay by that point.'

From their time in Spain, Alonso had known about Benítez's reputation as a determined manager, one who would not bend to satisfy common opinion. Alonso was arguably Liverpool's most popular foreign player, his name sometimes sung before Steven Gerrard's on match days at Anfield. In a pre-season friendly against Lazio, when rumours were circulating about Alonso being sold to finance Gareth Barry's move to Liverpool, the roar from the terraces was deafening when Alonso's name was read out. 'You can shove your Gareth Barry up your arse,' the Kop chorused. Jan Mølby, the Danish midfielder who had starred in Liverpool's greatest teams and someone Alonso had been compared to due to passing range, spoke out about the possible move, stating it would be Benítez's worst decision since taking charge. Though Alonso remained, the reality is, had Arsenal or

Juventus matched Liverpool's £18 million asking price, he would have departed sooner than he did.

He uses the word 'professional' when describing his connection with Benítez thereafter, insisting that he did not harbour a grudge, 'because I'm not that type of character'. I suggest to him that it could not have been nice – as it would not be in any working environment – to discover your boss does not rate you as highly as previously believed.

'I was surprised,' Alonso admits. 'I was disappointed too, because I was very happy in Liverpool. I could walk down the street and people would beep their car horns and wave. I went for meals in restaurants with my wife [then girlfriend] and everybody was very polite and courteous. When my family visited from San Sebastián, we could explore the city without any fuss being made of us.

'None of this would matter to Rafa, of course, but why should it? He was the manager. He is always under pressure. He has his way of doing things. He has never changed. He probably won't. He was that way at Tenerife. He was the same at Valencia. Then at Liverpool too.

'I played against Valencia for Real Sociedad and his team was like him: extremely organized, you could say quite stubborn. He wasn't afraid to make big decisions and I respect his opinion as a coach because his way has been successful in many places.'

The last thing Alonso probably wants to do now is endanger the bond he created with supporters and team-mates alike by being seen to put the boot in. He is smart enough to recognize that both he and Benítez remain popular on Merseyside. Yet judging by the way he speaks, it seems inescapable that Benítez instilled a sense of resentment that made Alonso's departure inevitable.

'Yes, I can admit that my relationship with Rafa wasn't as good as it had been in the first year,' he says. 'But I didn't ask to leave because of that. I had been five years at Liverpool. I had the feeling it was the right thing to do. At the end of the season, the same thought was running through my mind: *Do I move on or do I keep doing the same thing?* You can be happy and restless at the same time: eager to try something different, intrigued by another project. Moving from Liverpool to Madrid was the most difficult step to make in terms of the decision. I was doing well at Liverpool. My family were settled and happy. But I felt that I had new things to learn, new challenges to take. You only live once. Life, for me, is about experiences. The only thing I regret is not winning the Premier League with Liverpool. I'll never know how that feels and experience the reaction of the city, as I did after Istanbul. It hurts because I know the people want the league title more than anything.'

Alonso talks like a manager and it is imaginable that one day he will follow that path. Having worked under Benítez, José Mourinho, Carlo Ancelotti and Pep Guardiola, he must have so much to pass on.

'People ask me all the time: what links these four guys? It sounds simplistic but, fundamentally, they are all leaders,' he says. 'They are the ones who, at their best, know how to take the pressure and worries away from the players.'

For the time being, only playing motivates him.

'I know these are my last years and because of that I want the success even more. I want to be productive. I don't look back at what I've done in the past or how I've got here. I only look forward and at ways of maintaining my levels.

'I am committed at Bayern until 2017. I want to win the Bundesliga again. I want to win the cup. I want to win the Champions League for a third different club. I want to win everything there is to win.

'And maybe then I will stop.'

CHAPTER EIGHT

cultzeros.co.uk

ALBERT RIERA,
Winger

ON LJUBLJANSKA CESTA, THE COLD RAIN BOUNCES OFF THE
concrete and the tin roofs of low-rise buildings with
such intensity and such a din it suggests winter will not
be leaving the Slovenian coast quietly this year.

From a food kiosk beneath the Bonifika Stadium,
a balding man called Daki sells different variations of
börek and the aroma of melting garlicky cheese blows
out from across the counter, enveloping customers in a
lardy plume.

The doughy snack is a reminder that Koper is a staging

post between Italy's north and Europe's east. Inland, the H-6 motorway roars south and old wagons carry produce like hams and milk to mysterious kingdoms such as Macedonia and Albania. Out in the Adriatic Sea, cargo ships from places like Venice, Bari and Split come and go from Koper's port, blasting their horns.

Daki speaks English and is keen to test it out. 'Not many people from your nation pass here,' he tells me. 'Yes, in Slovenia we have tourism but the people, they go to places like Bled or maybe Ljubljana. Koper? They get on the ferries or the cruise ships and leave almost straight away.'

Daki does not know I am here to meet Albert Riera, the former Liverpool winger who recently signed for the town's football team. Between unfamiliar men, however, the topic of football usually acts as an icebreaker, and so he proceeds to tell me about the current situation in Slovenia, where there are ten clubs in the league. 'Koper are tenth,' he frowns, pinning blame on the 'unhealthy' regime of the previous president who was ousted two months before.

I look at the *börek* as he slices it up with a large knife before handing it over to me on greaseproof paper. Surely nothing can be as unhealthy as this, I think inwardly, because Daki is speaking again and nothing is stopping him.

'We have new owners,' he continues. 'There is a guy from Belgrade and a guy from Zagreb: businessmen. They are doing better things. In January, Koper signed seventeen new players. This is what needed to happen. In December, the team was terrible. We were going down.'

Koper is not Riera's first Slovenian club. Towards the end of 2015, he signed for NK Zavrč, based way out towards Hungary in Slovenia's eastern borderlands. Zavrč is a village outfit and in 2009 they were operating in the sixth division, around the time Riera was playing in victorious Liverpool sides against Real Madrid and Manchester United. Improbably, Zavrč rose another four levels before reaching the top flight in 2013.

I had chosen to meet Riera because it intrigued me how and why he has landed in this unusual place, out on the fringes of European football. Rafael Benítez had spent £8 million to bring him to Anfield in 2008 and although he contributed towards Liverpool's best domestic campaign of the decade, playing in forty games that season, he is not remembered for any single moment or even particularly fondly. He finished his second season – the worst of the decade for Liverpool – suspended by the club after allegedly telling a Spanish radio station that Liverpool was a 'sinking ship' under Benítez. It was reported that the comment followed a fight at Melwood with a teammate. In more recent times, a photograph circulated in the British media of him supposedly enjoying himself in a casino while one of his more recent clubs, Udinese, were playing.

While I wait for Riera to finish a training session, I sit with the press attaché of FC Koper, and he is just as comfortable as Daki in telling me all the gory details about the club's previous ownership and that things are changing with the 'guys from Belgrade and Zagreb'.

Matej Babić has only recently celebrated his twenty-second birthday. He is tall, slim and is wearing a smart unbranded shirt, jeans and heavy boots. He explains that he has taken a year-long sabbatical from a law degree at the University of Ljubljana and that he might abandon education altogether because football is his greatest passion and what is happening at Koper is exciting him.

Matej originally got involved at Koper because his mother had contacts at the club and was able to arrange work experience for him. The two businessmen from Belgrade and Zagreb recognized his almost perfect command of English and Croat as an asset, especially when there are only ten people from top to bottom running the club on a day-to-day basis, and that includes the manager and his coaches.

'Attendances have gone up because of Riera, two hundred at home to two hundred away,' Matej tells me proudly. 'He came from Zavrč but so did several other players. In Slovenia, Koper is the third biggest club behind Maribor and Olimpija. We should be doing better than Zavrč but Zavrč were fifth and we were bottom. That's why we had to look at their squad and act.'

Matej says that at Koper, everyone has to muck in, doing things that would not be asked of them at English Premier League clubs where the organizations are huge. 'Multi-skills is the term they use in England, no?' he asks. Riera is not immune and it later becomes clear that this made Koper more attractive to him. Having played in six different countries, Riera had encountered many different people and therefore had many different contacts in the game. At Koper, the offer was not just to be a player but to learn how to be a sporting director as well.

When Riera arrives at the door, he is accompanied by Zlatan Muslimović, the thirty-five-year-old Bosnian international centre-forward who has also recently made his way to Koper from Zavrč, having spent most of his career swapping between Italian clubs before a couple of seasons in Greece and then China. An intense discussion begins. Riera and Muslimović are Koper's senior players and, like Riera, Muslimović is entrusted with off-field responsibilities, helping out with recruitment.

Riera is still in his training gear and applying an ice pack to his hamstring. His meeting at the door carries on for more than fifteen minutes and there is a sense it comes to an unsatisfactory end for Muslimović, whose voice lifts several times during the discussion. Riera greets me apologetically. 'Football,' he says, raising one of his eyebrows. 'Always issues to deal with, especially when you are not just the player. Everyone has an opinion on the way things should be . . .'

After Bonifika's redevelopment in 2010, Koper's headquarters were installed in a stand behind one of the goals. The stadium can hold just north of four thousand spectators but the day before my visit only seven hundred or so turned up to witness the defeat to Rudar Velenje, another club with relegation concerns.

Riera's flip-flops slap against the tiled porcelain floor and he jangles a set of keys in the left pocket of his shorts as he leads me to another office where he conducts operations every day after training.

'I am at work here until six or seven p.m. before I go back to the hotel where I am staying,' he tells me. 'There is so much to do. My wife and children will move here soon and we'll buy a house. I haven't found the right place yet. I'd like to live very close to the sea, like I did in Mallorca and like I did in Liverpool!'

His office is spartanly decorated, painted all in white. A crack extends across the ceiling and down one of the walls. There is a new computer, a new television, a new chest of drawers, a new printer and a 2016 calendar with some telephone numbers written on different dates.

Riera begins by telling me how he came to Koper. The two businessmen from Belgrade and Zagreb, it transpires, are former footballers who became agents. Riera knew Dušan Petković from his playing days at Mallorca and his business partner is Andy Bara, a retired Croatian defender who spent most of his career in Poland. The president at Zavrč had asked the pair to work with him and the relationship explains how Riera ended up in Slovenia in the first place.

'Clubs from Dubai and Qatar came to me. That was the type of move I was looking for: easier life, slower pace of game, sun. But Dušan called and spoke to me about Zavrč, about the opportunity to be a part of something very different. When he explained that he wanted me to be involved in everything, to have the possibility to call a player and try to convince him to come and play for us, I realized this was what I wanted to do. It was my idea to become a sporting director after football but Dušan made me realize this opportunity was unique. I could play, but I could be a sporting director at the same time. So I said, "OK, let's start now."'

Riera says the relationship with the president at Zavrč was good until the issue of contract renewals arose. With

Koper's situation becoming increasingly perilous both on and off the pitch, Riera and Petković saw another opportunity to start something afresh, where they would have all of the control.

'A new president arrived in Koper. He called Dušan and said, "I want to make a new club – everything to be different, a new project." He wanted to give me, Dušan and Andy all of the responsibility to create what we thought was necessary. The money? OK, it is not so good. Other offers were better financially but that is not my priority at this stage. Making my family comfortable is the key, because I've moved around so many places and now is the time to find somewhere where I know I will be for a long time. My wife is Russian. I am Mallorcan. We need to find a middle ground somewhere.'

The contract at Koper is the lengthiest Riera has signed in a fifteen-year career. It will keep him in Slovenia – if everything goes well – for the next five seasons. And yet the highest paid player at Koper (not Riera) is on less than €800 a month. 'My salary is nothing,' Riera says. 'I am certainly not here for the money.'

Rather, he relishes his newfound responsibilities. It means that, usually, he is the first person in to work and the last to leave.

Having grown up in Mallorca before living in urban cultural centres like Bordeaux, Manchester, Barcelona, Liverpool, Athens and Istanbul, I suggest to him that Koper seems a bit primitive.

'Maybe, but where else would I get an opportunity like this one?' he asks. 'To run a club, you need big money. I saw an interview with the Indonesian owner of

Inter Milan last week. He wanted €100 million for 20 per cent of the club. Here in Slovenia, I have an opportunity to start a project from the very beginning and to learn about something new where the pressure is not quite the same.

'If I had the opportunity to go back in time and change what I have done, I would not take that opportunity,' he continues. 'All of the decisions I have made – to move here, to move there – the decisions were made with my heart. The decisions were true to my thoughts in those moments.

'I had the same feeling about Koper as I did about Liverpool. OK, Liverpool is huge, one of the big European clubs. Koper is small. Outside Slovenia, few people have heard of Koper. The attraction of Liverpool was the history, the ambition and the expectation. When I was twenty-six, that was what I wanted. Now I am nearly thirty-four. I am thinking about the rest of my life.

'I have a lot of friends who have stopped football and they don't know what to do. You have a period after retirement where it is difficult for a footballer: *bop*, the end. How do you replace a routine that has been there for twenty years?

'I realize I cannot go on for ever. After every game, it takes longer to recover than it did before. My muscles ache. You realize time is catching up with you. I do not want to experience this period where I retire and I have nothing to do. I don't like the idea of relaxing, because after a while it becomes boring. A footballer's life is very short and I am satisfied by my career but there is so much more to do, more life to live. OK, thirty-four is old for a footballer but it is not old in life.

'The day I cannot play for Koper, straight away I know I am working for the club. It is nice, because I don't have to think about the future too much and it means I can enjoy playing without the fear of what happens next. I will be honest with myself. The day I cannot dribble past a defender is the day I will stop. Maybe I will be unsuccessful as a sporting director and I will have to change my idea, who knows? But I feel like I have to try.'

I question Riera about whether it is difficult getting Koper's squad to trust him. He trains and plays alongside the players but ultimately his say will dictate whether they remain.

'From the outside, I know people will say, "How can you be a player as well as a sporting director?" But it's so easy. My message to the guys in the dressing room was very clear from the beginning of our relationship: "Listen, here I am just a player. If I do something wrong and you are unhappy about it, you shout at me like you would any other player. I am at the same level. I am not more than you. I am not less than you." I want the same thing as them: to win games. When I walk out of the dressing room and up to the second floor into my office, only then do I think about the issues that can influence the team to improve.

'We are a completely new group. Seventeen new players is a huge number and usually it would be considered unworkable. But Koper needed a new chapter, for everything to be clean and everything to be transparent. We are careful financially and will not spend what we don't have. Of course we would like to bring in fantastic players but at the moment that isn't a possibility. We have to do it little by little.

'What we really want is to play in Europe. If you play in Europe, there are more possibilities: to earn more money, to bring in better players and improve the infrastructure of the club so that fifteen or twenty years from now Koper is leading in Slovenia and respected abroad as a small but well-run club.

'Immediately, the aim is to escape relegation. The people in Koper, they have never experienced an expectation like this. In the past, they have had the opportunity to sign some Croatian or Bulgarian players, because those countries are so close. But never Spanish, never French or Italians. If everything goes to plan, I am convinced that next season we can finish in the top three for sure – I am convinced.'

Amongst Riera's first big decisions was one to reduce the squad from twenty-five to twenty-two players, and then he had to inform Ariel Ibagaza, a former teammate at Mallorca and Olympiacos, that he would not be able to sign him, despite the Argentine's determination to move to Slovenia. 'Believe me, Ariel can still play,' Riera says. 'He called me on the last day of the transfer window because a deal to re-sign with Mallorca did not happen. But I could not justify changing everything for him, just because he's a friend. Our team is mixed between experience and youth. The next six months will reveal whether the young Slovenian players are good enough. I believe they are.'

There must be wanderlust in the Riera family. Albert's

younger brother Sito plays in Kazakhstan, after spells in Greece and Ukraine. He thinks it is strange that both of them have followed less-trodden paths, especially when he thinks back to a happy childhood in Manacor on the Balearic Island of Mallorca, a town best known as the birthplace of tennis great Rafael Nadal and his uncle, Miguel Ángel Nadal, an international footballer whose fierce defending earned him the nickname 'the Beast' during eight seasons at Barcelona.

'I guess you could say we are only the second family in Manacor,' Riera concedes, smiling. Riera's parents led modest lives: his father as a wood craftsman and his mother in a shoe shop. He thinks it is strange that he and Sito became footballers, because football was not in the family before.

'I never had any pressure to play,' he says. 'I remember my first game with Mallorca's first team. Not even one member of my family was there. You see some young players and every day they have a father or an agent pushing them. This was not the case for me. Maybe if my parents had pushed me, I wouldn't have become a footballer. I have always liked to make my own decisions. I was good at maths at school and one day my mother told me she wanted me to become a doctor. From that day, I wanted to be everything except a doctor. Had my father pushed me as a footballer, maybe I would have ended up hating it.'

Riera does not offer platitudes about the game like other footballers. He admits his motivation to become a player stemmed from liking the idea of being paid to get fit. 'I am not typical,' he says, revealing that the bug of football only really seized him when he was sixteen or seventeen years old, with part of the reason for his interest being the resurgence of his nearest professional club. Mallorca had bounced between the top and second levels of Spanish football until Argentine Héctor Cúper became manager in 1997, leading them to the final of the European Cup Winners' Cup two seasons later. Miquel Soler, Vicente Engonga and Carlos Roa were the team's main players but it was Jovan Stanković, the Serbian winger, whom Riera admired the most.

'I had the chance to be close to him and learn. He was my example. I had the opportunity to play with him. He left for Marseille and I was selected as his replacement. A big responsibility.'

Riera was exposed to the ruthlessness of football from an early age. Mallorca's progress was stunted when the club moved to a new modern ground on the edge of Palma. The results of before did not follow, attendances dropped and financial problems plagued his first two seasons as a professional. Riera was twenty years old.

'I was very, very happy, living at home, around people I love. The club came to me and said, "Albert, we have sold you to Bordeaux – the offer was good for the club." They told me to fly to Barcelona and sign the contract. I could not believe it. I wanted to stay in Mallorca. There was an offer from Atlético Madrid but my heart and mind was in Mallorca and I was too young to go. It showed me that in football, your life can change very quickly. If you become too attached, your heart can be broken.'

The move to Bordeaux was successful without being

spectacular. He went back to Spain with Espanyol and when that did not work out initially, he signed for Manchester City on loan.

English football supporters probably do not realize the esteem in which the English game is held abroad.

'For me, England is the home of football,' Riera says. 'I liked playing in England the most. People ask me whether I miss the weather in Spain. I always say, "Sunshine is for when we go to the beach. A wet pitch is for football."

'Real Madrid and Barcelona are the two biggest clubs in the world and maybe they always will be. But the best football is in the Premier League because you are competing every weekend. There is intensity in England – sometimes animosity – but also a respect. I played on the wing. The terraces were close to me. I liked playing close to the line. You can feel the crowd, hear the noises. In England, you can smell the soup! You experience every sensation: the sound, the scent, the taste of the football. At corners, the fans get very excited. The anticipation that something was about to happen was enormous. You don't get that in other countries. In Spain, I sometimes think the fans would ban corners if they could. In France, we would not even practise attacking or defending corners. In England, it is like a goal.'

Riera returned to Espanyol, where he resurrected his career under Ernesto Valverde, a manager who 'appreciated the value of traditional wingers'. Riera helped the team to the UEFA Cup final, only to lose on penalties to Sevilla at Hampden Park in Glasgow.

'Everywhere else I went, the managers wanted the

wingers to defend or cut inside to help the number 10. When that happens, you are no longer a winger. My strength was getting chalk on my boots and stretching the opponent's defence – focusing on the attack. Valverde let me do this.'

Upon signing for Liverpool, Riera can remember recognizing the step up in standard within five minutes of starting his first training session at Melwood, largely due to the presence of one player in particular.

'Steven Gerrard was sliding into tackles as if it was a game and he was playing Manchester United in the FA Cup final. He was the first at running and his passes always hit the mark. The level of commitment was clear: he was the example of the standard you had to meet every day. Otherwise you wouldn't be good enough to play for Liverpool.'

His first season, as he describes it, was like a 'dream'. The team spirit amongst Liverpool's players was fostered by results on the pitch and then reinforced on the golf courses of Merseyside. Each week, between eight and ten of the players would enjoy a round together, with Gerrard and Pepe Reina acting as the organizers and others like Daniel Agger and Dirk Kuyt usually following. Kuyt, an unconventional Dutch forward, was fashioned as a winger by Benítez and, according to Riera, he played golf as he played football: 'a strange swing but the ball usually appeared on the green'. Riera moved on to the same luxury housing estate as Reina and Fernando Torres and he formed a close bond with Reina and his wife Yolanda. When the couple's second son Thiago was born, Riera became the godfather. Riera's relationship with the goalkeeper grew on the drives to Melwood, sharing lifts. Reina was superstitious and would pay a visit to the same petrol station before games even if his car did not need filling up. 'If it needed four pounds, that would be his excuse. He did not want to change anything: same dinner, same socks, same underpants. Pepe's mad.'

Riera says Liverpool's players were individually of the highest level. What defined the strength, though, as they scored four goals against Manchester United, another four against Real Madrid, before five against an emerging Aston Villa side, all in the space of twelve days, was the organization of the team.

'Everyone knew what to do. Everyone knew their job. We played the same way in every game. I remember watching the video of our victory in the Bernabéu. We looked like machines – robots! The movements, they were the same time after time for ninety minutes plus injury time. I was against Sergio Ramos and Arjen Robben: world-class players. Robben touched the ball only a couple of times in the game. This was because of Rafa's plan. Everything was done before the game. He came to us: "Robben, if he does not get the ball, we have no problems." I had to stop Ramos. So I chased him all night.

'From the outside, the journalist might say: "Riera – he did not play well. He touched five balls; he did not give the assist for the goal." My job was to stop the pass from Sergio Ramos to Robben; it had to be delayed for as long as possible. I was running, running, running all of the time. I know this game was not my best creatively.

I could not say I enjoyed it. But it was so satisfying, leaving the pitch as a winner in the Bernabéu. Not many teams do that. We did. We had some great players. But the team mattered most. Benítez takes the credit.'

Off the pitch, conflict was never far away. By this point the club had been sold to Americans Tom Hicks and George Gillett, but the relationship between the two men had broken down, while trust issues lingered between Benítez and Rick Parry, the chief executive. It could not have been easy for Benítez, managing Liverpool and reaching quick conclusions with important decisions. Yet it was his choice to try to sell Xabi Alonso in the months before Riera arrived. Though the midfielder stayed, by the summer of 2009 – after Liverpool finished second in the league behind Manchester United – Alonso was ready to go.

'You lose a player like Xabi and it is like losing almost 50 per cent of the creativity,' Riera says. 'You lose a player who is strong in the dressing room, who is well respected by everyone, but also someone who makes it easier for everyone else to play to their levels. He gave balance, tempo, aggression and rhythm to the team – everything. [He was] a perfect player for Liverpool, the way we were playing.'

Wingers are often criticized in England for not influencing the game consistently. Benítez demanded that Riera stayed wide and assisted the left-back behind him. His contribution in an attacking sense would be determined by the service he received.

'For wingers to be effective, a lot depends on the middle of the pitch: the balance and identity of the players. These guys need to understand your movements and when to play faster, to be able to give you the ball in a situation where you can create for the next person. Xabi was intelligent and had a quick mind. He gave possession very fast, so I was one against one rather than two against one.

'In that first season, we had Xabi who could do this. We had Mascherano, who was aggressive. We had Stevie, who could release Fernando [Torres]. The spine was so powerful, so quick and so creative. When Xabi left, everyone missed him. The base was gone, the first pass.'

Riera cites the departure of Sami Hyypiä as being significant as well. The Finnish defender was Liverpool's captain before the responsibility passed to Steven Gerrard. After a decade of service, Hyypiä was disappointed in Benítez for not telling him face-to-face that Philipp Degen, a new Swiss right-back, was being selected ahead of him in his Champions League squad. Although Hyypiä was registered again after qualifying for the knockout stages and performed strongly in key games, the rejection made him consider his options and eventually he decided to join Bayer Leverkusen.

'Sami was very strong in the dressing room, another leader, trusted by everyone,' Riera adds. 'Another one: gone.'

Benítez was promised more money by the owners to improve other areas of the squad, and had that money materialized he might have made better buying decisions to enhance the squad. It was his decision, however, to replace Alonso with Alberto Aquilani, an Italian with a dubious fitness record, someone who arrived on Merseyside with an injury.

'People like to analyse football using statistics and theories. Often, success and failure is determined simply by the standard of the player: how you buy and how you sell, and the consistency within the squad,' Riera says. 'From a position of strength, change as little as possible, only buy. In the first year, everything was perfect: players, atmosphere and the organization. The feeling amongst the group was more important than talent or quality. But three players [including Álvaro Arbeloa] were allowed to leave. It took time for the replacements to settle. Maybe they never settled. The mood changed.'

Liverpool's decline was swift. An expected title challenge did not materialize and as 2009 became 2010, they were struggling to qualify for the following season's Champions League, having been knocked out of the present one at the group stages. Riera was out of the team.

'It was a special moment because it was before the World Cup in South Africa. I was not playing. Rafa was trying other players in my position. The trust wasn't the same as it had been the previous season. I wasn't sure whether I was being left out of the team because of my efforts in training and in the few games I played in, or for other reasons. I went to Rafa and said, "Rafa, I don't want any favours from you but if I deserve to play, please put me on the pitch."'

Riera's frustrations spilled over on the training pitches of Melwood. Left behind while Liverpool played an away game, he was involved in a fight with Daniel

Pacheco, the twenty-year-old forward. Riera describes it as the 'standard' thing that happens when frustrations and emotions are running high. Pacheco was a friend of his but he'd said something that upset him in the aftermath of a pass being short.

It was the start of what he says was a 'strange' period. Marginalized from the team, he gave an interview on Spanish radio. What Riera insists was a constructive evaluation of the season came across as a stinging attack on Benítez, with only a few words from a longer discussion being released, thus allowing the comments to be taken out of context.

'They asked me a question about Rafa's commitment to training. I told them he was not there every moment of every day because his office overlooked Melwood and he could see from there if he really needed to when we were doing physical sessions and the fitness coach was at work. They made a headline out of that: Rafa is not there every day.

'Of course Rafa was angry with that and I could understand why. I went to him and apologized, explaining that my words had been twisted. Rafa is a very strong character and he did not accept my version of events. He was under pressure and a situation like this only increased his problems.'

Riera describes his relationship with Benítez before the confrontation.

'Not really close, not really far away – it was somewhere in the middle. You are OK if you accept the situation and see it like Rafa. He wants to control everything. You cannot ask him not to have an opinion on your diet or what you are doing in the gym, because that's his way: he has an opinion. You have to respect what Rafa likes. If you accept this, then everything is going to be good.'

Now he is older, Riera believes he is able to see the bigger picture. Back then he admits he did not find it so easy to make concessions – 'to listen to the reason of others'.

'If you want to work with Rafa, it requires you to be objective,' he says. 'You have to realize he is managing not just one person but a group, a team and a club. The expectations on him are massive. He lives and dies by his decisions. That means he can only do things his own way. He cannot afford to make many concessions. Being the football manager of Liverpool, it is like being the prime minister of England or the president of the United States. The pressure never goes away: every second of the day, the pressure is there.

'The problem is, players are selfish. I was selfish. You are desperate to do well. You want to play. You don't always think that Rafa's job is more than just about you. I think I have learned a lot of details from Rafa. You realize you cannot make decisions that everyone will like.

'I have to look at myself. I realize now he did not put me on the pitch because I did not deserve to be there. As players, we are selfish. We try to think we have reasons to be angry. But I had no reason at that moment. For sure, he was not doing anything to hurt me or Liverpool. It was one point in my life where I look back and think, *Maybe it was me*. I did not accept Rafa's opinion but I did not analyse why Rafa was thinking this way. I did not look at myself. If I had been playing perfectly, would he have put me on the pitch? For sure he would. I did not finish the season playing and I missed the World Cup. Spain won the World Cup. I regret it.

'I do not have anything really bad to say about Rafa. Everyone is different and it would be boring if we were all the same. He is one way; I am another. I have a strong character and sometimes it is not the best way to be. I react so fast without considering the consequences. Sometimes you have to think. Rafa will stop and think – maybe too much.

'OK, maybe I would not go with him for dinner and maybe he does not want to go with me! We have no friendship. But that doesn't really matter. People always look for the bad things and the criticisms and they make you forget the good moments. Rafa was the perfect manager for Liverpool. We always ask questions about managers: who is the best one? The question should be: which manager is better for your club? Rafa was perfect for Liverpool and I would say Luis Aragonés was perfect for Spain too. I say this because of their intensity and their attention to detail. It is what the people of Liverpool demand and it is what the people of Spain demand. As a player, I never stepped on the pitch not understanding what was expected of me.

'Rafa, he also brought me to Liverpool and for that I am grateful. The first season was probably the best in my career, the most enjoyable. The second? Maybe the worst. It doesn't mean I only have to look at the bad parts. As a society, that's what we tend to do a lot.'

Liverpool's seventh-placed finish contributed towards Benítez getting the sack in June 2010. By then Riera insists his relationship with the manager had improved and he was confident of getting another chance to prove himself. With Benítez gone, however, his prospects became bleaker with the appointment of Roy Hodgson. Christian Purslow, Liverpool's managing director, had a list of players he wanted to sell and Riera was amongst them alongside Lucas Leiva, the Brazilian midfielder, and Emiliano Insúa, the Argentine left-back – both Benítez favourites.

'Hodgson, he was clear with us in the pre-season. He said, "I want 80–85 per cent of my team to be English." Rafa had been there for six years, something like that, so it seemed to me that Liverpool wanted to start again, to follow a different route. Hodgson wanted to start a new culture from the first day. I said, "OK, I respect your decision" but I didn't agree with it. In football, a mix is good. Sometimes you need something different. I felt I still had qualities to offer the team and the decision was purely based on where I came from.'

Riera went to Olympiacos, spending a season there, before moving on to Galatasaray.

'I made my Liverpool debut against Manchester United and we won [2–1]. Maybe the noise wasn't as loud as the derbies in Athens or Istanbul but noise is not the only detail that matters.

'In Athens, I can remember seeing Djibril Cissé shielding himself from stones being thrown by the Panathinaikos fans. You think, *If the fans do that to their own players, what are they going to do to us?*

'The only time I was scared in my life was when we won the league in Fenerbahçe's stadium with Galatasaray. We finished the game at nine o'clock and at five o'clock the next morning we were still in the dressing room, hiding. The police told us to stay. People were waiting for us. When we finally got out, it was like a film. For five kilometres until we reached the Bosphorus, the police vans were there: in front of us, behind us and by the sides of the coach. You could see the guns. You could see fire. The Fenerbahçe fans were burning everything: cars and buildings.

'It was the first and the last time the Turkish federation decided to finish the league with a play-off. The game had to be stopped six or seven times. The atmosphere, it was something different. A few months ago, the Fenerbahçe supporters tried to shoot the driver of the Galatasaray bus as it crossed the bridge. They were trying to kill the whole team. This is not normal. OK, as players we are paid a lot of money. But we should not have to deal with this.'

Riera signed for Udinese on a free transfer in 2014 and these proved to be some of the darkest months in his career. When a photograph appeared in a national newspaper of him in a casino on a match day, it portrayed a player not taking his responsibilities seriously, yet Riera says nothing was really as it seemed.

'It was not on a match day,' he insists. 'The club had not selected me or paid me for six months and I wanted to leave because of this. But I also thought the club should honour their commitment to me. When I signed, I did not put a gun to their heads. And they did not put a gun to mine. And suddenly, as if by magic, this photograph appears in the press . . .

'It was a very bad experience. I gave up fighting and went back to Mallorca because it was making me unhappy. I wanted to enjoy my life again.'

At Mallorca, though, he returned to a club with 'no clear objective' under a German owner where 'football is not the most important thing'.

Riera reasons that he has moved clubs so many times because of restlessness.

'If you are in the right place and you have everything that you need, why would you want to move? I admire the player that stays his whole life at one club, because it is so difficult. You see so many players and after two or three years their motivation disappears. These players need something else to [help them] switch on again. I see players like Jamie Carragher and Steven Gerrard in the same way Real Madrid supporters view Raúl or Roma with [Francesco] Totti. I wonder whether the pressure of remaining is actually greater than that of leaving.

'I would have liked this to happen in my career: to play for Mallorca for ever. Unfortunately, Mallorca wasn't able to win trophies. They needed the money and sold me even though I didn't want to be sold. Maybe I wouldn't have earned enough money at Mallorca to sustain my life after my football career was over. By moving clubs, it has taken financial concerns away. Stevie at Liverpool, he had everything. Totti at Roma, he had everything as well. Maybe they could have won more league titles at other clubs but if that comes at the expense of happiness and reputation, I don't think it is worth it.'

Riera has gone from playing in front of ninety thousand spectators at the Bernabéu to just a few hundred at the Bonifika.

'You have to accept the situation,' he concludes. 'The motivation remains the same otherwise I wouldn't be here. The pressure comes from within yourself: the desire to carry on and make a contribution towards a victory. There is no better feeling than the moment at the final whistle when you win. That still gives me immense satisfaction.

'The atmosphere is different, of course. It is more beautiful to play in front of a lot of people. In the big English stadiums, you cannot hear your teammate fifteen metres away because the crowd is shouting.

'In Slovenia, the stands echo.'

cultzeros.co.uk

JAMIE CARRAGHER,
Endurance

THERE IS AN IMAGE OF JAMIE CARRAGHER THAT WILL ENDURE for eternity, one where every strand of sinew in his body is surrendering to the physical torment of the event and only his soul would not submit.

This is a footballer who as a child witnessed his father order the breaking of a crossbar to get a game abandoned when his team was losing. On a different occasion, Merton Villa were in desperate need of physical reinforcement so Philly Carragher instructed his best mate, Bucko – a substitute that morning – to 'go on and sort out' the best midfielder on the other side. Though Philly had meant for the opponent to be stopped by sporting means, ninety seconds later Bucko had his tracksuit on again, banished to the touchline for headbutting.

In Istanbul, it was past midnight and into Thursday morning. Liverpool were still playing a Champions League final, having somehow hauled themselves from three goals down to draw level against AC Milan. Near the end, Carragher looked up to the scoreboard, wishing for time to hasten and for Liverpool to take the encounter to a penalty shoot-out. Carragher could barely walk; it was as if he'd experienced a death march. Jackknifed with cramp, he rose again. As the crosses were delivered towards the Milanese strikers, he kept defending, stretching his legs as far as he could, somehow repelling the danger.

'I've got a pretty good memory but that fifteen-minute period is a blur,' Carragher says. 'It was pure instinct to carry on. Coming off in a game of football, I saw it as a sign of weakness even if I was injured. There was no way that was happening.'

Carragher admits to 'taking a few clips around the ear' from Philly in his youth for asking to be substituted when, as a seven year old in a game amongst eleven year olds, his team were losing amidst a storm of hailstones on Buckley Hill, the pitches exposed to the wild elements in Netherton, Liverpool's north end. Later, at home in Bootle's Marsh Lane, he did not have to admit to feigning injury. His pupils were dilated with fear.

'I don't want you to think my dad's a bully, because

he's not,' Carragher continues. 'I owe a lot to him. He's the type of guy that offers you the shirt from his back. But there's no getting away from it, I grew up in a generation where if you did something wrong, there were consequences. I realize it's different now. That morning, my dad knew I'd bottled it because he'd seen so much football in his time. He was as obsessed as I became – if not more so. I can confidently say I never bottled it on a football pitch again.'

That Carragher played 737 games for Liverpool and is second on the club's all-time appearance list behind Ian Callaghan owes much to his mental fortitude. Ability propelled him into Liverpool's first team but passion and dedication kept him there. He possesses a spirit that underpins the greatest Liverpudlians and, indeed, the greatest Liverpool players. He agrees with Graeme Souness when the former captain and manager says that the moments he misses most are those in a tunnel in the minutes before kick-off.

'Gérard Houllier used to tell us that we were going to war. That stayed with me and I loved it,' Carragher says. 'I'd see teams walking out for cup finals at Wembley and the players would be waving at their wives and girlfriends. When we played ours in Cardiff, Houllier used to remind us, "No waving at family – you see them later." He wanted us to play as if it was the last thing we'd do.

'Players now, they're hugging and kissing before a game. OK, some of them might be from the same country, so it's understandable to a point. But for me, no: I was going to war with these people. You might think it's a strong analogy but I had to be like that. I was focused because I had to be. I couldn't afford to take it easy otherwise I wouldn't have been good enough. In the tunnel, I was going to war with them: it was life or death.'

The rule of combat was not exclusive to matches. Carragher is retired now and admits to not missing the training mainly because it was the longest part of the week. He took preparation so seriously that there was rarely an emotional let-up during the course of a football season.

'They're your teammates, not your mates,' he says of those he shared a working environment with. 'I'm still in contact with Stevie [Gerrard], Michael [Owen], Danny [Murphy] and Jamie Redknapp. Didi Hamann was sound and I liked John Arne Riise too. He was the one everyone took the piss out of because he was ginger and a bit daft.'

The rest he refers to usually by their surname, reflecting the distance. 'I was competing with Ziege for a place in Houllier's team for a while; I was competing with Finnan for a place when he first arrived. There was [Rigobert] Song before him too. Then Agger and [Martin] Skrtel. The different managers may have claimed otherwise but managers don't buy players to put them on the bench. But I also knew that they wouldn't be able to train to the standard that I did every single day, 250 times in that year. I just knew it. I knew eventually I'd wear them down. I knew that based on my intensity in training, the manager couldn't afford not to pick me. Most players want a day off but not me. Every day it was bang, bang.

The intensity never dropped. I never took it easy. I knew mentally I'd be too strong for the other players in the squad competing for my position. I trained as if it was a game. Even though I feared for my place, I knew that if I was at it day in, day out, I'd play.'

For a long time, Carragher roomed with Michael Owen, sharing secrets and frustrations. When Owen left for Real Madrid, Steven Gerrard took his place and for nine seasons the pair shared hotel rooms on away trips. They now speak once a week.

'It's down to circumstance with Stevie, really. Everyone has their own lives, don't they? Going in different directions. He's in LA at the moment. I liked a lot of the lads and the better players – the ones that stuck around. I think they liked me. I never shit on anyone and I wasn't a snake. I didn't sneak. I think everyone knew where they stood with me. I always tried to be straight. At the beginning of my career at Liverpool, I was a bit of a joker if I'm being honest. I loved a laugh. I still do. As I got older, I became more serious – maybe less pranks.

'I was desperate for the team to do well, let's not forget that. I tried to help people, especially early on when they'd just signed. The example is [Fernando] Torres. At first I thought, *God, I'm not getting much out of this one*. He didn't say a word to anyone and was struggling in training for the first week. So I bought my son a kit with Torres's name on the back. I brought James into Melwood to try to make Torres feel a bit better. James was only four years old and didn't have a clue. Torres obviously proved himself as a very good player but I thought he needed a lift, so I did what I could. The club made a huge investment in him. I cared about the club but most of all I wanted Torres to score the goals that would win us games.

'The Spanish players under Benítez were more outgoing than the French players we had under Houllier. You could mix with them a little bit. There were other characters that I got on well with straight away. Xabi Alonso was one. Pepe Reina was another. Pepe was larger than life and very popular, the typical mad goalkeeper.

'I hope my teammates liked me. But, being totally honest, I don't care if they didn't. I'm not a sensitive person. I was confrontational with people during games and in training but I'd forget about it quickly afterwards. We were there to win. We weren't there to be mates.'

When Liverpool did not win, it cut through Carragher's consciousness like a wound. As he grew older, he discovered how to disguise the face of pain. Yet inwardly, losing embarrassed him, it made him want to stay indoors rather than go out. Losing meant he cancelled planned meals out with his wife Nicola. He dreaded picking his kids, James and Mia, up from school. There was a temptation to go underground. But he always found a way to reappear above the surface – he'd never postpone an interview, even if it was scheduled for the morning after a bad loss.

'That's one big thing I enjoy about not playing: not suffering the disappointment,' he says. 'The low of the disappointment was more extreme than the high of the victory. When you did well, you felt only relief. You were happy that your head wasn't going to be battered for a week. You could get on with your life, take the kids to school – everything was fine. It wasn't as if you were buzzing. The worries went away for a short time. When we lost, I only felt enormous guilt. It was horrible.'

The guilt explains why Carragher is not ready to become a manager, instead choosing to work as a leading pundit for Sky Sports. When their enemies were at the gates, the Romans would suspend democracy and appoint one person to protect the city. It wasn't considered an honour; it was considered a public service. Carragher describes the position of Liverpool manager similarly, calling it 'a civic duty'.

At Liverpool, he played under six managers at first-team level, starting with Roy Evans and ending with Brendan Rodgers. He is put off mostly by the changes in character that inevitably happen because of the pressure. None of Liverpool's managers in his time left as heroes. Instead, they stayed long enough to see themselves become the villain. Liverpool makes mincemeat out of managers, chewing them up and spitting them out.

'The best Liverpool managers were the ones that weren't afraid to make big decisions,' Carragher says. 'Both Houllier and Benítez were like that, especially Rafa. I never looked at Rafa and thought he bottled making a decision in terms of his team selection or substitutions. I didn't agree with him taking Stevie off at Goodison Park [in 2007] and I don't know really why he did it, but Liverpool ended up winning the game, so he was vindicated. Then he took Torres off at Birmingham and he took a lot of criticism for that. Other managers wouldn't have done it. But he had the balls.

'You hear a lot of people discuss the art of

man-management. I would say not fudging a decision is a big part of that even though it gets overlooked. Big decisions can send a message to the squad. The squad thinks, "That could be me if I'm not careful."

'I felt sorry for Roy Hodgson. He must have wanted to drop Torres in those first few months. I wouldn't say he bottled it, though. He had no choice. David N'Gog was the only backup. Torres was playing so poorly and in training he couldn't get going. I remember watching Hodgson trying to butter Torres up and get the best out of him. I looked at that and thought, "Is this what management is?" I'd probably have grabbed Torres by the throat. But Hodgson had to put up with it all because he had nothing else to fall back on. He had to tell him he was doing well when he wasn't, try to find some confidence and enthusiasm in him.

'People say to me, "You'd be a good manager of Liverpool", and they get really excited about it. But I wonder if the modern player would match my passion and if not, how I'd react. You see some of these managers now and they're all calm and collected in the post-match interview even after a defeat. They probably are passionate inside but they know they have to put on a front. Listen, I know I couldn't go running around like a lunatic fighting with people but I just think I'd get frustrated with players that don't want to win as much as me.'

It is an oversight on Liverpool's part that Carragher is employed by Sky rather than the club he represented for so long. He possesses an understanding of Liverpool's idiosyncrasies and nuances. His passion is not senseless.

It is measured. At the very least, he would make a great adviser or administrator.

Listening to him, it is easy to forget that he grew up as an Evertonian, travelling to away games with Philly when he was as young as five years old.

'Like a lot of Evertonians, I suppose I was obsessed with Liverpool,' he laughs. 'I saw Liverpool's teams, especially in the early 1980s, winning trophy after trophy. Now, people might disagree but I think it's a myth when it's argued that Liverpool played flair football. When John Barnes was there, they did. Before he arrived, though, Liverpool had not had a natural winger since Steve Heighway's retirement. Liverpool's most successful teams were very powerful and strong. Everyone did the right thing. There was none of this open fancy football. It was playing the game with your head. Liverpool were men – real men; they knew what to do at the right time and knew when to play. They were streetwise. People say, "Look at Alan Hansen bringing the ball out from defence." But he never played in the wrong areas.

'I wasn't born then but I know about the UEFA Cup final with Borussia Mönchengladbach in '73 when the first leg got abandoned because of rain. The next night, they started the game again and Bill Shankly brought John Toshack back into the side at Brian Hall's expense. He changed the team to bring a big man in. He spotted a weakness in the opposition and exploited it by knocking passes up to Toshack. That was the Liverpool way: finding a way to win.

'Remember, my guidance at Liverpool started with

fellas who'd been in the Boot Room, fellas like Ronnie Moran, fellas around Shankly every day of their working week. Liverpool was a club that played passing football but without unnecessary risk. Ronnie never said, "Let's get it down, lads, and start passing it." There were no short balls or long balls; there was only the right ball. If they've got a weakness, you go for it. Ruthless. It was like, "Let's turn them and see if their defenders can run by knocking it in the channel." Liverpool didn't play unbelievable football. They played the right way and didn't do stupid things. You find a way to win. You have to be defiant, because that's the way Liverpool people are. Liverpool people identify with defiance, and when belief is generated from that, it becomes too much for opponents.'

I interview Carragher at the end of high summer across three sittings at different restaurants in Crosby. He lives in nearby Blundellsands now, a prosperous suburb in northern Liverpool. He bought land there a decade ago and has been building a home to his and Nicola's taste ever since. The latest development is the installation of a proper lawn. Previously it had been synthetic, so James could play football without dragging mud across the carpet. Carragher is back from a boxing session at the Rotunda gym when we first meet, which is situated a mile down the hill from Anfield.

'I go there every day,' he says. 'I could never be one of those people who does the school run and then sits on the couch watching Sky Sports News all day – oh my god, no. I've not done that once since retiring. I need to be out of the house, keeping fit, having a laugh with the lads, having a bit of lunch afterwards. By the time I've finished, it's nearly time to pick the kids up from school again, making their tea, then taking Mia to dancing or James to football.'

James is at Liverpool's academy. He plays as a centre-back, the same position as Jamie. James seeks advice from his father.

'We all have insecurities, don't we? He knows deep down whether he's had a good game or not. I was the same. Quite often, you're looking for a bit of reassurance. *I was OK, wasn't I?* I remember when our James was seven and he was having a bad game. He looked across at me and I glared back at him, "Come on . . ." Afterwards, I was angry with myself. What could he possibly gain from that? He was looking towards me for help . . .

'My dad didn't say much to me at all, even if I did well. You hear people say, "My dad was my harshest critic." I couldn't think of anything worse, coming home after a bad performance when your head's battered and your dad starts having a go. There are enough critics out there. Don't get me wrong, there have been times when I've pulled James to one side if he hasn't given it everything he's got. But not if it's passing, if he's made a mistake or missed a header. That's just football. I always want to see him switched on, to be alive. I tell him if he does that, he'll be all right.'

Carragher met wife Nicola at primary school and their houses were only a couple of streets apart in Bootle, an area of Liverpool that will probably always struggle to shake off a dubious reputation in the consciousness of the British public. The Strand Shopping Centre, where James Bulger was abducted by two other children in 1993 before being left to die on a nearby railway line, is a five-minute walk from the area of town where Carragher and Nicola lived.

A perception exists that Toxteth, or Liverpool 8, is the poorest part of the city, even though it never has been. That would be on the north side, in and around the hinterland behind Bootle's docks, which was economically savaged by the gradual closure of Liverpool's mighty port, despite the resistance by one of the most stalwart movements in British labour history.

Bootle began its history as a large, well-defined village completely separate from Liverpool. As the city expanded, Bootle found itself well placed during the expansion of the industrial revolution. It soon bulged with incoming labourers, who took advantage of the tram and rail networks to get to work at the docks, and became packed with trade buildings.

Carragher's childhood encompassed the whole of the 1980s, a decade where Liverpool's docks were sent into decline under Margaret Thatcher's Conservative government. From his bedroom window, Carragher could see the blue cranes of Seaforth's Freeport, a place where unemployment rates soared. Stepping outside his front door, he could whiff the stench of a considerably sized grain silo further down the coast in Kirkdale. Around the corner on Derby Road was Quadrant Park. 'The Quad', as it was affectionately known locally, was an abandoned warehouse and, along with Cream and the Paradox, was home to Liverpool's rave scene from the late eighties until the mid nineties. Nearby, old dock workers' pubs like the Chaucer were lively, spilling out on to the streets at night-time. That the Chaucer is now closed and has a tree growing through its collapsed roof might be a metaphor for the difficulties that Bootle has faced. Carragher recognizes it as a tough place but insists his upbringing was no more challenging than that of the majority of other footballers.

'I remember Gary McAllister coming to me with a paper and there was a story about the places with the lowest life expectancies. Bootle was fourth and the place he grew up in Scotland was third! We had a laugh about it and Bootle is tough, yeah. But in every footballer's auto-biography it says they came from a tough area. Bootle is no less tough than areas of Manchester, Newcastle, London or wherever, other working-class cities. People in these areas all face the same problems.'

During an interview before Carragher had his testimonial for services to Liverpool in 2010, we walked together around Bootle's streets. His presence attracted attention but not the kind Steven Gerrard might get if he went back to the Bluebell Estate in Huyton. There were no requests for photographs, just interest in the welfare of his family. Everybody called Carragher by his first name, James – as if he were still the young kid that kicked a football against the wall or the one that nipped into his dad's pub, the Salisbury, for glasses of Coca-Cola. They certainly knew Philly.

'I love Bootle,' Carragher says. 'I love the people there; I love the humour. I love getting together with my mates and my dad's mates from when I was growing up. If I think about the perfect celebration, whether it's a party or a wedding, I don't picture it at a fancy do in London. It's in Bootle on Knowsley Road, with people I know, where I can get pissed, I can get on the karaoke, I can get up and dance, I can do what I want, and no one's bothered, no one's watching.'

Bootle is also one of the safest Labour seats in the country. Carragher is a Labour voter. It is uplifting to hear a footballer talk about political issues. He can understand why few footballers do.

'I'm not going to sit here and say what we should do about immigration, housing or foreign aid. I haven't got a clue, really,' he begins. 'I watch *Newsnight* now and again, and sometimes I watch *Question Time* if there's no Thursday-night footy on the TV. But all I know is, where I came from people had fuck all and they've still got nothing. You go down Marsh Lane and it's hard. My parents split when I was a kid and I know lots of one-parent families and kids that have gone off the rails.

'I'm lucky because I've been a footballer and I work for Sky now, going to and from London on the train, wearing a lovely suit on the TV and it looks great. But I don't think you should ever forget where you come from. My background is working class. I always say to our James, "Son, you don't know how lucky you are." He can get new football boots if he wants. Mia can go dancing and, financially, it's not a problem. It's a case of whether she's got the time, whereas some of her friends can only go once a week because their families don't have the money. I'm reminding my kids about this constantly and I hope it's getting through, because they'll grow into better people if it does.

'Politics to me is simple. The Tories are for the people who have got a few quid and Labour is for the people who haven't. Now I'm in a position where I have a few quid. With the 23 Foundation [Carragher's charity], we give away food hampers at Christmas because some families can't afford a dinner in Liverpool. They can't afford to put clothes on their kids' backs.

'The attitude I've always had is, if there's a fella not playing well in your football team, you get around and help him for the greater good. What's the point of sitting in the pub having a bevvie if nobody else can afford to join you? What are you going to do, sit there on your own?'

While the whole of Bootle is undoubtedly Labour, the Marsh Lane area of the Liverpool suburb is also undoubtedly Everton. Liverpool is not a city where supporters of its football clubs are found bunched in particular districts. Marsh Lane is the only one and at the Brunswick Youth Club, known affectionately by locals as the Brunny, most of the kids wear Everton shirts. Carragher used to be one of them.

'We were all Evertonians, my dad especially,' he grins. 'You go into the pubs around Marsh Lane and you see pennants on the wall. The Everton games are always advertised and for the fellas who can't make it to Goodison Park the pubs have the games on TV. There is a sense of community.

'My brothers were mad Evertonians and my dad would take us to all the home games and a few of the aways.

My dad was known in the area as a big Evertonian. He ran on to the pitch at Wembley in the 1977 League Cup final to have a go at Gordon Lee, Everton's manager. Then, in 1984, he was pictured on TV kissing Graeme Sharp when Everton beat Watford in the FA Cup final. If somebody told him then that I'd play for Liverpool and he'd become a Liverpudlian, he'd never have believed them. But Bootle is the type of place where blood is thicker than water. He's a mad Red now. He drives all the Evertonians crazy.'

Because Carragher had grown up as an Evertonian, the Merseyside derby was more important to him than any other fixture.

'I was very intense. I thought about games days before. I was like that as a kid. You build yourself up all week into a frenzy. Ahead of the derby, you'd read the papers and see fans on the street. You'd get wound up. You desperately wanted to beat them. I mean, playing at Goodison – fuckin' hell. It was my favourite place to play an away game and win.

'I'm not blowing mine or Stevie's trumpet but the two of us were so up for those Everton games, their players couldn't match our will and aggression. So our record was very good. Before Stevie and I were in the team, Liverpool used to get bullied by Everton. That certainly stopped. We bullied them. Everton were a very good team. We usually finished third or fourth and they were fifth or sixth. But they struggled to beat us. I think David Moyes did it twice in the league [actually three times] in the whole of his time there [eleven years]. It became a mental thing for them. It got to the stage where they didn't believe they could beat us. They'd beat United, Chelsea, City and Arsenal. But against Liverpool they fell apart.'

Carragher believes both genetics and nurture offered him the platform to become a footballer.

'I achieved what I did because I was up for a fight, I had that drive,' he explains. 'Very few players have got it. I was born that way. I was the best player in Liverpool's youth team but I also had the most determination. My family don't stand back. My dad's got a short temper and I've got one. Paul, my younger brother, is probably the worst. Then there's our John who works on the [oil] rigs. We're all lively.

'I think my desire comes from my parents. I'm a mix of my mum and my dad. When my mum was pregnant, she was told that I might have spina bifida. They knew there was something wrong with me but she wasn't quite sure until I was born. I spent the first six weeks of my life in Alder Hey Hospital. My mum must have been pretty determined.

'In football, winning was always more important than performance. Don't get me wrong, if you play badly every week the chances of losing go up and you'll get dropped. But I grew up as a five-year-old kid seeing my dad hit a referee with a corner flag through anger about a decision he felt was wrong. George Cain was the official and he ended up refereeing in the Football League. My dad got banned for that. My family would do anything to win, even things that others might find unacceptable. You find a way.'

Carragher's childhood memories are filled with

weekend mornings spent at Chaffers, Brook Vale and Buckley Hill – amateur league pitches in Sefton – kicking in the goal at half-time or practising penalties with other kids. In the distance, he could hear Philly shouting at his team, whether they were winning or losing.

'I love this story and it probably sums up Sunday football in Bootle. Like me, my dad is an obsessive and as manager of Merton Villa he went to watch a rival team called the Cabin, who were run by two brothers. One of them played and the other one ran it from the sidelines. The one playing was completely taken out by an opponent, so the manager goes to a sub, "Get changed." The sub thinks he's getting a game. "No, get the fucking lot off – I'm going on." He was going on to take care of the fella. And he did!'

Carragher wriggles with laughter when he thinks back to the day his dad offered to give a referee, who lived in Bootle, a lift by car to a cup final being held in Kirby, several miles away. When Merton Villa lost, Philly decided to leave him behind.

Carragher was known around Bootle as the best young player and his talent was so obvious that he was regularly selected three years above his own age group for district sides. Playing as a centre-forward for Bootle boys', he scored more than fifty goals in one season, an achievement that led to him being asked to train with Liverpool, where he signed forms.

This was an era where the best young players in the country spent time at the Football Association's centre of excellence at Lilleshall in Shropshire. At home he still has the match programme of a game between England

and Italy schoolboys, where he scored past Gianluigi Buffon, who would become one of the greatest goal-keepers of his generation. Yet Carragher emphasizes that anyone who thinks his ascension to the top was a smooth path is wrong. He chose Liverpool over Everton because Liverpool's youth system was producing more players than Everton's at the time and his father recognized it before making a cold decision. At Liverpool, the standard was simply higher.

'My first years at Liverpool were very difficult,' he says. 'I think people thought, "This kid's coming back from Lilleshall, what's he about?" I wasn't physically ready to train every day and play competitive matches against older lads. At Lilleshall, you only played against lads your own age. At Liverpool, it was a free-for-all. You could be with the reserves or players younger than yourself. I wasn't prepared for the change in routine. My football ability kept me at Liverpool. If they had judged me on my physicality, I might have been let go.'

The structure at Liverpool followed the same pattern as that at many other clubs: the first team came first, followed by the reserves, then the A and B sides. The A side was open age: the best eighteen-year-old players plus reserves and occasionally a first-teamer working his way back to fitness. The B side included those aged eighteen and under.

'Anyone who was on a YTS contract and doing really well was in the A team. I was in the B team for the whole of my first year apart from one game against Everton where I was taken off at half-time after struggling play-ing right-midfield. I'd never played there before. Tony

Grant played in the middle of the park for Everton and ran the show. He later played for Everton's first team. We got beaten 2–0 and I couldn't keep up with the pace of the game. I wasn't ready for it. It was tough. I had doubts.'

To put it in context, David Thompson – who later played fifty-six times for Liverpool – was in the reserves aged sixteen, a level Carragher did not reach until he was nearly eighteen.

'It's not like today, where sports science can help a club predict how a player will grow. I don't think anyone was fighting my corner, saying, "Carra – he'll be OK in twelve months' time." I had to get on with it. It was down to myself to prove to them I could do it. I was playing out of my skin with the B team. But people looked at the B team as kids' football.'

Liverpool's youth structure was well established by the time Carragher joined and run by a group of men who'd long worked together, which meant there was a clear direction at the club running from top to bottom. Liverpool's B side was managed by Dave Shannon, Hughie McAuley was in charge of the A side and Steve Heighway was the overseer of the entire system. Heighway, recruited by Liverpool when Bill Shankly was manager in 1970, had won almost every trophy there was to win as a player, and many academy graduates credit him with playing a key role in their development. Heighway was educated to a university standard and an intelligent person.

'To be honest, most of the lads won't say a bad thing about any youth coach, because the ones you're interviewing are the ones that made it!' Carragher says sharply. 'But there's no doubt Steve had an authority about him. He was stern. You were a bit scared but in a good way – it wasn't as if you were petrified with fear. He would tell you if you weren't producing. When you describe someone in football as a schoolteacher, you automatically think negatively about the person. But with Steve, he was convincing and you didn't want to upset him. He trained with us and always looked the part. He could still do whatever he was asking of us.'

Heighway was most critical of Carragher and David Thompson.

'If we were getting beaten, it was always our fault even when it wasn't. We were strong characters, so we could take it. But I think he was thinking, *You two are the best players, so sort it out.* He'd tell us sometimes that he was only doing it for our own good. The others weren't good enough, so there wasn't any point in having a go at them because they weren't going to improve.'

Carragher believes it was guidance rather than coaching that helped Liverpool's young players the most.

'Dave, Hughie and Steve wanted us to be streetwise, to make decisions for ourselves. If we made a mistake, it was OK so long as we learned from it and didn't do it again. It's not a criticism of Liverpool's academy, but at every academy now a lot of the players seem the same.'

Carragher grits his teeth, clenching his fist, his speech becoming a lot quicker.

'I don't see many who have what I had or Thommo had. You'd always notice us whether we were playing well or not. We'd be loud, we'd be aggressive, arguing with each other, arguing with the referee. I'll be watching a youth game and all they want to do is pass the ball nicely.'

When Carragher was a teenager, Everton's best player was a midfielder called Peter Holcroft.

'He didn't have a career in football but back then he had a lovely left foot; he could run a game. You'd be thinking in the dressing room, "I've got to do him here." Maybe that sounds bad but I knew in my own mind that he was going to get it as soon as he received the ball for the first time. At that level you had to hit someone with an axe to be sent off. So he was getting it.'

There is a theme about those who became professional footballers and those who didn't.

'Look at Steven Gerrard, look at [Wayne] Rooney, look at me; Michael Owen was a nasty little bastard as a kid, let me tell you. He had a clean-cut image but when you look at some of the tackles he put in, especially early on in his career, he had no fear. Remember the one he did on [Peter] Schmeichel when he was eighteen or nineteen? That's why I like Jordan Rossiter at Liverpool now. No fear. He keeps it nice and simple; he's alive, he's on his toes, ready to fly into a tackle. You can see it; you can smell it. He's got something about him. [Rossiter has since been sold to Glasgow Rangers] There are plenty at academy level who are neat and tidy and nice to watch. But where is the personality and character? I get infuriated thinking about it.'

Beating West Ham United in the 1996 FA Youth Cup final helped propel Carragher and Michael Owen into Liverpool's first-team reckoning, an environment where the mood was not as professional as it could have been. In the 1990s, Liverpool's team became known as the Spice Boys and many of the club's players appeared as much on the front pages of newspapers as they did on the back. Liverpool's players were talented but they often fell short of meeting expectations at key moments, leading to the impression that they were not as focused as they should have been.

In the early part of the decade, Graeme Souness was sacked largely because of poor results but behind that was the fact that Liverpool's players refused to buy into his strict new rules, which limited drinking and changed eating habits, searching for healthier alternatives to steak and chips. His replacement Roy Evans looked to the past for answers, trusting players to bond socially and form a connection that would help contribute towards a positive camaraderie on the pitch. This happened at precisely the moment football was accelerating in the opposite direction, becoming an industry where extreme discipline and fitness were sacrosanct.

Carragher admits that first-team habits were confusing. Steve Heighway's discipline was unbending. It was not so intense with Roy Evans.

'It doesn't matter how the first-team players act, you look up to them because they're the stars,' he says. 'I was training with John Barnes and Ian Rush – competing with them.'

This was a time where a footballer's day was not scheduled like it is now. Like workers in other industries, an hour's lunch presented an opportunity to break free from Melwood, and the Liverpool players would walk over to the Sefton public house, a few roads away in West Derby, and during pre-season it was not uncommon for some to enjoy a relaxing pint or a roast dinner.

It was only when Gérard Houllier came in as manager that attitudes began to change. At the beginning of his reign, Carragher was censured for his antics with a stripagram at a Christmas party when photographs made the papers. On other occasions, he was caught out drinking with his mates from Bootle.

'I think I was always going to work well with Houllier because, although I liked a night out with my mates, he didn't have to make me train better. I'd always trained well and he loved me from day one because of that. Maybe it wasn't the case with other players. There's no doubt, though, that Houllier came at the right time. He was all over me. I was a bit-part player under Roy Evans but as soon as Houllier arrived I was in. He was talking to me all of the time and one of the first things he did was sort out a new contract for me with Rick Parry. He'd only been there a month. I think he loved my aggression and intensity compared to the others. He probably thought, *He's someone I can work with and improve.*'

Not everyone took to Houllier. Captain Paul Ince challenged him in a team meeting and was sold to Middlesbrough soon after. Robbie Fowler, who was en route to becoming Liverpool's greatest post-war goal-scorer, was also allowed to leave for Leeds United after clashes, as was David Thompson, who went to Coventry City. Each of them have since made public their views on Houllier, citing a lack of understanding on the manager's part. Yet Carragher explains the breakdown in relationships as being a result of something even simpler than that.

'You know what, there's no trait or no science behind it when a player doesn't like a manager. Ninety-nine per cent of the time it's because he doesn't play. It's very simple. You hear players say, "We didn't see eye to eye." No, no, the manager didn't rate you as highly as the other person he picked. If he'd picked you, then you'd have liked him. It's the same at any level of football or in any industry. If he puts faith in you, you'll have faith in him. Any other argument is irrelevant. If you were playing every week like I was, like Danny Murphy was or Michael Owen was, you'd like the manager.

'When Houllier came in, he didn't miss a trick. As soon as he saw something, he was on to it. He was comfortable taking on big characters at the club. Nobody was getting in the way of what he wanted to do in terms of discipline. Sometimes a manager might bend the rules for a star player or a captain and they say it's good man-management. But Houllier ruled with an iron fist. It was like, "No – this is what we're doing and this is how we'll do it." He took on Paul Ince. I remember him picking out [Jason] McAteer for saying something in a newspaper. If you did that, Houllier would pull you up in front of everyone. "It's a lack of respect for your teammates," he'd say.

'Houllier was massive on the team. Nobody would stop him creating a spirit. He used to do this thing with pencils to emphasize his point. He'd get one pencil and snap it. Then he'd get eleven pencils and say, "Try to snap that." You couldn't. The strength of eleven pencils was greater than one.

'His team meetings were unbelievable. I'd never seen anything like it before. I was in awe of him. Even someone like Gary McAllister, who was thirty-six, said he'd never seen a manager speak with so much passion. Before every season he'd do a big presentation, mapping out what he wanted to happen, explaining his values. It wasn't done by PowerPoint. It was a really aggressive, rousing speech.

'Jamie Redknapp didn't get on great with Houllier. But I always remember him saying that if Liverpool had had Houllier in the mid nineties, they'd probably have won the league and wrestled back the initiative from United.'

The narrative of Houllier's reign as Liverpool manager has been covered in other chapters in this book. The success achieved by him was underpinned by a powerfully built team, one that knew what to do tactically.

'It wasn't the easiest side on the eye,' Carragher admits. 'I know Houllier used to get upset with that, pointing out that we'd scored 127 goals in the 2000–01 season. He should have embraced it and celebrated the fact we were resolute. We loved going to places in Europe, playing shite football, drawing 0–0 or winning 1–0. When we were at our best, we could go anywhere and do a job. It didn't matter who the opposition was.

'If you'd looked at that Liverpool team without knowing who was in charge, you'd probably think it was a British manager. The size and power: we had four centre-backs in defence. [Markus] Babbel played right-back and had been a centre-half at Bayern Munich and I was at left-back and I later developed into an established centre-back at Liverpool. Babbel got forward more than me but I certainly wasn't a flying full-back. Then you had [Didi] Hamann in the centre of the park along with Stevie [Gerrard]. [Emile] Heskey was a big lad too and up front he helped it stick. Deep down, Houllier must have known he'd created a bit of a monster. He should have celebrated it!'

Houllier lasted six seasons at Anfield before departing in 2004. Twelve years later, he remains the most successful manager to have taken charge of Liverpool in a quarter of a century. Of all the managers Carragher worked under, his fondest memories are those with Houllier. It makes it easier to analyse where it went wrong for him, and Carragher admits that after Houllier suffered a heart attack in 2001 he was never quite the same.

'Towards the end, Houllier wasn't as aggressive, decisive and clinical. He wasn't himself. There were things that he wouldn't have let go a few years before. Maybe he realized he was clinging on to his job and needed people on his side. It happens to a lot of managers. When they go into a club, they know they have a certain amount of time to shape things. They can be combative. But as time passes, you probably need to be more of a politician while maintaining your integrity. Otherwise the politics of the club can drag you down. You become paranoid and lose your focus.'

Carragher looks back on Houllier's years in charge with great fondness. Yet the period was not without its frustrations. He thought about leaving Liverpool.

'Yeah, it got to the stage under Houllier when it felt like he was continually buying players in my position, so I considered it. I got wound up when Finnan came in. There was a constant mental battle to prove yourself. It was like, "I've been here seven years, I won the treble – do I still need to do this?" Then Benítez's first signing was a right-back [Josemi]. I thought, "For fuck sake, here we go again." I'd finished the previous season really well, even though Houllier was on his way out. I was like, "Yeah, I'm sorted now." Then a new manager comes in and gets a right-back straight away. Your mind begins to go. It was pissing me off. Mentally, it's hard to keep going season after season. In the previous years, I'd started each season thinking at the start of pre-season, "This person won't play ahead of me." It was on my mind all the time, every training session. It was exhausting. There's only so much you can take of that, being in a zone where you're so wound up.'

Carragher had finished Houllier's reign as a centre-back and played well. It was soon clear that Rafael Benítez wanted him to remain there.

'He was talking to me a lot in the early training sessions. He saw me as an organizer. I have to be honest, I thought my days at centre-back were over, really. [Igor] Bišćan had played there under Houllier ahead of me and somebody had said that I was too small. It got into my head that I was a full-back. I didn't look at Bišćan and Djimi [Traoré] and think, "Wait a minute, that should be my position." I was player of the year in Houllier's first season as a centre-back [1998–99] but had a few bad games the following season and was moved out. Maybe his way of thinking got into my head as well. I wasn't going into Benítez's first year with any guarantees.'

Carragher was not alone in wondering what it was like away from Liverpool. In successive summers, Steven Gerrard had thought about moving to Chelsea. In 2004, shortly after Benítez's appointment, Michael Owen followed through with the idea and went to Real Madrid.

'I roomed with Michael at the very beginning of my professional career and later I was with Stevie. We'd lie awake talking about things: our hopes, our fears. Stevie was thinking seriously about Chelsea and I'd say to him, "Yeah, but Liverpool is one of those clubs you can't walk away from. How does a local lad leave Liverpool?"

'I look at the career of Steve McManaman, who was a brilliant player and later proved himself at Real Madrid as world class. But is anyone really that bothered about it around Liverpool? Not really. McManaman won two cup finals for Liverpool on his own but because of the way he left, it gets forgotten. I'd lie there late at night with Stevie, because he'd have offers every summer to go elsewhere. "Remember McManaman," I'd tell him. "You might go and win something but in Liverpool nobody will be arsed about it." On the flip side, if you stay too long you get people saying, "You're shite, you're finished" as soon as you hit thirty and have a few bad games.

'I thought a lot about my reputation. Even now I do. Since I've stopped playing, I've worked for Sky and have a column with the *Daily Mail*. You get offered loads of different things for money and you think, "Bloody 'ell, it's good money that." But it wouldn't look right. Betting shops have been in touch asking me to do their advertising. It isn't me, so I turned them down.

'Players might not admit it but I'm sure if Michael could turn the clock back he would have stayed at Liverpool. McManaman is slightly different because he went to Real Madrid and won two European Cups. Deep down, I think most footballers want to feel loved. That's more important than anything to me. If I was advising a young player, I'd tell them to think about their legacy – how you're thought of at the end of your career.'

Carragher told Gerrard that if he were to leave Liverpool, it should only be for Real Madrid.

'Look at Ian Rush: he goes to Juventus then comes back to Liverpool. We had these conversations where I'd say, "If I was in your position and you don't think we're doing well, you have to go to Real Madrid." I didn't think Barcelona would have suited the way he played. Stevie was more dynamic. Look at what [Cristiano] Ronaldo did for Madrid; he probably couldn't have done that at Barcelona because the demands are different.

'I'd tell Stevie that if he was going to go to Real Madrid, it had to be when he was in his prime. Of course, we wanted him at Liverpool when he was in his prime but going there then would have given him the time to come back. If you go to Madrid at thirty-one, there's no way home. At twenty-seven or twenty-eight, it would have been ideal for him to do the foreign thing for three or four years.

'What I'd really say is, he couldn't sign for another English club, although I think he knew that. Especially being a local player. He'd come home from Chelsea with three or four Premier League medals but when he was forty, where was he going to go for a pint or a meal in town? Nobody was going to ask him about them because Liverpool people wouldn't be interested. In fact, we'd be fuming about it.'

Carragher believes Gerrard remained at Liverpool because, deep down, he appreciated all of this. In the years where he could have left, it was felt that Liverpool were close to being where they wanted to be: reaching cup finals in Europe and at home, winning a few, getting a bit closer to the league title. It was enough to keep Gerrard, despite the efforts of opponents like Raúl, who asked Gerrard to sign for Real during a 4–0 victory at Anfield in 2009.

Carragher admits Gerrard was more emotional than him, despite a public persona that suggested he was always in control.

'Considering how good a player he was, Stevie would worry. I know the Lampard–Gerrard thing used to annoy him [where the two midfielders' performances for England were constantly cross-examined]. It didn't get him angry but it would be inside his head. It boiled down to his desire to be the best. He didn't want to fall behind. He didn't want Liverpool to fall behind.'

Gerrard is not alone in his insecurities. Carragher has the same impression of Graeme Souness and Roy Keane, midfielders with similar reputations – characters he's since worked with for Sky.

311

'No player is brilliant at absolutely everything. Everyone has a weakness or something, at least, they're not so good at. The greatest players, I think, use that insecurity as motivation. It drives them on. You think about Souness and Keane, you see them on the TV and think they're superhuman. But when you talk to them, you realize there is a sheen to their personality. Chip away and maybe they're not as confident as they seem. Put them on the football pitch and it's like they put a tin hat on and power through. The determination to be the best and the insecurity drives them.'

Carragher says he isn't aware of any other clubs making offers for him and wonders whether it's because he made it known how happy he was at Liverpool through the press. During a television interview in 2006, when asked whether he'd ever sign for a bigger club than Liverpool, he responded incredulously and emphatically: 'Who's bigger than Liverpool?'

'I nailed my colours to the mast so much, I wonder if it put other clubs off,' he says. 'Maybe they thought I wouldn't leave. Sometimes I probably undersold myself. If I'm being totally honest, when I was at my peak – for four or five years – I could have played for anybody. I don't want that to make me sound like a big-head. Maybe Barcelona or Real Madrid would be taking it too far because of the unbelievable type of football they played, with full-backs flying everywhere. But in that period, I was playing for a team that was featuring in the semi-finals or the final of the Champions League. There was me, John Terry, Rio Ferdinand, Carles Puyol, [Fabio] Cannavaro and [Alessandro] Nesta. I wouldn't say I was any better than them but I was competing at the very highest level.'

Carragher says he sympathized with new signings trying to fit in at Melwood, as it was a process that he never experienced elsewhere. He began to realize that those who made a positive first impression would often end up being a success at Liverpool, though it wasn't always the case.

'You know pretty early but not always. [Momo] Sissoko's first week in training was horrific. But he ended up being a good signing for us. The really good ones, you get an idea with on the first day. When Xabi Alonso came in, you could see immediately [that he was talented] because of the way he passed the ball. I'm not talking about 60-yard passes, I mean 10-yarders: *bang* – punching it in. He looked the part.

'I remember looking at [Igor] Biščan and he had a pair of Copa Mundials on. His laces were done so tight, you're thinking, *What top player does that?* He just didn't look right. How was he going to kick the ball properly?'

Didi Hamann was one player who did not impress Carragher initially in his first season only to improve drastically in the second and thereafter.

'It sometimes happens the other way, where you get kidded someone is a good player by the way they start, having five or six good games early on. You think, *We're on to someone here.* Josemi was one of them. He was aggressive, getting stuck in in training and playing well. Then in his third game, someone ran away from him at Bolton and suddenly you think, *Hmm, that's a bit worrying*. As the season goes on, you realize the truth.'

There are a few signings Carragher believes Liverpool should have made. Damien Duff from Blackburn was one under Houllier.

'We finished second and as a player you think about the players you've faced who could win us the league. We didn't have a top wide player and Duff was playing really well for Blackburn. We beat them 4–3 at Anfield and he was brilliant. Realistically, you're also thinking about who you can buy. Duff had grown up with Blackburn, which isn't too far away. Sometimes I look back and think, *I wish I was the manager back then; why did you not do that?*'

Under Benítez, Liverpool's spine was as strong as it was under Houllier. The problems, again, were in the wide positions.

'We used to ask Rafa a lot about Joaquín [the Real Betis winger]. Rafa was adamant his mentality was wrong. Maybe he was right, because he probably didn't fulfil his potential. But sometimes a player comes to a club and it clicks, even if it makes a difference for one season only.

'Simão was another one. I'd marked him against Barcelona in the UEFA Cup semi-final at Anfield in 2001 [which Liverpool won 1–0]. He was so wide on the pitch, right on the touchline. I was permanently worried about where he was. He was really clever with his movement. I think he might have been a good one, because I like those wide players who can play on both sides. The story goes that we missed out on him but if we really, really wanted him, why was the deal only being finalized on the last day of the transfer window? I wanted us to get him but when the deal fell through I was wondering whether he was a panic buy because it was so late. If he's your man, put a bid in in June or July.'

The purchase Liverpool made that surprised Carragher the most was Peter Crouch.

'I couldn't believe it when we signed him, being totally honest. It was a strange one because we had [Fernando] Morientes at the time already and I was thinking to myself, *Morientes can't run; Crouch can't run – how's this going to work?* Initially, I think Rafa wanted to play the two of them together, because he told me about the option of playing Morientes in the hole. It looked really slow to me, that, especially when you consider Rafa sometimes liked to play counter-attacking football away from home. Who was going to run?

'Crouchy, though, was a brilliant player for Liverpool. People go on about his height [Crouch is 6 ft 7 in.] but it was his finishing that set him apart for me. Look at the different types of goals he scored. Whenever he had a clear sight, he slotted it coolly. He was a brilliant finisher: volleys, overhead kicks, headers. He was never going to win us a league but the job he did was very good. He was a great lad to have in the dressing room too.'

Under Benítez, Carragher says British players generally struggled to make an impact.

'The ones that had been there before were OK because we were used to the intensity of the training under Houllier, where the game at the end of the session was at match pace with tactical responsibilities and positions. Jermaine Pennant and Craig Bellamy weren't used to this, for example. It's fair to say Craig didn't like Rafa at all. Rafa is someone who breaks your game down and tells you exactly what he wants you to do. For a defender, it's not so bad, because it's black and white: when a ball goes in a certain area, you've got to be there. I can understand why a forward might find it frustrating, especially when you first join because you're desperate to start scoring goals and play a bit off the cuff. Robbie Keane later had the same problem.

'I've realized that you have to deal with attacking players differently to the way you deal with defenders. With strikers – or creative types – you have to treat them like you'd treat your daughter. With your son, you can be a bit more forceful – *liven yourself up* – but with your daughter you have to check they're OK and make them feel valued. Going back to Torres, that's what I tried with him.'

It is fascinating listening to Carragher open up about his relationship with Benítez. He credits the Spaniard with helping him establish himself as one of the most consistent high-performing defenders in Europe. Despite what critics think, Carragher believes Liverpool's run to the Champions League final in 2005 would not have been possible without Benítez in charge. And yet, within twelve months of his appointment at Liverpool, their bond had loosened. By the time Benítez departed in 2010, it had broken. They have not been in contact since.

'When Rafa came in, it was like Houllier all over again – he took to me straight away. He'd won two La Liga titles with Valencia, a team I knew all about. I'd played against them twice and watched them loads on TV. When Rafa was appointed, I thought, *Yes!* What a team, and he was the manager of it. I was made up. It was really bold of Liverpool to go and get him.'

Benítez's first hurdle was convincing Steven Gerrard to stay at Anfield.

'It quickly became clear that Rafa's not the type of fella you have a laugh and a joke with. He's not like the father figure that Houllier was. He was serious about football and that's where conversations ended.

'Stevie needed a bit of persuading that Liverpool were moving in the right direction, because Chelsea had made an offer. Rafa was very straightforward. He'd just met him for the first time and started going through the way he viewed his game, saying that he ran around too much. I was thinking it wasn't really the time for a breakdown of our best player's game. We really needed to get him to sign a new contract.'

Gerrard remained but a rapport never developed between him and Benítez beyond discussions about training sessions or games. In his autobiography, Gerrard said that Benítez did not like him as a person but that he never understood why, calling him 'emotionless' and 'distant'. Gerrard wrote that he could pick up the phone to any of his other managers but not Benítez. Like Carragher, he has not spoken to him since 2010.

At the beginning, the dynamic was slightly different.

'Rafa probably used me to try to get through to Stevie,' Carragher explains. 'I was in Rafa's office once a week at the start of that first season. He was trying to put his thoughts and beliefs into me. "This is what we're trying to do; this is what we did at Valencia. We're struggling because of this and we're going to sign this player." I've never had more information out of a manager. He'd tell you a lot of things. It made me feel great because it suggested that he fancied me as a player.

'It was only over time that I realized he was trying to influence me a bit by getting me on side. Most of the conversations led back to Stevie. He knew Stevie and I were mates. He probably wanted to know what he was thinking and saying about him.'

Benítez needed Carragher as an ally in those early months in charge. In the 2004–05 season, Liverpool lacked the physicality to convince in the Premier League and stumbled through the Champions League group stages, winning two from five games until the final fixture came along. The victory over Olympiacos was settled by a Gerrard blockbuster in front of the Kop as injury time approached.

Liverpool steamed through the knockout rounds, a process where Carragher says Benítez's influence was defining, despite what rival managers and critics like Sam Allardyce claim.

'Allardyce said in his book that winning the European Cup had nothing to do with Benítez. I mean, come on! How can you win a European Cup without the manager playing a major part? Sam embarrassed himself saying that. Anyone who says Rafa was lucky probably hasn't won a European Cup before, because along the way of course you need a bit of luck, especially if the team isn't as talented. If Rafa's lucky, then that makes me lucky too.

'Liverpool won the European Cup for a number of reasons: Benítez's tactics on the way to the final and for the final itself, Stevie's brilliance and the contribution of other key players. Then there was the crowd. We fed off the crowd. You can't quantify how important the crowd was, because there are no statistics. That's not me paying lip service because the supporters might like it. Against Chelsea [in the semi-final], the crowd inspired us as players but it affected Chelsea's players too. You could say the same against Juventus and then Istanbul.

'In the final, we were 3–0 down at half-time. Rafa was brilliant here. We were getting battered, everyone was panicking and two players had had to go off injured. We could have lost our heads completely but Rafa remained cool. Rafa's a thinker. He's not a motivator. Yet his finals became emotional occasions. We probably ended up winning because you had Rafa being a pragmatist on one end of the scale and me and Stevie playing like kids in a schools' cup final at the other. I started the move that led to the equalizer, didn't I – how many times has that happened?

'People then say Rafa made a mistake with his team selection in the first place by choosing Harry Kewell and not Didi Hamann. I'll admit, I thought to myself, *That's bold*. But if he'd brought Didi on and kept the formation the same, I think we'd have lost. It was the tactical change – going three at the back – that made the biggest difference in the end.'

In the aftermath of Istanbul, Carragher returned to Melwood to see the club's doctor. An unscheduled meeting with Benítez, who was there planning for the

319

following season, proved to be the moment where the reality of their relationship was exposed.

'I was told Rafa was upstairs, so I thought I'd go up and see him and say hello. We spoke about the players he was trying to sign and everything seemed great, I was really encouraged. "About your contract," he said. I immediately thought it was strange that he was bringing up the subject, because I'd only ever dealt with Rick Parry about contracts. None of my previous managers had got involved.

'Rafa goes, "We can't lift your wages, because I'm trying to buy other players." I was shocked. The last time I was due to sign a contract, I broke my leg at Blackburn but Rick still honoured the agreement, so I signed it when my leg was still in plaster while I was still a left-back. Now, I was a centre-back and we'd won the Champions League a few weeks before. Then I felt like he was taking me for granted. I was imagining him going to Rick Parry, "I've got Carra on side here. He trusts me. I'll sort this one out, Rick. It's only Carra." He even asked me, "Are you thinking about money or football?" as if I wasn't the sort of character to focus on football for the next four years. It was the first time it hit home that with Rafa, football was business.'

Carragher eventually committed himself to Liverpool but two years later a similar impasse developed.

'Five players had contracts that were due for renegotiation. Liverpool usually handed out four-year contracts to their best players and would discuss terms again halfway through. I knew I'd sign. I didn't want to go anywhere else. Some of the others might have been looking at what was on offer elsewhere.

'Rafa calls me into his office and says, "We're going to sort yours out last." I asked why that was. "Because I know you won't leave." So, I was the most loyal in Rafa's eyes but I was getting put to the back. Now listen, it was probably the right thing for the club, as obviously you don't want people who are more likely to leave to go. But again it felt like he was trying to capitalize on my closer links to the club.'

Graeme Souness had attempted to follow the same path as Benítez in dealing with player contracts before appreciating he had taken too much on and realizing that the process only led to resentment between player and manager.

'People reading this interview might say, "Yeah, well, Carragher, he's paid lots of money, so it shouldn't matter." Others will realize that it's an issue of fairness and respect that would affect any person at any work place.'

Carragher was driven by torment, self-reproach and a daily churn of fear. Steven Gerrard drank from the same reservoir of insecurity. Carragher thinks again about all those hours spent together in hotel rooms, sharing their impressions.

'Stevie's more high profile than me, yet he's more introverted than I am,' Carragher says. 'I was louder. He's a little bit of a worrier, although we all are; it's how you hide it. No matter who you are, you have insecurities. I've listened to him in the room thinking, *Stevie, you're one of the best players in the world.*

'In the periods where I wasn't playing well, I'd be more nervous going into a game. You put an act on, whether it's in the changing room or with the press. People might see Stevie and I as players who can blank it all out but I can say 100 per cent that neither of us ever took our place in the team for granted. I remember when Kenny [Dalglish] bought Charlie Adam and Jordan Henderson. We were already well stocked for midfielders. Stevie was injured and he goes to Kenny, "'Kin 'ell, where am I playing?" He said it as a joke but, knowing him well, he really meant it.'

To a large extent, the success of Carragher's and Gerrard's careers was driven by fear: the fear of losing, the fear of letting people down, the fear of being dropped.

'It's a good thing to have, fear. You should never lose it. Because when you do, that's when you start getting complacent. We never took anything at Liverpool for granted. When I retired, Alex Ferguson wrote a letter to me. Michael Owen got in touch, asking for my address. So I wrote back to Ferguson, thanking him. We ended up meeting over a meal. You have rivalries with these clubs and people but once you stop playing, they go. Look at me with Gary Neville [as Sky pundits]. I used to go away with England and didn't really bother speaking to the United players because a few weeks later we'd be kicking shite out of each other. But when you finish, it's like two boxers at the end of a fight.

'Ferguson was top class to be honest. I enjoyed his company. He told me he wrote another letter to Brendan Rodgers when he earned promotion with Swansea. The one piece of advice he gave him was not to lose the fear. I thought then, *You know what, I've had that my whole career*. This was coming from a manager who has won everything there is to win. It makes you think. What he probably meant was, "OK, Brendan, you've got Swansea promoted but don't think you're the bees' knees now." It always makes me laugh when a player says he's got nothing to prove. You've always got something to prove. Every day in training you have to prove to your manager that you've still got it. You've got to embrace the fear. I had that without ever really thinking about it until it was over.'

Carragher is a man driven by passion. That does not mean he was a rebel of the dressing room. Pepe Reina, Liverpool's Spanish goalkeeper, mentioned in his autobiography that he was surprised both Carragher and Steven Gerrard acted in such a dignified way when the club's financial future seemed in peril towards the back end of the decade under American owners Tom Hicks and George Gillett, a period where Benítez's politicking accelerated.

'It wasn't the Liverpool way to speak out against the club,' Carragher reasons. 'It bothered me deeply that things weren't as they should have been. I thought a lot about the future of the club, the direction it was going in, the way it was run and how it was perceived from the outside. There were things that Liverpool should have been doing in a certain way, the correct way. You associated class and dignity with Liverpool. Everybody else was fighting. If the players got involved, what's left?'

Carragher had already released his own compelling autobiography by then. In the nicest possible way, he'd likened Benítez to a 'pub bore' – a man with an answer to everything. It was a bold statement for Carragher to make, considering Benítez was still his manager.

Outwardly, Benítez's and Carragher's relationship continued to work: Liverpool won the FA Cup in 2006, reached another Champions League final in 2007, a semi-final in 2008, before mounting a title challenge in the Premier League in 2009.

Yet behind the scenes, a feud between Steve Heighway, the academy director, and Benítez had resulted in an impracticable situation where nobody benefited. It was symptomatic of the dysfunctional working relationships at Liverpool.

'When personalities don't like each other, they hope the other person doesn't do well. Do I think Rafa wanted Liverpool to win the FA Youth Cup? Probably not. Did people at the academy really want Liverpool to be flying under Rafa? Probably not. When a relationship breaks down like that, the club suffers. At the end of the day, who's really missing out? The kids.'

The 2009–10 season proved to be Benítez's last. Results at the beginning were bad and after a home defeat to Aston Villa, a summit was called at Melwood.

'Rafa had said in the press that some senior players needed to start taking more responsibility. He later said it wasn't aimed at me and Stevie but I thought it was a careless thing to say bearing in mind Stevie and I had probably taken more responsibility than any of the players in the league since Rafa had taken over, not in terms of performance or playing really well, but in terms of being available week in, week out – never hiding. I didn't even miss the Carling Cup games. I was thinking, *I'm there every single game.*

'It was the only time in my career where I felt like I could have done with a bit of reassurance. I knew I wasn't playing well and I looked towards the manager and thought, *You know what, I've done all right for you for five years, just pull me to one side and, rather than going through what I've done wrong, say something positive.*

'We had a meeting and, in fairness, most of the squad had their say. It reflected the bad feeling that had built up after Xabi Alonso left, because Xabi was a really popular character. I don't think Rafa ever really recovered from that meeting. I'm surprised it never got out in the press, because it was quite eventful. Even [Javier] Mascherano spoke out, though I'm pretty sure he was angling for a move to Barcelona at the time. Like a lot of the South Americans, Mascherano had been really close to Rafa.'

There is an overriding feeling that Carragher respects Benítez the coach, but Benítez the human being not quite so much.

'Yeah, I thought Rafa was a brilliant coach,' he says. 'I realize he was managing Liverpool at a difficult time when the owners were at war but he rubbed too many people up the wrong way and it caught up with him in the end.

'It didn't stop me going into work every day and trying to learn from him, though.

'I was like a sponge under all of my managers. I

listened to every word a manager said to me. Sometimes I saw other players and they weren't concentrating. They weren't even looking at the manager. I'd have hit them for that if I was the manager. I put myself in the manager's shoes and made sure I always looked at them in the eye, even if I thought what they were saying was bullshit.'

There is a common narrative that runs through Carragher's career, one which says he would not have emerged as a top-class defender had it not been for the intervention of Benítez.

'Yeah, Rafa had a big role in my development, there's no question about it,' he says. 'But what I hate is a manager or a coach taking total credit for players doing well; I hate it with a passion.

'You hear scouts claiming glory for spotting someone. Yet ultimately it's the player that has to go and play. Don't get me wrong, Houllier took me to a certain level, then Rafa took me to another level by playing me in my best position.

'OK, Rafa takes a lot of credit. Fair enough. But when we were doing defensive sessions and I was picking things up and carrying out exactly what he wanted, Josemi was involved in those sessions too. He didn't improve. Kromkamp was doing them too. Where did he go? It wasn't as if the coaching was one-on-one training. The manager put a session on for the defenders and because I was clued up, listened and took things in, progress was made. OK, thank you for the information but I had to take it off you and implement it into the game. It's not all about me and you've been a great help, but don't tell me otherwise.'

He continues. 'You hear coaches at academy level take all the credit for a player's development. "They came through with me," they say. Well, if it's all about you, why didn't twenty-five other players come through in that year as well? That kid's got ability, you helped him – that's it.

'I don't want this to be misinterpreted as me criticizing Rafa, because I'm not,' Carragher concludes. 'I have huge respect for what he's done in his managerial career and especially what he did at Liverpool. He just wasn't a manager you could have a long-term relationship with. Many are like that now, partly out of circumstances, because management is a tightrope. When I really think about it, I don't particularly want to have a relationship with any manager anyway – just pick me every week, which he did. Sound.

'What I will say is, Rafa knew lots about defending and he helped my game enormously. He wasn't the type to crack a joke but he got results. In the end, the results dried up and that's why he left the club.'

Mention of Benítez's legacy returns Carragher to where he is now: away from the club, and not as a manager anywhere else. Has the game lost something?

'People say, "Have a go at management, go 'ed, have a go!" Then I look at someone like Rafa and see how successful he's been, look at what he's won. Very few managers can match that. But even he – with all of the big clubs he's been at – is having to justify himself. You see every manager who has lost his job and they're talking about what they gave to a club. It must be going around their heads all of the time.'

There is a sense almost that Carragher loves football too much to become a manager, a job he realizes can make a person become 'bitter and twisted because it eats them up'. He wonders whether managers ever find a way to relax: 'I see them and think, *Just go and have a bevvie!*

'The best teams are always a reflection of the manager,' he continues. 'Look at Mourinho – Chelsea had a winners' attitude. People say Roy Evans was too nice, his team were too nice. Ferguson – he was a gambler, wasn't he? He backs the horses. Well, his team were gamblers, weren't they?'

And Benítez's teams? 'Defiant . . . or stubborn. Stubborn – really, really stubborn.'

It is impossible to see another player in Liverpool's history being like Carragher or, indeed, Ian Callaghan: one-club men; men carved out of hard stone from the Mersey riverbed. Carragher never became the PR-moulded, bland character we now expect – but loathe – of our Premier League stars. His searing honesty is the reason Anfield identified with him more than any other player of his generation.

And yet, because he stayed at Liverpool his entire career, it was difficult for him to enjoy the moment. Bill Shankly referred to the quest for success when the responsibility is with you as being like a river, 'Something that goes on and on.'

'You can't take a break because if you have a break, you're fucked,' Carragher says. 'Someone else would try to take your place. Winning wasn't really a joy, it was a relief. Sometimes you weren't even happy you'd won.

You were happy you'd stopped someone else winning. I remember beating Everton in the FA Cup semi-final in 2012. It wasn't a case of, *Great, we're in the final*. It was, *Christ, I'm made up they never won*. Can you imagine the build-up to the cup final if Everton had beaten us? A whole month of it in the *Liverpool Echo* and on the phone-ins; the reminders being there day in, day out; flags and scarves hanging out of car windows.

'Honest to god, it terrified me.'

CHAPTER TEN

cultzeros.co.uk

RICK PARRY,
The Chief Executive

'ON THE ODD OCCASION, YOU'D COME ACROSS PEOPLE YOU hadn't seen since school. They'd inevitably say, "Blimey, you've got the best job in the world." You'd pause for a minute and only then would it dawn. "I suppose I have, actually. Thanks for reminding me!" It didn't always feel like that.'

Rick Parry was Liverpool's chief executive for twelve years. He was a supporter of the club and therefore felt it more when times were bad. He appreciates that it was 'far from a hardship or the type of drudgery others

331

experience'. Yet for Parry, seasons were seemingly ever-lasting. His years mirrored those of the football manager; breaks – time to stop and think – were rare. There was the day-to-day running of Liverpool, with a planning cycle geared towards the following game, where transfers and commercial deals fitted in somewhere. Then there were long-term projects: the prospect of a new stadium, which he believed would shape Liverpool's prosperity for the next twenty-five years, as well as the potential sale of the club, a choice made by chairman and owner David Moores in 2004, the magnitude of which Parry describes as a 'for ever decision'.

Parry tried to run Liverpool on good faith. A hand-shake meant something. He still believes it's possible to build a football club and make it thrive around the best intentions, care and consistency even if the money is not as readily available as it might be elsewhere.

'Yes,' he says forcefully, without a moment's hesitation. 'It's challenging but I think it's absolutely possible and far more rewarding. That's the model that interests me the most rather than simply throwing unlimited funds at it and buying success. For me, it's about sticking to your values and principles no matter what the situation. There were a lot of testing times.'

A perception now exists of the business people that run football clubs as uncaring types, self-preservationists – ruthless vipers whose sole intention is to look after number one, not stopping at anything as they climb to the top of the greasy pole. But it is hard not to like Parry when you meet him. He does not use new-fangled corporate language to describe his work. He clearly understands the mechanics of football. While his successor Ian Ayre boasted about the shirt sales of a failed player being a reflection of his decent work, Liverpool won almost everything there was to win while Parry was in place.

Parry talks with authority but is nevertheless quite shy, delivering his thoughts quietly, almost secretively – taking you into his confidence. You begin to understand that he is left-thinking as he speaks about Liverpool being a community and that 'everyone should have the opportunity to bask in the glory when it is almost in sight'. When Liverpool reached the Champions League final in 2005, Parry insisted that all staff at the club had access to tickets and was then criticized because the following morning nobody was present at the Anfield megastore to capitalize on sales following the most remarkable of victories. He admits that the claim he should have done otherwise annoys him.

'Is that what football is supposed to be about?' he asks sharply. 'The sale of a few shirts that morning was never going to determine the future of the club. That was the ethos of Liverpool: everybody shares. The Cardiff cup finals, we took everybody there too. Just because Istanbul was a long way, we didn't decide to say no because it was more expensive. Are we saying that because the shop was closed the morning after, people would never come back again? If it meant we deferred a few sales, it was worth it. I would do the same thing a thousand times again. Is it the right thing to say to a group of people, "We've got to capitalize on the success and therefore you're not coming to share in the glory?"

Or do you maintain your values and say, "We're in a final, so everybody is on board"? For me, it's an easy answer. Besides, if you look at our retail sales from that year, they were pretty impressive. The glow of Istanbul has lasted for ten years. And it will continue for a while yet.'

For nearly a decade, Parry made many of the biggest decisions at Liverpool. His signature would be on every significant contract: from the steel purchase that was supposed to create a new Anfield to the finest details of a signing, whether it be a manager or a player.

Perhaps he was defined by the conclusions he did not reach. In the final months of the 2003–04 season, Liverpool had again been close to qualifying for the Champions League under Gérard Houllier. Yet the mood had slumped inside Anfield, mainly because Liverpool were more points behind the Premier League's first-place team than they had previously ever been at that stage of the campaign while Houllier was in charge.

Parry can recall the day when there was an unexpected knock on his office door at Anfield. It was late morning on Tuesday, 9 March 2004 and he did not have any meetings scheduled until the afternoon. A Portuguese agent had been on Merseyside discussing potential transfers with Houllier.

'Porto were playing Manchester United in the Champions League quarter-finals that night,' Parry remembers. 'The agent represented a lot of players as well as José Mourinho. He asked whether he could have thirty minutes with me in private and, although I thought it was unusual because it was completely unannounced, I agreed.'

The point of the meeting was made quickly.

'The agent told me that José Mourinho was very interested in managing Liverpool and asked whether Liverpool might be interested in appointing him for the following season.'

Parry was surprised by the suddenness of the approach.

'It tasted badly,' he says. 'The agent had been to meet Gérard trying to sell him players with one hand but then moments later was ostensibly trying to get him fired. It was classic football. There has to be a more dignified manner, surely?

'I said, "Look, we do things a certain way and we are not going to make an appointment behind Gérard's back, a) out of respect to him, and b) because we are still in contention for the Champions League and we do not want to make a decision in March." Had we done so and it had derailed the campaign entirely, we might not have qualified for the Champions League that season and twelve months later we mightn't have had Istanbul under Rafa Benítez.'

Later that evening, Porto beat United and Mourinho reacted to Costinha's equalizer, which secured progression to the next round, by running down the touchline to join in the celebrations with his players.

'We all share the euphoria of beating United and nobody [feels it] more than me. But one of our core values was respect and that includes treating other clubs and people with respect,' Parry says. 'There are limits and ways of doing things. Seeing Mourinho celebrate like that reinforced my initial belief. The way he behaved sewed another seed of doubt. Of course, I'm sure he'd have been a great manager for Liverpool – there is no doubting his qualities. But was he really a *Liverpool* manager – did he characterize the club's values?'

Ultimately, Parry chose not to pursue Mourinho because the timing wasn't right.

'Simply, we did not want to be railroaded into a quick decision about something so important. We hadn't decided to get rid of Gérard at that point, so how could we advance talks?'

Parry and Houllier shared the strongest of bonds. Parry says his and David Moores' happiest moments in football were spent in what they called 'the bunker', the night before an away game in the team hotel after the players had gone to sleep. Houllier would join Parry and Moores at the bar, where they would discuss the possibilities of the following day with the rest of the staff over bottles of wine. Moores would pay for the round.

'It was David's big thing, the only thing he ever wanted to do. The payback for his commitment to the club was to travel with the team, to be around the players in those hours – never to interfere. Gérard embraced that completely and made him part of it. They were great times.'

For Houllier in 2004, his era at Liverpool was near an end. Parry now underlines his memory for detail as well as his aptitude for making the toughest of calls if the circumstances needed it.

'The season 2002–03 was a massive disappointment,' he explains. 'The year before, we finished second with an exciting young squad that should have gone further in the Champions League. Yes, in 2002–03 we had the lift of beating United in Cardiff in the League Cup final. But we finished nineteen points off top position and outside the Champions League on sixty-four points. Twelve months later, we got back into the Champions League but finished on sixty points, a huge thirty points behind the champions, Arsenal. We were winning less than one game in two.

'For all the good in terms of the legacy you create and the values you instil – and Gérard certainly achieved that – Liverpool will always be about winning. Finishing thirty points off the top wasn't where we wanted to be. Separating with Gérard was cruel. But football is demanding and there is a stark reality that has to be recognized. That's why the change was made.

'When you arrive at Liverpool, the excitement is the expectation. Yet it's also the millstone around your neck. But hey, why would you want to have it any other way? Why would you aim for mediocrity? The price you pay when you don't achieve is a heavy one.'

Parry organized meetings with captain Steven Gerrard and his deputy Jamie Carragher to discuss Houllier's successor. The initial instinct was to appoint an experienced British coach with a track record of reasonable success. But neither Charlton Athletic's Alan Curbishley nor Southampton's Gordon Strachan compared to the ultimate candidate.

'The process was relatively straightforward,' Parry explains. 'We wanted to win the league. So the first credential we looked for was someone who'd won one. There were only two people around with experience of winning the Premier League: Alex Ferguson and Arsène Wenger. Neither of them were going to come to Liverpool. So we then looked further afield, at people who had experiences of winning leagues in Germany, Italy and Spain. That brought us to Rafa Benítez. If you analyse what he'd achieved in Valencia, there were parallels with Liverpool in terms of not having the riches of the clubs they were competing with for trophies. Valencia had played against us in Champions League games as well as in pre-season and they'd played us off the park. They were very attractive to watch, despite the limited resources. There wasn't much else to it. Rafa ticked all the boxes. He stood out.'

In the next five years with Benítez in charge, success followed. Yet in that period, Parry and David Moores made the decision to sell the club to new American owners, Tom Hicks and George Gillett. While Moores took a backseat, Parry continued in his role at the club and the relationship between chief executive and manager would be tested in the most extreme circumstances. It is a common belief that the pair did not get along. Parry admits it wasn't easy.

'A lot of the stuff with Rafa has been overplayed because of the situation Liverpool found itself in,' Parry says. 'The bottom line is, the five years I shared with Rafa included a Champions League win, another Champions League final, a semi-final, a quarter-final, an FA Cup win and finishing second place in the league. Upon my appointment, I was told that the most important thing was to make Liverpool as competitive as it could be both on and off the pitch. I'm not trying to take any credit away from Rafa whatsoever, because the biggest pressure was on him when it came to the matches. Yes, we had our ups and downs but the ultimate concern for everyone involved at Liverpool was the results of the team. That's the way it should always be. When I was there, I think they were pretty commendable.'

I meet Parry over breakfast twice, once in Liverpool's city centre and again in an Italian restaurant in Chester, the historical walled town he grew up in. As a child, many of his weekends were spent with his grandparents, who worked as doctors across the River Mersey.

'They lived on St Domingo Grove in the shadow of Anfield,' Parry remembers. 'Some of my earliest memories are of being in a pram listening to the sound of the Kop, and then wondering why every Saturday we couldn't find a parking space. I was fascinated with Liverpool Football Club even before I understood what football was.'

Parry smiles at the thought. He explains that his father, a lecturer in physical education, warned him away from following the same path. 'I wanted to be a footballer but I wasn't good enough. Teaching PE seemed a natural compromise but my dad told me regularly about the drain of the job – being on muddy pitches at the age of forty wasn't so good for the old knees.' Instead, after progressing from Ellesmere Port Grammar School, he obtained a degree in mathematics at the University of Liverpool.

Parry's subsequent career path did not happen by design. But it did not happen by accident either.

'It was a combination,' he continues. 'I had aspirations and dreams. You try to make the connections and try to create opportunities, although the chance of reaching your goal can seem pretty remote. I was never focused on becoming the chief executive of Liverpool. But I always wanted to work in sport. I tend to think that the more connections you make, the more things fall into place. It certainly wasn't a linear path, though life never is, I guess.'

Parry trained as an accountant and progressed from there. He became involved in Manchester's Olympic bid for 1996, which was eventually awarded to the city of Atlanta in the United States. It was a role that nevertheless 'opened up doors across the north-west'. In 1986, he was taken on as a consultant for the Football League, which led to relationships being made with its management committee, including Graham Kelly, secretary of the Football League, who progressed to chief executive of the FA in 1989.

Parry remained with the Olympic bid committee until 1990, a role he describes as 'great fun', despite Manchester losing in the process by a considerable voting margin.

'I was at a crossroads and needed to reflect. I could have remained with Manchester, who wanted to bid again for the 2000 Olympics, which eventually went to Sydney. A friend of mine had been made redundant by ICI [the chemical company] and he recommended I read a book called *What Colour is Your Parachute?*, which focused on self-analysis. So I spent three days filling in A3 sheets. What it essentially does is match your skills to what you enjoy. The charts concluded that my ideal job was running the Football League. I figured that was ridiculous, as only one person could do that and the job certainly wasn't available. So I chucked all the charts away. I then went and spoke to another friend who was in TV. I explained that I'd completed this exercise that was a monumental waste of three days. He'd done the same thing. He told me the day he stopped worrying, he quickly found a new job that he loved. So I decided to take that approach and the next morning the phone rang. It was Graham Kelly, who wanted me to work as a consultant for the embryonic Premier League.'

It is not too dramatic to suggest that with that phone call, football probably changed for ever. Parry, though, was not initially convinced the Premier League would get off the ground. 'I thought I'd do it for three months and it would be over. But we were on to something.'

Today, the Premier League is seen as a slickly run beast that stops for nothing. At the beginning, however, it was a completely different story.

Despite the significant success of English football clubs in European competition during the 1970s and 1980s – especially Liverpool – the era marked a low point for the game in the country. Stadiums were crumbling, supporters endured poor facilities, hooliganism was rife and English clubs were banned from European competition for five years following the Heysel disaster in 1985. The English First Division fell behind rival leagues such as Italy's Serie A and Spain's La Liga both in terms of revenues and attendances, and it resulted in an unprecedented number of top English players moving abroad.

'Football was tarnished,' Parry says. 'It certainly wasn't flavour of the month with Mrs Thatcher, with the membership schemes and ill-thought-through measures that were played around with under her governance. The idea that football would in the future be talked about at the dinner tables of the chattering classes was ludicrous.'

The year 1990 was crucial. The Taylor Report, published in the aftermath of the 1989 Hillsborough disaster, where ninety-six Liverpool supporters died, proposed expensive upgrades to create safer all-seater stadiums. England's run to the semi-final of the World Cup in Italy then injected the game with a feel-good factor.

Television companies spotted the shift. The Football League received £6.3 million for a two-year agreement in 1986 but when that deal was renewed in 1988, the price had risen to £44 million over four years. During negotiations, ten clubs, led by 'the Big Five' (Arsenal, Everton, Liverpool, Manchester United and Tottenham Hotspur), threatened to leave and form their own 'Super League' but were eventually persuaded to stay. The main obstacle, as they saw it, was their affiliation to the Football League, which had organized league football for over a century.

The common basic narrative thereafter reads that in 1991 the Football Association ratified a plan to set up a Premier League. Starting in the 1992–93 season, its long-term aim was to reduce the number of games for top players to help the England team and to take maximum advantage of the commercial opportunities that an elite competition would bring.

In 1992, First Division clubs resigned from the Football League en masse and formed the Premier League as a limited company working out of an office at the Football Association's then headquarters in Lancaster Gate. According to Parry, who was appointed as the Premier League's chief executive in the February of that year, it was a chaotic period.

'Ken Bates, Doug Ellis, and Ron Noades – there were some big personalities involved in the initial meeting and arriving at a common agreement was challenging to say the least,' Parry remembers. 'Disagreements were breaking out about the way the new league should be run and Sir Philip Carter of Everton acknowledged that a chair should be appointed in an attempt to try to bring a level of decorum. Unfortunately, I did not duck my head quickly enough.'

Parry produces a photograph on his mobile phone of a piece of Ernst Young letter-headed paper, which became a legal document detailing the agreement between the founder members. Parry says agreement was only reached after two chairmen from Premier League clubs had 'chased each other around the room', arguing with one another as they tried to find a resolution.

'Symptomatic of the lack of trust, someone suggested we should write down what had been approved and have everybody sign it before we left the room. So I wrote out the constitution – one page of eight points, simplicity. You see the problems that FIFA have had in recent years and a lot of that is down to the sheer complexity and opacity of how the sport is run. The constitution of the Premier League was very transparent and revolutionary in world football in as much as that each club had a vote on key issues and there were no subcommittees; it couldn't have been simpler. It was completely logical and the sort of thing you'd do if you were starting with a blank piece of paper. It was so eminently sensible, it was bound to work – although we didn't expect results overnight.'

The division of money from any forthcoming television deal was the constitution's most significant point.

'You might forget that the concept of regular live football had only started on British television in 1983,' Parry explains. 'For the first half of 1985, because of a fall-out between the Football League, ITV and BBC, there wasn't any football on television at all. There was a total deadlock over the contract. When you think now of the coverage, it's incomprehensible that such a thing could happen. It was a warzone, with clubs arguing over how the money should be split, bigger clubs wanting a bigger slice of the pie, one fudged decision after another. I realized we had to find a way to satisfy everybody's interests. The big clubs still wanted most of the money because they drove the audiences, while the smaller clubs, the Wimbledons for example, argued that the Premier League should be like the NFL, where the money is shared equally. The opinions were opposite and unrealistic. The solution was to share 50 per cent of the TV revenue between all of the clubs, 25 per cent would be shared on the basis of the number of appearances on TV and the remaining 25 per cent based on league performance. It's a pretty smart formula and I can say that with confidence because it has remained unchanged. Few things in football remain unchanged.'

Terrestrial station ITV were favourites to win the new deal.

'The bigger clubs were wedded to ITV; the smaller clubs were opposed to ITV,' Parry says. 'When we had the final vote for television rights in May 1992 – just three months before the launch of the Premier League – it went through 14–6, instead, in favour of Sky, which is the bare minimum you need for a majority vote in the constitution. Had it been 13–7, I don't know what would have happened. The remarkable thing is, two clubs abstained. It turned out to be the biggest decision for English football in modern times yet two decided not to vote. It was a secret ballot, so I have no idea about the identity of those clubs, although I have my suspicions, as one chairman chose to send his secretary instead, which I suppose reflects priorities. I often wonder where football would be today had the vote gone against Sky. It was the tightest of decisions and there was a lot of resentment and bitterness between the clubs. The big clubs were not at all happy.'

Parry believed that Sky presented the better option for the future of football, even though it meant that its coverage was pay-per-view.

'Previously, ITV had bought 100 per cent of the product and thrown 95 per cent of it away. If you've got rights, you should always have obligations and responsibilities as well. ITV showed just eighteen live games a year and the ITV season did not start by definition until September or October. From the start of the season and for the eight weeks that followed, there was no live football on television. How can that be right? At the very least you have to have one live game a weekend if you're going to tell the whole story. And then you ask: what did they do in terms of promoting the game? The only football show was *Saint and Greavsie*. Sky promised us they'd create a channel devoted to sport. We'd never seen anything like that before. Sky only had two hundred thousand subscribers but they were ambitious and very convincing. And they delivered on their promises.'

Parry was aware of the way football was viewed. The Conservative government feared its union-like power to mobilize lots of people.

'Remember, football was on the verge of getting beaten into submission by Thatcher. Its reputation was really, really low. The other big challenge the clubs had was the Taylor Report after Hillsborough, which meant that stadiums had to be all-seater. Where was the money coming from for that? Football was on a downward slope. The clubs were losing money; there was hundreds of millions to find. You have to remember it wasn't as if Sky invented the Premier League; we were already there. We were looking to transform and take control of our destiny.

'Sky were a risk,' Parry continues. 'They were on the verge of going bust. They were haemorrhaging cash and looking for something to give them a boost. What could be better than football, a live unscripted drama, to boost your ratings? They really gambled the house on the

Premier League – an all or nothing bet. Sam Chisholm, who was first chief executive of Sky, a great character, a hewn-out-of-granite New Zealander, described the relationship between Sky and the Premier League as the greatest corporate romance of all time. And he is probably right.'

The first deal Parry helped broker with Sky as well as the BBC, who took the Premier League's highlights package, was worth £42.5 million a season between the twenty clubs. The previous one, across all ninety-two league clubs, which included coverage of the League Cup, was worth just £11 million. When a second deal was agreed in 1996, the fee soared to a whopping £170 million a year, a 400 per cent increase.

'They were astonishing step-changes,' Parry admits. 'We were much pilloried at the time and I became public enemy number one – something that I had to get used to. The Premier League was the pariah of Europe for having sixty live games on pay-per-view television. This was going to be the end of football. UEFA used to call it the "so-called English model". It's pretty rich now when you think nearly every game in the Champions League – a competition organized by UEFA – is on pay TV.'

That the Premier League's inaugural competitive season was conducted without a sponsor was indicative of the other problems Parry faced. Ken Bates, the notorious Chelsea chairman, gave an interview where he claimed he was going to his farm to spend time with his pigs, a 'better class of people', after the biggest clubs formed a voting block, with Chelsea left on the outside of that group.

There were fierce debates on the issue of Sky screening live Monday-night football. Parry said Liverpool were strongly against the idea, with David Moores arguing it was against the interest of supporters. Oldham Athletic were one of the clubs in favour.

Parry learned diplomacy.

'I'd never describe myself as a politician,' he says. 'What you had to be was a good listener. What you couldn't do was fudge and compromise, try to please everybody. That's why I certainly wasn't a politician. Otherwise, the Premier League would have imploded before it even began. You have to stick to certain principles while trying to cajole and persuade those who are doubtful. [You have to] get everybody to see sense, the greater good.'

He gets asked all of the time if he feels any sense of pride in the way football is covered by Sky now, with the astronomical sums of money involved. In 2015, Sky won a major power battle with BT Sport as the Premier League broadcast rights were sold in a staggering £5.1 billion deal for three seasons.

'Sometimes you look back and think we created a monster, with the twenty-four-hour news stations. Sometimes with the countdown to the transfer deadline, it's so over the top you think, *Just leave it*. But if we were going to transform football, we needed to take it to new audiences and there's an inverted snobbery about how it shouldn't appeal to other people. Why not? Why shouldn't it be universal? Why shouldn't we have different cross sections of society inside the stadiums? Why shouldn't there be a safe environment and capacity

attendances? I only wish live football was more accessible to children.'

Arsenal were favourites to win the first Premier
League title. Instead, Manchester United overturned
twenty-six years of fallow league history by lifting the
new trophy for the first time in May 1993. Gallingly
for Parry, he handed over the trophy to United's captain
Bryan Robson at Old Trafford. Video footage shows the
cranes behind the Stretford End. United were ready to
capitalize on their accomplishments in a way Liverpool
never were.

'Liverpool were very much part of the Big Five who
were driving the change. David Dein of Arsenal was
unquestionably the main voice and the most persistent.
He kept cajoling the Big Five. Liverpool were right in
there but it was tricky for them because Sir John Smith,
the chairman, was on the Football League management
committee. So Peter Robinson and Noel White were
the leaders and totally, totally supportive of the drive
towards Premier League football.

'Yes, United cottoned on to the change more rapidly.
Martin Edwards deserves a lot of credit for transforming
United but you have to still bear in mind he was on the
verge of selling to Michael Knighton in 1989, a deal that
fell through at the eleventh hour. It wasn't as if United
had a strategic plan. They said, "Let's see which way
this goes; let's form a public company and float it."

'United rode a perfect storm; they did it at exactly
the right time. Were they smarter, with more foresight
than anyone else? I don't think so. I remember speaking to Martin in those early days and looking out

349

across Old Trafford. He was telling me how they were buying up land from the Trafford Park Estates. They were investing in space, enabling them to make the stadium bigger. This was one of the things that held Liverpool back for so many years, with Anfield being in a residential area and the ownership issues surrounding that. United were better placed because they were surrounded by wasteland rather than family homes. But they did at least have the foresight to appreciate that.'

At the Premier League, Parry knew he had a prime job for as long as he wanted it, having completed the two biggest television deals in history. He was missing something in his career, though. Saturday was a day off and usually he attended games as a guest. 'I saw the buzz of winning and losing, the excitement of being at a club at the sharp end of results. The greater challenge.'

Parry was approached by an unnamed Premier League club and was close to being appointed as their chief executive. 'But then I thought, if I am going to join a club it has to be Liverpool. I knew Peter Robinson really well and he'd told me that he realized one day he would have to plan for his successor. So I called him out of the blue and said, "Peter, I'd quite like your job."'

Robinson was respected as one of football's most efficient administrators, having run Liverpool on a day-to-day basis since Bill Shankly's time as manager. So much needed doing at Anfield, however. In the aftermath of the Taylor Report, the stadium had been upgraded yet there remained a desire to expand. The club wanted to revolutionize its youth system, moving away from the old Vernon Sangster sports centre and playing fields in the shadow of Anfield to a modern site elsewhere. The team also needed rebuilding. By 1997, there was a feeling on the board that it might be time to replace the manager, Roy Evans, a son of the fabled Boot Room.

Privately, Robinson had decided to retire in 2000 but that was still three years away. At a board meeting, Robinson suggested that it might be prudent to recruit Parry, admitting that although his farewell would be long, a gradual changeover would be beneficial to both Parry and the club.

Parry's first defined project was dealing with the academy.

'Liverpool had already bought the land in Kirkby and in my last year with the Premier League I'd worked with Howard Wilkinson on the charter for quality, defining the expectations for new academies. As I'd written the rules, it was logical that I'd take this on. Liverpool invested more than £12 million in the project, which was a huge sum of money, greater than any figure they'd spent on a player. Liverpool had seen the great work that Steve Heighway had done previously, bringing through Steve McManaman, Robbie Fowler, Michael Owen and Jamie Carragher. Rightly, the club had a lot of faith in Steve and wanted to back him as much as they could.'

There were no other specific mandates.

'But it was made clear that the target for the club was to win the Premier League,' Parry says. 'The requirement was to at the very least be a contender. We did not want to be out of the running in November. There was no financial brief of how much money the club should earn.

David [Moores] wanted to win the league because that was the point of the club's existence. Every day's work was geared towards making that happen. Silverware mattered. We took the cup competitions seriously and wanted to win trophies as well. It wasn't good enough to throw everything at the Premier League.'

Within twelve months of Parry's appointment, Parry and Robinson would not be the only pair sharing a job inside Anfield. The chairman, David Moores, had agreed to remove Evans as manager only to change his mind at the last minute.

'Nineteen ninety-seven to ninety-eight was a disappointing season, although to be fair to Roy [Evans] it would have been considered a very pleasing season today, with Champions League qualification being secured – although the basis for sealing that has changed completely since then and that cannot be ignored. We were way off being where we wanted to be. So we discussed at length – over weeks and months – what we were going to do to get back up there rapidly and stay there. Chelsea and Manchester City did not have lots of money. The playing field was a lot more even than it is now. At least every club was deriving revenues from football rather than massive influxes of investment. Getting into the Champions League was easier and we saw that as a launch pad rather than a goal.

'The original thinking was to try to bolster the existing staff. Ronnie Moran was retiring, so it was a chance to bring in new ideas and refresh the coaching. The debate evolved into one about making a further step. We looked at the impact of the Champions League and how the game was developing internationally and realized we needed someone with a Continental pedigree as manager.'

Tom Saunders was the first person to mention Gérard Houllier as a candidate who could help improve Liverpool. Saunders had served in the British army in North Africa during the Second World War and after returning home he became a head teacher at West Derby Comprehensive, close to Liverpool's Melwood training ground. When, in 1968, he became youth development officer at Anfield under Bill Shankly, it was the first appointment of its kind in English football.

'Tom was very much the wise elder statesman. He offered tremendous football knowledge and at that time was the link between the boardroom and Melwood. He was the greatest of individuals. He recognized Gérard's achievements in France and was convinced that he was up on current trends: what was happening in Europe, identifying the key players abroad.'

Parry knew Houllier through his work with the Premier League and had travelled to Paris to canvass opinion on Continental youth-development programmes.

'Gérard was always unfailingly helpful and sparing with his time. I was a massive fan of his. It was very important too that he was an Anglophile. [He] spoke the language, knew Liverpool, had lived and taught here, and most importantly understood the values of the club. That was massively important. Gérard was a great find.'

The recruitment of Houllier was complicated because he'd already received offers to manage Celtic and Sheffield Wednesday. Initially, Liverpool were only prepared to offer him a coaching role.

'Gérard clearly favoured Liverpool but he was also clearly keen to come in and manage. He didn't want to be an assistant and he didn't want to sit upstairs.'

Parry speaks about the managerial job-share that followed as an 'experiment that ultimately failed'. He pauses in order to find the answer as to why it did not work out and why Roy Evans eventually approached the board first about resigning.

'Liverpool being Liverpool, I think it was a genuine attempt to bring in something new while preserving the best of the old. I guess for a variety of different reasons it became clear early on that it was going to be, to say the very least, challenging to make it work between Gérard and Roy. But let's be clear: nobody was trying to make it not work. Nobody was trying to sabotage it. Nobody was trying to undermine it. It just didn't work.'

Houllier needed financial backing to reshape the Liverpool squad. These were nervous months at Anfield, with Sky willing to inject Manchester United with huge sums of cash if a proposed takeover proved to be successful. The move would have accelerated United's sprint into a different financial league, leaving Liverpool behind.

'How could you have the Premier League's broadcaster owning the most successful and glamorous club?' Parry asks. 'It would have created a monopoly and, thankfully, the commission looking at the deal recognized it.'

Granada came to Liverpool with an offer.

'In order to compete, we needed investment in the team. But we also realized the need to be smart. We didn't want to go a long way down the line with Granada only for the deal to be thrown out by the authorities.'

Parry says Liverpool were not just behind United commercially but other clubs as well.

'Granada had a lot of expertise in this field. So it wasn't just a case of money being ploughed into the club. We wanted to harness their knowledge and make Liverpool stronger in the long term.

'The board agreed to sell 9.9 per cent of the club to Granada and the following year a new £22 million deal was brokered for 50 per cent of the club's media rights, which eventually led to the creation of an in-house TV station, LFC.TV. Immediately, all of that money went into strengthening the squad to give us the platform that we hoped would make us successful.'

In the meantime, media partners proposed a break-away European Super League. Liverpool and Parry were 'uncomfortable' with the idea.

'It was permanent membership. There was no promotion or relegation, which for me betrayed the ethics of football. I was never in favour of an exclusive club. Barcelona weren't either. I was invited by UEFA, along with the president of Barcelona, to discuss what could be done with the Champions League – how could it become more attractive? In the end, UEFA decided to follow a similar constitution to the Premier League in terms of sharing the money between all the clubs who appear in the group stages. Getting into those group stages became very important indeed. We realized that a consequence eventually would probably be that around sixteen clubs would emerge from the pack and an elite group would form. Liverpool simply had to be in that group.'

It took Houllier two and a half seasons to propel Liverpool from the mid table of the Premier League to treble cup winners and Champions League participants. In that period, he signed twenty-two new first-team players and sold or released twenty-five. That four of the sales were earlier recruitments made by him reveals that he was able to admit he was wrong in the early days.

Parry enjoyed working with Houllier. Their under-standing was at a friendship level.

'Gérard had great qualities as a human being as well as a manager,' Parry says. 'He was a relentless modernizer, which we needed because there was a lot to do. He was decisive. Gérard had a passionate belief in preparation and attention to detail, giving the players the best conditions to succeed. He used to say, "You can't plan success but you can programme for success." If you give the very best training facilities, if you work hard and if you travel in the right manner, everything will be set up and there are no excuses. I mean, we didn't even have a kit man when Gérard arrived. Previously, Ronnie [Moran] and Sammy [Lee] used to pack them on a Friday afternoon, then Roy and the others would carry the skips into the dressing room from the team bus.'

Of Houllier's principal strengths as a manager, Parry believes there were two outstanding features.

'The first was his strong commitment towards having

an English – preferably a local – heartbeat to the team. Gérard's idea was to use local talent when he could and supplement that by signing players with the right ability and attitude: professionals and good people. If you look at the bare facts and analyse what his 2001 squad was built on – Gerrard, Owen, Heskey, Fowler, Carragher, Murphy, [Nick] Barmby and Redknapp – you realize he achieved that. Even in Gérard's final season, many of those players were still there. He didn't shift his approach and stayed true to his convictions.

'People ask me regularly which game I look back fondly on. Many are surprised when I tell them it is Liverpool 7, Southampton 1 in January 1999. Our scorers that day were Fowler [with a hat-trick], Owen, Thompson, Carragher and Matteo: five academy graduates. The great thing about our graduates was they were all local. They weren't bought from elsewhere. Had it been possible, they'd have stayed at Liverpool for ever.

'The second thing about Gérard was his core values and the way he lived them: to be a winner, think team first and to be a top professional. People talk a lot about the discipline that Gérard installed: the fines for using mobiles at Melwood, being regulated for poor time-keeping. The rules were not arbitrary. They related back to the core values, where the aim was to improve communication, modernize and bring fresh thinking.

'He believed in respect and instilling that right across the club. It was the essence of the Liverpool way and he got it. When Liverpool won everything in sight in the decades before, it would be inaccurate to say the club was always loved by everybody. But it was always respected for the way it did business and treated people. I'll always remember having a conversation with Frank Lowe, the advertising guru, who was a big Man United fan. He recognized that United were simultaneously the most loved and most hated club, which isn't great from a brand point of view. He realized too that people never hated Liverpool but always respected them. That for me was the Liverpool way: to respect and to be respected.'

The League Cup, the FA Cup and the UEFA Cup were all lifted during the 2000–01 season, followed by the Charity Shield and the European Super Cup. Liverpool also qualified for the Champions League. The club was back in the business of winning trophies. And yet spells where the team played twelve games in thirty-six days took their toll. The search for success must surely have had an impact on Houllier's health. For Parry, the good times did not last long.

'They were over almost instantly,' he says. 'When I left the Premier League and first moved to Liverpool, one of my good friends in the game, David Dein, told me that I should really savour the good times because the bad are always just around the corner. I thought he was exaggerating. But he was dead right. The good times in football are like your wedding day – you should never let it pass you in a blur, because it is over so quickly.'

With Liverpool slipping further and further away from the Premier League title, by 2004 it was time for Houllier to leave.

'The day I took over from Peter Robinson [in 2000], I went to Gérard's apartment and we started planning the future straight away. The first thing he said was, "You and I are friends. There will come a day in football where we'll have to part. When that happens, we have to make sure we part as friends." I thought that was a really nice thing to say. And he's been true to his word. Gérard's a sensible man. He knows tough decisions are made in football. The wisest people know where the pressures lie and what needs to happen when things aren't working. It's the nature of the beast.

'Yet I think Gérard harboured a belief that he could turn it around. It certainly wasn't a knee-jerk decision to let him go. In 2002, we were seven points off the title. In 2003 we were nineteen points away and in 2004, although we came fourth and got into the Champions League, we were thirty points behind. There were more than ten defeats in each of those seasons and we had won less than half of the games. Bearing in mind it was our aspiration to be winning, or at the very least be contenders, to be in a position where by Christmas we were out of the running for the title was unacceptable. There was nothing to suggest that trend was going to turn.'

Rafael Benítez, a two-time La Liga-winning manager with Valencia, was appointed as Houllier's replacement. He was walking into a club where not everything was as it seemed. Privately, David Moores had decided to sell Liverpool, fearing the takeover of Chelsea by Roman Abramovich would heap even more financial pressure on himself.

Though Moores had been in charge at Anfield since 1991, the Moores family had owned the club for more than fifty years. They had made their fortune from the Merseyside-based Littlewoods pools and shopping empire and while it made them one of the wealthiest families in the UK, their pockets were nowhere near as deep as those of Abramovich, whose arrival in English football was as transformative as Sky's, considering the number of foreign owners who followed him.

Moores did not want Liverpool to fall behind and so admitted to Parry that if the right buyer could be found, he would step aside. At the same time, Moores also realized the capacity of Anfield desperately needed to be increased. Alternatively, Liverpool could move to a new stadium.

The Taylor Report's dictate that football grounds in the English top flight must be all-seated arenas led to major changes at Anfield. In the space of a few years, the Kop was razed and replaced, the Kemlyn Road became the Centenary Stand and the old Anfield Road stand developed a second tier. The only terrace that wasn't altered considerably was the main stand.

'It was perfectly understandable that something major needed to be done in terms of safety,' Parry says. 'But one of the weaknesses of the rush towards building new stadiums within the old was that many, like Anfield, were too small and were in areas of the city with little room for future expansion. Had we been able to spend time thinking it through, analysing the revenues that could have been made from the Premier League, the clubs could have built bigger. Liverpool – understandably, and I must stress that – had to move quicker than most to get it done. The money had to be invested quickly. In the nineties, there was no alternative option.'

The possibility of exploring a new site closer to Liverpool's waterfront on the Dock Road was there towards the end of the nineties but Parry advised there would not be much room to go beyond a fifty-thousand-seater stadium. He preferred the idea of staying put.

'I genuinely wanted to see Anfield as a catalyst for the regeneration of north Liverpool. But we also saw the need to become better neighbours and build better relationships. The mistrust with the residents was enormous. When you don't have communication, people leapt to assumptions about what the club was going to do behind everybody's backs, none of which was true. When you spend time talking with residents, you realize their needs are not overcomplicated and their demands are not unrealistic. They expect the neighbourhood to be clean and tidy and don't want people peeing in the garden. It's all perfectly reasonable. When you talk to them about enhancements and regenerations, they don't want the Sydney Opera House. They want a post office and a launderette: perfectly sensible and pragmatic demands.

'We worked with a group called Keep Britain Tidy and got involved in other initiatives to try to build the relationship. We invested a lot of money in rebuilding houses on the road behind the Centenary Stand and tried to set an example. But then nothing happened to the stadium itself and that created suspicion.

'The finances for the stadium were tight. It's not the borrowing of the money that is difficult; it's the repaying. There was a fine line because obviously you're generating a lot of additional revenue [by increasing Anfield's capacity] but a lot of that is dependent on how the team performs. The assumptions for the financial model were that we'd be in the Champions League for three seasons out of five, the UEFA Cup one year out of five and out of Europe for one year, which back then looked fairly conservative. David, of course, asks, "What happens if we have a blip? Where does the money then come from to rebuild the team? That's the most important thing." He'd seen what had happened at Leeds United, where they'd qualified for the Champions League and done really well before the whole thing imploded.

'Sure, we could have borrowed,' Parry continues. 'We had the same consortium of banks that backed Arsenal [in building the Emirates Stadium] lined up. We could have done it in-house without selling the club. But David had decided to sell. His mind was made up in early 2004. It wasn't just the concern about the stadium. We were not having a terribly good season and he was worried that he would be criticized by fans. David certainly wasn't arrogant like other chairmen. He wasn't thick-skinned either. He really cared and it hurt him if even two letters appeared in the *Liverpool Echo* criticizing him. He'd be genuinely upset. He wanted the very best for the club. He was really concerned by Abramovich coming in and all the money Chelsea were spending. David didn't want to hold Liverpool back. So in 2004, he decided it was necessary to make a change.'

On the night of Rafael Benítez's first game in charge of Liverpool against Grazer AK in Austria, Parry says Steve Morgan – the owner of Redrow Homes, and a major shareholder – 'came within a whisker of acquiring the club'. Morgan even met Benítez after the game to discuss his plans.

'David was worn down to the position where he decided it was right to sell to Steve, because they did not get on very well,' Parry explains. 'David agreed a price with him, which was way less than we eventually sold the club for, but when Steve went to complete due diligence he sent his accountants in only to change his mind about the price. I'm not sure whether it was a negotiation tactic or whether he had reservations about the cost of the proposed stadium redevelopment. With David, when you shake hands on a deal with him, you've done a deal. Having been beaten into submission to accept Morgan's offer by other board members, he wasn't in the mood to start another round of negotiations. So David called the whole thing off.'

While Morgan later bought Wolverhampton Wanderers, it is fair to say that Benítez achieved what appeared to be the impossible during his first season in charge: Liverpool, despite finishing fifth in the Premier League, won the Champions League for the first time since it ceased to be the European Cup, a trophy last collected twenty-one years before. Yet largely due to Liverpool's poor league performance, critics of Benítez cited the role of captain Steven Gerrard as being more significant.

'There's an extraordinary desire in football to narrow success down to a binary decision,' Parry says. 'Steven's contribution was immense in certain games. But so was Xabi Alonso's, so was Luis García's, so was Didi's, so was Carra's, and so, indeed, was Rafa's. It's all of those things coming together. It's wrong to say one is more important than the other.

'Rafa, to be fair, what he definitely brought to the club was not an arrogance but an inner belief. His attitude was, "You know, why can't we win it?" He got the players to believe that as the rounds went on. Suddenly when you beat Juventus, you think, *Blimey, I wonder* . . .

'The atmosphere inside Anfield in the semi-final against Chelsea surpassed anything I have witnessed before, even Saint-Étienne [before Liverpool won its first European Cup in 1977]. The following day, I could still hear the crowd ringing in my ears. I think it was Anfield's best night. What made it even better was the Eidur Gudjohnsen miss really late in the game, which was kind of a repayment for all of Chelsea's evil over the years. You just thought, *Great!*'

Under Benítez, Liverpool qualified for the Champions League five seasons in a row, winning the competition once, reaching another final, a semi-final and a quarter-final. There was also an FA Cup victory in 2006 and a second-placed Premier League finish three years later. The club reclaimed its status amongst Europe's elite and in doing so it became more attractive to a larger range of potential buyers.

Parry recognizes that Moores' decision to move aside slowed progress on the new stadium. Conversely, Moores did not want to sell simply to the highest bidder. He realized the stadium was key to Liverpool's future and that any new owner must be capable of solving that issue.

'Yes, we wanted to sell but it had to be to the right person or people,' Parry says. 'So we looked for someone with a track record in dealing with stadiums.'

Parry was keenest on discussions with interested parties from Dubai.

'Not that I had particularly close contacts with Dubai but I'd visited on quite a few occasions and had seen the way the city was developing. I knew people who'd worked for the Jumeirah Group and had seen the way they'd sprung remarkable hotels up from the ground, which were the best in the world, in a very short space of time. Dubai did things unbelievably quickly.'

Parry and Moores regretted a deal with Robert Kraft falling through. Kraft was the owner of the NFL's New England Patriots. He began negotiations a few weeks after Liverpool lifted the Champions League in 2005, gripped by the romance of the win in Istanbul.

'David and Robert really hit it off. Robert had developed a beautiful stadium in Boston and had a great record with the Patriots as well as New England Revolution in the MLS [Major League Soccer]. There were all sorts of good reasons to go with him but most of all David really liked him. He trusted him. It was a family thing. The Krafts were decent, proper people. David was devastated when Robert woke up one morning and thought, *No, I can't do this.* I think he pulled out for two reasons. The reason we were given was that a reality dawned on him that he's from Boston and already had his hands full with two institutions there. He questioned what his affinity with Liverpool actually was. The other factor was the lack of cost control and financial fair play. As an NFL owner, he was conditioned to revenue sharing. The idea of free-for-all expenditure in the Premier League was ludicrous to him. And I can understand why.'

Kraft pulled out while Parry was with the Liverpool squad in Tokyo as they competed in the Club World Championship.

'It wasn't months wasted but several months that had expired working with a party to no positive end. A take-over is another job in itself aside from the other stuff you're supposed to be doing. Throughout the process, we were still itching to win the league and get everything right on the pitch. Yet there was this prolonged uncertainty over investment. Are we going to get more? I was constantly telling Rafa, "Yes, we are still talking to new investors." When we brought Rafa in, it seemed the right thing to tell him that David was trying to sell the club. We warned him that there might be some uncertainty.'

Then came interest from Thaksin Shinawatra, Thailand's prime minister and a business tycoon who made his wealth in IT and telecommunications. Parry made two trips to Bangkok and Shinawatra invited his entire cabinet for dinner, attempting to reflect the passion for football and Liverpool within the country.

'His strategy was twofold. He wanted to do something for the people of Thailand. He had a concept of public ownership where the country's lottery fund would fund Liverpool. His advisers argued against that because they realized he would be too far oversubscribed. It could have led to massive disappointment if Liverpool were unsuccessful.

'He also had an economic vision for Thailand. His idea was to acquire a brand and produce shirts themselves rather than a counterfeit economy existing. He saw Thailand as a gateway to China and India. Had he been able to pull it all off, it would have been an interesting proposition.'

Shinawatra did not prove he had the funds and Liverpool walked away, and though Parry believes Shinawatra's proposal had some foundation, considering he later bought Manchester City, he was concerned about the perception of a sale considering the stories of human-rights violations in Thailand while Shinawatra was in control.

There were other groups and people who just wanted to make headlines.

'The main problem with selling a major European football club is that you have every Tom, Dick and Harry who never has any intention of doing it but wants their few minutes of fame and therefore makes an offer that isn't genuine. Suddenly, they become the person in years to come that "nearly bought Liverpool". Although in reality, they didn't. Of course, if you ask a wealthy person whether they want to buy Liverpool, they're obviously willing to talk about it. But are they really determined to do something?'

Discussions with Dubai International Capital (DIC), the investment arm of the Dubai royal family, were ongoing and the most interesting to Parry, even though negotiations had been disappointingly slow. But in the summer of 2006, George Gillett made first contact, an American businessman.

'He came along to Merseyside unsolicited and talked with great passion, speaking about values and explaining why he wanted to buy Liverpool for the right reasons. We'd spoken to so many groups by that point that we took it with a pinch of salt and didn't get too excited.'

Parry and Moores were invited to Montreal, where Gillett owned the Canadiens ice hockey team.

'George wanted to show David how he ran his businesses. It was a very impressive visit, although David was fairly guarded, having spent time getting close to Robert Kraft before he had a change of heart. George wheeled in his sponsors, key staff and the commissioner of ice hockey – a whole raft of people that would support his credibility. But to be fair to him he also invited us to wander round and speak to anyone we wanted to. He gave us the keys and, universally, everyone said good things about the way he ran the Canadiens and his commitment to Montreal. It all sounded good.'

While Gillett prepared to make an offer for Liverpool, DIC made contact with Parry again.

'George's interest was genuine but he was always playing catch-up because we'd known DIC for longer. David felt the weight of responsibility about making the right decision. Yet David had never been to Dubai. I figured that maybe DIC could arrange a visit and show Dubai off to David, make him realize the spectacular things going on there. George had done it with some style and had convinced David to travel even though he doesn't like long flights because he can't smoke. The fact that he was able to smoke on George's private plane was a bonus. We told DIC about the fact George had presented himself well. He had given us the keys to Montreal and had nothing to hide. He even sent us off to a Bob Dylan concert. What could DIC do to show they were serious?'

DIC could not arrange a private jet for Moores and Parry to travel in.

'So we rented our own and paid for it. That had no bearing whatsoever on the deal but when someone is determined to impress you they do everything they can to blow you away.'

Moores and Parry were checked into the Burj Al Arab, the world's only seven-star hotel and the fourth-tallest hotel on the planet.

'But we never got out of the hotel,' Parry says. 'We were supposed to meet Sheikh Mohammed but were told that he'd gone horse riding. So we didn't meet him. In fact, we didn't meet anyone important, not even the chairman of DIC. I was still really keen on Dubai because of everything else the place represented and delivered. But we had spent two days in a nice hotel without making any progress. The experience was a negative one and it was a fairly depressing journey home because it did not reinforce their credibility at all. We began to ask ourselves whether the people that really mattered in Dubai were serious about Liverpool.'

Moores and Parry overcame their disappointment. The year was coming to an end and, having had proposals accepted for the new stadium in Stanley Park, just across the way from Anfield, the club required an injection of more than £12 million for the steel to be ordered in January. Without that money, Rafael Benítez's transfer plans were potentially going to be affected.

'We made it clear to DIC and George that the sale of the club had to be done by the first week of January. George was adamant that his funds were in place and meanwhile we finally received a formal offer from DIC in November. By then, DIC had been considering what to do for eighteen months. We'd negotiated with them on an open-book basis. Steve Morgan's due diligence had only taken two weeks. What exactly did DIC need to know – or do – throughout that time?'

Despite the delays, Parry and Moores deemed that DIC's offer was the safer and wiser option to take.

'I had to phone George and tell him the bad news. I explained that ultimately we were going with a country with more resources rather than one individual. The broader deal was considered better. George must have taken that on board, because a few months later the outlook had changed and he altered his bid.'

By the end of January, the deal with DIC still hadn't been concluded.

'It was ridiculous. We then had to introduce DIC to the banks that we'd lined up to fund the stadium in the first place. Surely Dubai was funding this? Surely DIC is awash with money and has connections with their own banks? Why were we setting up meetings involving us, them and the Bank of Ireland? The whole thing was becoming decidedly odd and exasperating.'

February came and DIC's exclusivity period expired.

'David had shaken hands with them and, as I've said before, the gesture meant a lot to him. So he was insistent that he wouldn't solicit any other interest, although

George [Gillett] hadn't gone away. To George's credit, he didn't make a lot of noise about his disappointment. He didn't go to the media. Instead, he let it be known that he was still keen on Liverpool if it went awry with DIC.'

In January, a delegate from DIC had promised to underwrite the cost of the steel needed for the stadium. It was then revealed that the delegate had no authority to sanction such a proposal and Liverpool were left exposed.

'We had £12 million worth of steel that potentially we couldn't pay for if a takeover wasn't concluded swiftly.' It reached the point where Anfield's board shared reservations about DIC.

'George came back, explaining that he'd listened to our concerns about being a single family and that he'd found a partner to bring in. Did it alter the dynamic? At that point the board was being advised of its responsibilities to the shareholders and that it must accept the best deal. In the final analysis, George's offer for the shares was better than DIC's.'

DIC had also been evasive about how much cash it was prepared to invest in Liverpool's team.

'The answer always was along the lines of, "Well, we'll own it and we'll be fine." With George, it was all very detailed. He had pots of money allocated for lots of projects, which in fairness was true. The only problem was, it turned out not to be his money. It was the Royal Bank of Scotland's money.'

Liverpool were playing West Ham United when a board meeting was hastily arranged in London.

'The view of the board was, DIC have had long enough and we had to go with the solid offer from George and his partner, [Tom] Hicks. But even then, in David's position as the majority shareholder, he insisted that having given his word to DIC, he was not going to go back on it lightly. He wanted time to reflect on it for a couple of days.'

Moores made the telephone call to Sameer al-Ansari, DIC's chief executive, the following morning.

'DIC had been expecting the board to rubber stamp the deal with them and finally get it signed. I went around to David's house with his adviser Keith Clayton and listened while he called Sameer to tell him the news. David said, "Listen, we're in a bit of a quandary, we've got another offer on the table. The board's view is we should be accepting the other offer, although I wanted to think about it carefully before I make a momentous decision."

'If I'd been the chief executive of DIC, I'd have responded to that by saying, "David, I'll be on the next plane. I'll come and reassure you." What Sameer said was, "Unless you accept by 5 p.m. today, we're walking away." David's immediate reaction to that, being strongly principled, was, "Hang on, we're Liverpool Football Club. You don't treat us like that." David didn't talk about himself, it was "You don't hold Liverpool Football Club to ransom." He reminded Sameer that it was the biggest decision that he'd had to make in his life and all he wanted was breathing space to make sure he was doing the right thing. There was no way he was going to be bullied.'

DIC's ultimatum failed. At 3 p.m., news arrived from the Middle East that negotiations with Liverpool had ended. This left Liverpool FC in a vulnerable position. It was now obvious to Gillett and Hicks that there was no opposition. If Steve Morgan – a Liverpool supporter – had negotiated on price before, why wouldn't they do the same? Parry phoned Gillett.

'I told him that our stance had changed and that we were prepared to enter discussions with him again. But I also said we didn't want any fun and games over the price and that we wanted it done pretty damn quickly. To be fair to George, his reaction to that was, "Listen, you have my word. I've agreed a price. We'll get the due diligence done swiftly." The deal was completed within a week.'

Parry accepts that he should have taken more time in getting to know Tom Hicks, a Texan with a track record in leveraged buyouts where he used outside capital to purchase companies.

'He didn't say much when we met,' Parry says. 'He left a lot of the conversation to George, who had spoken well of him. But Tom, he soon started talking.'

Gillett and Hicks did enough to convince Liverpool's board their proposal was sound, stressing that the pair of them had worked together successfully before and that their business interests would dovetail to benefit Liverpool.

Although Hicks and Gillett insisted they would not 'do a Glazer' by loading Anfield with debt, as had happened at Manchester United, the *Liverpool Echo* reported that they proceeded to use loans rather than cash from their own personal fortunes to finance Liverpool. After paying

£5,000 a share in a total outlay of £174.1 million, they also borrowed another £11 million to pay banks and advisers and a further £44.8 million to absorb the club's debt. On top of this, another £70 million was added to the loan for the stadium project and to cover ongoing running costs.

Within twelve months, the owners took out a £350 million loan with the Royal Bank of Scotland and Wachovia. Of that, £105 million was immediately loaded on to the club's books, with the remaining £245 million being taken on by Kop Holdings, the holding company set up by Hicks and Gillett when they bought the club.

A spokesman for Hicks publicly admitted that the club would face interest payments of around £30 million a year on their borrowings. By the end, it was paying around £100,000 per day in interest.

'Our clear understanding was, it was while they reorganized their own finances,' says Parry. 'In the offer document, there was no debt on the club. It would not have to bear any costs. That certainly changed.'

When confirmation of the club's RBS refinancing arrived, the club statement carried only Hicks's name. In March 2008, just thirteen months after the takeover, Gillett told a Canadian radio station that the relationship between himself and Hicks had been 'unworkable for some time', stating that he was willing to sell his stake in Liverpool to Hicks.

'There is no doubt that you can have a perfectly rational and analytical relationship if you are investing in a meat packing company,' Parry continues. 'But when you get involved in sport, it is completely and utterly different. Because we needed to make a decision quickly, partly to meet the club's needs, I suspect they did not spend a lot of time on the legalities of how their relationship would work. There was a straight assumption that it would all work out fine.'

Parry is not trying to absolve himself of blame here. He reasons that Liverpool had been backed into a financial corner through the delays with DIC. Circumstance played a big part in the sale to Hicks and Gillett.

'To be fair, they did not attempt to chip away at the price. We could have started all over again but, having ordered the steel and with a huge bill to foot, god knows what would have happened. It sounds ironic now but we were still desperate to be in a new stadium by 2010. We were also desperate to win the league and to do that we needed the kind of investment that Hicks and Gillett were promising.'

One of Hicks's first significant public statements came ahead of the 2007 Champions League final with AC Milan, when he compared the purchase of Liverpool to buying Weetabix – another one of his leveraged buy-outs – admitting, 'It's just business' and saying that anyone eating Weetabix was essentially paying for his purchase of the cereal company.

'George, I think, genuinely did want to do things the right way and was trying to understand the club's values,' Parry says. 'I don't think it ever mattered to Tom. I don't think it bothered him at all.'

Under Hicks and Gillett, Parry continued as chief executive, while David Moores remained as a director, though his influence was inconsequential.

'When David was in charge, we scrupulously had a monthly board meeting. That stopped under the new regime. Occasionally, they flew in with an entourage and we'd have an agenda for the day. There were other meetings in New York but they were few and far between. Sometimes there were telephone conversations – occasionally with both but more often with just one. It tended to be more with George.'

The new owners' man on the ground in Merseyside was Foster Gillett. Around Liverpool, a perception existed that Foster was simply the son of a billionaire, posted out on secondment to one of his father's companies for experience. Towards the end of the Hicks and Gillett reign, Foster and his wife Lauren disappeared back to the United States without telling anyone.

'Foster was a decent person,' Parry says. 'He was good natured and respectful. He tried to understand the club's traditions. But then he went back for Christmas and we never saw him again. He left his lease car in the garage. I guess he was caught up in the family squabbles. It was difficult for him in that position.'

It was never established precisely what led to the decline of Hicks and Gillett's relationship. Both were contacted in the writing of this book and neither responded. But in one sense, the pattern of life inside Anfield and Melwood became regular thereafter, according to Parry.

'When George was supporting Rafa, Tom wasn't. And then vice versa. It must have been confusing for Rafa. One thing I passionately believe in is, if you are determined to establish a high-performing winning culture, you need a single philosophy from the top down, which we absolutely didn't have. There was a complete split at the top. How on earth we maintained a spell of relative success until 2009, I have no idea.

'The ownership issue was totally debilitating and distracting,' Parry continues. 'Certainly with David [Moores] we didn't have to even talk about values, because they were simply exercised in everything we tried to do. We lived it; we didn't have to debate it. Unfortunately, the two owners from America had two very different sets of values and very different mindsets. When you've got two owners with different philosophies, you can't have a single philosophy by definition. That makes life incredibly difficult. For me, Liverpool isn't just about winning – although that is the most important thing. It's also about being different and being special. I'm positive it still matters.'

Sympathizers would argue that Rafael Benítez was caught in the middle of the mess. Critics would say he exacerbated the situation by using the uncertainty to meet his own needs. Parry concedes that he did not share the same 'intimacy' with Benítez as he did with Houllier. The manager's closest relationship had been with assistant Pako Ayestarán, who had followed him from Tenerife to Valencia and then to Liverpool. The 2007–08 season was a few weeks old when an argument led to Benítez's long-time friend departing Anfield.

'Gérard had the same close relationship with Patrice Bergues before he decided to move back to France to manage Lens,' Parry says. 'They had been together long enough for Gérard to accept Patrice challenging him. Any manager needs a strong number two, albeit someone who is different in personality. Management is a very lonely position and you can start to believe the publicity, either good or bad, when you're stuck there on your own. When Patrice left, Gérard lost something very important.'

Although Liverpool recorded their best league finish under Benítez the season after Ayestarán's departure, perhaps he lost something too: a trusted pair of eyes and ears on the training ground but also, deeper than that, someone he could speak to about the challenges of working at a dysfunctional football club owned by Hicks and Gillett. Even before their arrival, though, Parry says he witnessed a swing in the way Benítez operated.

'Rafa's focus shifted away from his real strengths,' Parry says. 'When we brought him to Liverpool, we told him that we wanted him to use his knowledge as a coach to work with what we had and improve the abilities of the squad. We didn't have massive amounts of money, so we had to be smarter than Chelsea and work harder. In 2005, Rafa's attention to detail and preparation work helped get us to Istanbul. He was a tremendous coach.

'Ultimately, I think Rafa bought too many players. There was too much change. Even when you're on an upward trajectory, as we were because Rafa was producing great results, any signing is a risk. There are no certainties. Personalities, families settling – you can never tell until the player actually plays. There is always an element of gambling, so obviously the fewer signings you make, the less of a risk you're taking. Ideally, you're better off making one or two big signings a summer, who are really going to add to the squad. In the eighties, that's what Liverpool did.'

'It's tough being Liverpool's manager,' Parry continues. 'You see changes in a person's character. The weight of expectation is incredibly difficult to deal with. You get hit from all sides. Rafa moved his focus from being a coach to more of a wheeler and dealer, trading players. We had a bit of tension over that; there always is when it comes to money.

'Rafa knew on the day he was appointed that there wasn't pressure from the board to win the league immediately. We thought it would take three years. The message was: let's do this steadily and calmly. It was made clear to him that we were not going to fire him overnight and promised that he would have time to work independently and build gradually and, ultimately, sustainably. All managers want to do things quickly because they are motivated people. But maybe Rafa wanted it too quickly – making too many changes – and it caused him to lose a bit of focus.'

The challenge for Benítez must have been immense, operating in an environment where he did not know which owner to trust, in the same way as Liverpool's players did not know who to go to when Roy Evans and Gérard Houllier were in joint charge.

Benítez had got to where he was by going his own way: fighting up from the bottom. His initial period at senior level in football ended because of politics and control issues at Real Madrid. Having been appointed as assistant on a temporary basis to Vicente del Bosque in 1994, he returned to the club's B team when Jorge

Valdano was hired, and his last year there was marked by an awkward coexistence where, from above, Valdano would suggest he play certain players that he did not rate. There was Sandro, supposedly a classy midfielder from the Canary Islands, and Paco Sanz, who happened to be the son of Lorenzo Sanz, the vice chairman. Valdano saw Sandro as a footballer who needed to be free of tactical restriction, while Benítez demanded sacrifices from him. The disagreements would prove unworkable and from there Benítez knew it was only a matter of time before he would leave.

The intervening years had hardened Benítez. During their introductory press conference, when George Gillett infamously claimed 'there has to be a shovel in the ground within sixty days', in relation to the new stadium site on Stanley Park, both Gillett and Tom Hicks had argued about who was sitting where at the top table. Later, they went to Melwood, where they stood and observed training from the side of the pitch.

'Rafa was uncomfortable with that and told them,' Parry remembers. 'They reacted by making it clear that everything at Liverpool was their domain because they owned it, "all of it".'

Initially, Benítez was told he would have £20 million a year to spend on players.

'In 2007, George and Tom backed us big time in terms of Fernando Torres and in 2008, when the relationship had turned, they were still backing the team. There was a degree of game playing and Rafa would say, "Well, that was when we didn't get Florent Malouda." But we got Torres – he couldn't get every player he wanted to sign.'

Not everything was as it seemed at Liverpool. Parry too was caught in the middle. The owners were his paymasters, yet he also felt a sense of duty to Benítez. Benítez appreciated Parry had known Gillett longer and therefore would have more of an allegiance to him. If Hicks was promising Benítez a longer contract and more money to spend on the team, how could Benítez trust Parry to help him? Parry was spinning plates, trying to run a club on a day-to-day basis where the most significant decision makers were becoming over-whelmed by paranoia.

Parry's and Benítez's relationship worsened after it was revealed an approach had been made to recruit Jürgen Klinsmann as Liverpool's manager.

'Clearly Rafa was hurt and understandably so,' Parry admits. 'I think he was very hurt that I'd had an involve-ment. When I said, "Rafa, you know, I'm employed by these guys. If they tell me to go to New York and to attend a meeting, that's what I have to do." Rafa's response to that was, "Yeah, well, you should have come straight back and told me." It was supposed to be confidential, of course. That became a very difficult period.

'They weren't trying to do anything malicious in approaching Klinsmann. In football, everything gets blown up. They had a very straightforward mindset. Rafa was making a play in the media about the possi-bility of going to Real Madrid. So they took him literally and explored other options in case he did. They didn't think he was playing games and decide to ignore it. They took it at face value.

'One of George's best friends was Dr Richard

Steadman, who'd operated on Michael Owen's knee. Richard met Michael and listened to the stories about Liverpool. Later, Klinsmann went to see Steadman too and soon enough one thing led to another and George met Klinsmann too. In fairness to George, he was keen on learning more about football and initially the meeting was just about that: gaining knowledge. Eventually the question was asked, "Could this guy be any good as a manager if Rafa goes?" There was no more to it than that. Klinsmann was a proposed contingency but in the highly charged atmosphere that existed around that time, the story became Liverpool wanting to replace Rafa with Klinsmann.

'It was one of Rafa's initiatives that backfired. He was thinking if he threatened to leave, it might strengthen his position. Instead, it was the reverse: they thought, *Well, if he's got other plans, we'll have to do something else too*. It was a case of Americans being pragmatic.'

According to Gillett, he and Hicks received two thousand emails a week from angry Liverpool fans. 'Ninety-five per cent of them have been directed at some of the comments made by my partner. And five per cent were aimed at both of us: "Go Home, Americans!"'

Supporter momentum against the owners gathered quickly. Despite Dallas-based architects HKS presenting plans for an expandable sixty-thousand-seater stadium – complete with futuristic 18,500-seater Kop – which were granted planning permission, work would never begin. Hicks and Gillett simply didn't have the funds and when Liverpool revealed their annual accounts in May 2013, it emerged the club had spent £35 million on design fees, legal and administrative costs with regard to the unbuilt site.

If the challenge of running Liverpool was immense under David Moores, for Parry it became almost impossible with Hicks and Gillett. It says much about the pair that Hicks's name is always mentioned first, for he was viewed as the dominant partner even though Gillett was the one who initially wanted to buy Liverpool.

Hicks appeared the more combative figure, falling out with all of those around him at some point. He fell out with Rafael Benítez when he reminded him during a telephone conversation that it was his job to 'coach' the team rather than involve himself in the transfer business. Though the relationship was later salvaged, with Benítez agreeing a new five-year contract in 2009, Hicks then took on Parry by agreeing to a television interview at his ranch in Texas during which he condemned the work of the chief executive.

Previously, Gillett had flown to Merseyside, suspecting that Liverpool's new finance director Ian Ayre was reporting to Hicks. An argument ensued in Ayre's office and soon enough Parry then became a target of Hicks. With a fire roaring cosily in the background, Hicks infamously spoke at length on his misgivings about Parry, labelling his reign a 'disaster'. Hicks's lack of awareness was displayed by the fact he delivered the comments on the anniversary of the Hillsborough disaster. Hicks finished the interview by calling for Parry to resign, appreciating that he was in no position to fire him, because Gillett would have to agree and by then they agreed on nothing.

'I never watched the interview,' Parry says. 'Sometimes the only way to deal with it is to ignore it. Tom also sent me a letter, which I've never read, although my lawyer has. I can't think of any good reason why I would. There was no point in responding to him, certainly not publicly. Just because someone else doesn't operate with the same values, it doesn't mean you should stoop to their level.'

The interview increased the heat on Parry. Every supporter had a different opinion on his work anyway because of the stadium issue, the sale of the club, transfers that didn't happen – transfers like Dani Alves, who'd later become a great Barcelona right-back, someone Liverpool had ready to board a plane from Seville only for the selling club's president to call him back at the last moment. Somewhere in the narrative of transfer stories like these, Parry would be blamed.

'You can't let criticism distract you,' he says. 'I tried not to read the papers. When you ignore them, it's remarkable how much better you feel. You have to focus on what you believe is right as well as outcomes, rather than trying to please people or worrying about your own popularity. Supporters don't just have an opinion; they want to see everything in black and white. It has to be biro. It's a case of Rafa being a hero or a villain. It's a case of Steven Gerrard being the greatest or the worst. Actually, the reality is somewhere in the middle. Nobody is all bad or all good. Everybody makes mistakes; everybody does good things. Unfortunately, there is a culture in football – as well as in society – that everything is binary when really there is usually a shade of grey.'

It says much about the dysfunctional leadership at the top of Liverpool that Parry was able to remain after Hicks's public condemnation. In November 2008, Parry was told by advisers from both the Hicks and Gillett camps that the club was up for sale. Parry had sold Liverpool once. He hoped to be able to do it again. Yet by January 2009, the outlook had changed. He describes 'the insanity of Liverpool', mentioning a scene where Hicks arrived at a home game with his entourage in the directors' box while Gillett was left in the overspill seats usually reserved for scouting in front of the press box in the main stand.

'I went to George and said, "With respect, you don't look like the equal partner at the moment. You've got to do me one favour at least: don't leave me with that fella." At least I could finish with a bit of dignity myself.'

Parry did not hear from Gillett again. Instead, a week later Hicks contacted him to explain that he'd discussed it with Gillett and it was the one thing they could agree on: that a meeting should be scheduled to establish whether a termination of Parry's contract could be arranged.

'It was the only civilized moment of those few years. It was a relief when my departure was finally confirmed,' Parry says. 'The thing that hurt the most was that the club was not being run in the correct way, with the right values. I'd like to have left when the outlook at Liverpool was healthier.'

Parry's exit was presented as a victory for Rafael Benítez, who signed a new five-season contract extension soon afterwards, albeit one that he would complete just one further season of. Parry believes this is a myth that needs debunking.

'Yes, Rafa and I had disagreements but that does not explain all of the ills at the club. I was involved in previous negotiations over Rafa's contract where I said, "Listen, if it helps for me to go, it's not a problem." But Rafa and his people assured me that wasn't an issue at all. There were big issues over how much power he wanted, who was in charge of what and how things should be done. But it was never a personal thing between him and me. There was even lots of talk about me having an office at Melwood and spending more time there with him.

'The idea of my departure being the result of a power battle between me and Rafa isn't true,' Parry concludes. 'We still speak and in his own inimitable way – because he'd never admit to being wrong about anything, ever – there is definitely a sense that he realizes you should maybe be careful what you wish for, even if it's fleeting. He made a point of writing that in his book and when it was released he ensured that David and I received signed copies.'

CHAPTER ELEVEN

cultzeros.co.uk

FERNANDO TORRES,
The Kid

WHEN THE CLOAK OF DARKNESS FALLS UPON MADRID IN THE weeks before spring's arrival, the temperature drops suddenly and gusts blow across the city. Yet over on the banks of the Manzanares River, at the Vicente Calderón Stadium, there is a flame that always burns.

To understand what Fernando Torres means to supporters of Atlético Madrid, imagine the family of six who have driven two hours on a school night from a town in La Mancha, where the windmills are immortalized by Miguel de Cervantes in the novel *Don Quixote*.

Torres has not been introduced, having only been selected as a substitute, but with Atlético 2–0 ahead at half-time against Real Sociedad, he takes to the pitch and begins to warm up.

One of the young boys, no older than eight, spots him. 'El Niño Torres!' he yaps. 'Look, El Niño Torres!' His brothers break from an argument and stare out across the verdant field in front.

Before kick-off, when Torres's name was announced, the raucous cheers bounced off the ramparts of this tattered football ground, which sits in the working-class south of Spain's capital, not too far from where Torres grew up. Arganzuela is an industrial neighbour-hood and such is the volume of noise it would probably have been enough to conceal the rumble of the M-30 motorway, which runs beneath the west stand while operational on non-match days.

It is a challenge to explain exactly how much of a hero Torres is at the Calderón, where the goal that won the 2008 European Championships, Spain's first inter-national tournament in forty-four years, was believed to be Atlético's, not only because Torres scored it but also because he celebrated the achievement that night, and then the World Cup in 2010, by decorating himself in an Atlético flag. By then, Torres had left the club and yet soon after his departure in 2007 Liverpool shirts were worn inside the Calderón.

Back home now, after seven and a half seasons away, Torres's presence is not required. Atlético end up winning 3–0, squashing Sociedad with a display of considerable physical strength and unity. Not one of their players is a real star. Under Diego Simeone, the team is king.

In fact, there is a sense Atlético might not need Torres much longer. He is not really El Niño (the Kid) any more and, rather, a near 32-year-old father of three with his best years behind him. Because Torres is on loan from AC Milan and because, at the time of our interview, Atlético are under a transfer embargo, he might have to go somewhere else when his contract ends in Italy in a few months, whether Simeone wants him or not.

When I meet Torres the following day, the prospect of leaving Atlético for a second time – the club he grew up supporting, the one where he made his debut at seventeen and became the youngest captain at nineteen – does not appear to concern him too greatly, largely because he is not considering the future as much as he did when he was younger, something which, he explains, contributed towards an acrimonious exit from Liverpool to Chelsea. 'Day by day – I have realized that in life you should look no further,' is one of the first things he says to me.

At Atlético, the love for him is unconditional because when he left, he moved abroad and the supporters understood why he had to do it. The destination of Liverpool was acceptable because Liverpool are not rivals and, as Torres later reminds me, 'Liverpool beat Real Madrid in the 1981 European Cup final', and Real Madrid are Atlético's enemy.

At Liverpool, no foreign player in modern times has appeared to understand the club and the city as much as he did. As captain of Atlético, he wore an armband that bore the words 'You'll Never Walk Alone'. In his debut season at Anfield, he scored thirty-three goals in forty-six games. In 2008, when Liverpool became the European Capital of Culture, his presence helped it feel like an even more cosmopolitan place. That summer, an advert for his boot maker Nike included shots of a house in Anfield being painted in the red and yellow colours of Spain, along with the parking lines on the streets below. There were chip shops advertising all-day tapas, street markets selling paella pans and increased numbers of women at salsa lessons. The world famous Cavern Club became the Caverna Club. The final scene included a modestly dressed Torres walking his dog across green space on Everton Brow, retrieving a football for a group of lads involved in a game. Although injuries interrupted the next two and a half seasons, his name was sung even before Steven Gerrard's in the pubs before matches. Torres was the working-class hero from another country who simply got it all.

But then he signed for Chelsea, a club whose injection of riches since 2003 had seen them win more than Liverpool, as a new rivalry developed. Torres says that when he closes his eyes and forces himself, he can remember driving through the gates of Melwood for the last time as a Liverpool player. A gang had congregated, ceremoniously burning his shirt in front of television cameras. John Aldridge, the former Liverpool centre-forward, worked for radio and could not bring himself to utter Torres's name thereafter, referring to him as 'the other fella'. His debut for Chelsea came the following weekend and, as fate would have it, Liverpool were the opponents at Stamford Bridge. Visiting supporters greeted him with a couple of banners with clear messages:

'He who betrays will always walk alone' and the slightly more obscure 'Ya paid 50 mil 4 Margi Clarke'. Torres was hit by a cigarette lighter thrown from the south-east corner of the Shed End and, to complete his indignity, Liverpool won 1–0.

It was a surprise that Torres agreed to meet me. He does not do many interviews and has never before given his side of the story about his departure from Liverpool to Chelsea. The discussions with Torres's representatives in order to secure time with him were, however, relatively straightforward. They appreciated this as an opportunity to set the record straight over some issues, particularly those that led to his £50 million-pound sale from Liverpool, a British record. I flew to Madrid sensing that not everything was quite as it seemed.

My brief was to be at the Cerro del Espino from noon, the day after Atlético's easy win over Sociedad. Set in the town of Majadahonda, the training ground is fifteen miles north-west of Madrid and higher up on the Castile plateau, so the air is cleaner. It is a wealthy area of plush shopping arcades and impressive-looking apartment complexes with gardens. In the distance, the snow-capped mountaintops of the Navacerrada are visible. As Torres finishes his training session, rich smells of fresh bread from a fancy bakery breeze across the car park.

First to arrive is Antonio Sanz, Torres's long-term adviser. I first met him in the months after Torres joined Liverpool. Football agents tend to be viewed suspiciously but I liked Antonio because of his jolly nature and straight talking. On the day Torres left Liverpool, I spoke to him in the reception area at Melwood and detected some sadness that it had come to this. Before I could ask what was really happening, his mobile phone rang and by the time he had finished his conversation I had been directed somewhere else for another interview with Liverpool's latest signing, Luis Suárez. It felt like a sliding-doors moment for Liverpool fans – what could have been had both been there at the same time . . .

Until any interview takes place, you never quite know what you are going to get. It is a relief when Antonio tells me that Torres had decided it was a good idea to do this one straight away. 'Ask him anything you want, anything at all,' he says. 'There are some things he would like to say.'

Torres has showered and changed into a jumper, jeans and trainers when he appears soon after. His film-star qualities remain: his thin freckled face and, though it is shorter than it was when he was at his best for Liverpool, there is the striking mop of blond hair. A firm handshake makes you trust him that bit more and, despite being shy, he makes consistent eye contact when introducing himself.

We are led into an anteroom next to a press canteen that serves empanadas and juices. There is a wooden table, two wooden chairs and one tiny window at the top of the dimly painted back wall. Jokes follow about it feeling like a set for interrogations and, though I'd like the conversation to be serious, I don't want him to feel on the back foot straight away, so I open with a few questions he might find it easier to deal with.

I suggest to Torres that it must have been a big decision to leave Atlético for Liverpool in the first place. He leans on the table, joins his hands and begins to speak slowly in a deep, staid voice.

'Well, I had offers from different English teams a few years before I moved to Liverpool,' he says. 'Manchester United were one of the clubs that came. But I never took the decision because it was very hard for me to leave Atlético. When I was a kid, I did not see further than Atlético. I wanted to get the chance to play for the first team, to score a few goals, stay there and win trophies. It was everything I dreamed about. I never thought I might leave.

'The situation was difficult for the club at that time [from the moment Torres made his debut in 2001]. We were in the second division and went back to the first division. There were a lot of financial problems. I'd never even played in Europe. So my aim became clear: to help the team qualify for Europe and after that maybe think about leaving. It would be the best for me but especially the best for the club, because I felt like they were building a team around me, which I don't think is the way to become a stronger team. I was sure if I left, they could use the money to build a side the fans could be proud of, rather than just one individual. With time, I saw that this was the conclusion, so it was a relief that it worked this way. OK, it was good for me but it was especially good for Atlético.

'We qualified for Europe. Then Benítez called me. At least I was leaving the team in a good situation. Liverpool had played two European finals in three years. Benítez was there, Alonso and Reina. It was a club where I felt it would be quite easy for me to adapt. The relationship between the fans and the team was also something I was looking for. It was difficult to leave Atlético. But it was not difficult to choose Liverpool.'

From his early teens, Torres was projected as the average boy from the average town who became a supremely talented footballer and did not change. That's why supporters of Atlético love him so much. It was part of his appeal on the terraces of Anfield too.

Torres was raised in Fuenlabrada, half an hour by train from Madrid's Atocha Station. I have been there before and it is unremarkable, featuring row upon row of identikit housing blocks. It could have been the outskirts of any major European city had the weather not given an idea of the location away. Fuenlabrada is classic Spanish suburbia: an arid place of tall concrete and shadows. The pace of life is slow. In a smoky room in Café Padilla, I was greeted by strange looks from old men who preferred to engage in their brandy glasses rather than conversation. One of them emerged from the miasma to ask me what I was doing there, and when I explained it was for research into Torres's early life, the man with lips like bloodied hacked meat scoffed. He was a Real Madrid fan and took pride in informing me that Atlético were the second team in Fuenlabrada, like everywhere else near Madrid.

Torres lived in Parque Granada, the type of barrio where everyone knows everyone else's business. His parents had moved there from Galicia when his father José was relocated as a policeman. During summer holidays, they would return to Spain's rugged north-west coast and it was there that Torres met Olalla, his childhood sweetheart, to whom he is now married. They have three children named Leo, Nora and Elsa.

The Torres family resided in a flat on Calle de Alemania and his primary school was 150 yards away from the front door. By the age of seven, Torres's gift was obvious from the number of goals he scored in small-sided *fútbol sala* games, 'sometimes fourteen or fifteen,' remembers Jose Camacho, a family friend who owned the sports shop where Torres bought his first pair of football boots.

When Torres scored his hundredth goal for Atlético in February 2016, he gave the shirt to an 84-year-old man called Manuel Briñas. Torres first met Briñas twenty years earlier when he turned up for a trial on the gravel pitches of the Parque de las Cruces in Carabanchel, the prison town, more Atlético turf than Fuenlabrada. Briñas had been tasked with rebuilding Atlético's youth system after it had been disbanded by Jesús Gil. Along with around two hundred other kids, Torres played eleven-a-side games split into twenty-minute halves while the coaches gave marks out of ten. 'Give him ten,' Briñas said when he saw Torres. 'In fact, give him ten and a bit.'

Torres was already an Atlético supporter. His induction to the club as a player consecrated the relationship. Offers later came from Real Madrid, and Pedro Calvo, his first coach, can remember approaches being made by sporting directors at Inter Milan and Arsenal. Financially, those moves would have been rewarding but Torres would not depart because he felt aligned to what he describes as the '*sentimiento de rebeldía*' or a sense of rebellion. His distaste for Atlético's rivals does not lay hidden.

'It is difficult sharing a city with one of the most successful clubs in history when you support the other club,' he says. 'When I beat Real Madrid with Liverpool, it was my first time, you know? With Atlético we could not beat them. Ever. The satisfaction of going to the Santiago Bernabéu and winning as a Liverpool player was huge. Then the next week they came to Anfield and we beat them for a second time, 4–0. I could not help myself, celebrating a goal in front of their fans. It was special. Beating them with Atlético [as he had done the weekend before our meeting] tastes different. There is a lot of pressure here in Madrid when you don't beat Real for eight years, which happened in my first period here as a professional. I was the main man at Atlético and the one getting all of the blame.'

Michael Robinson, the forward who played for Liverpool in the 1980s before emerging as a famous football commentator on Spanish television, described Atlético as 'the dog with fleas'. 'You can't help but love them,' he said. 'Atlético can defend well, they can attack well. But they're not particularly brilliant at anything other than giving everything they've got. They're irresistible.'

Despite the pressure and despite his dubious record against Real before he left for Liverpool, Atlético supporters worship Torres for dragging them out of the second division after they had been relegated for the first time since 1934 in the season before his debut. They love him too because he left to master the world but never forgot them and was true on his promise to return one day.

I ask Torres what Atlético represents to him.

'Atlético means everything to me,' he says. 'When I was a kid, I only watched Atlético games, none of the others. I was the kid going to the stand with my grandparents and my dad and brother. I would go by myself sometimes, getting the train and then the metro for one hour from Fuenlabrada. And then I would travel home by myself.

'My life and education has been Atlético. Everything that is happening now to me – the records, the games – it's so emotional because it makes you look back and consider what has happened since the first day I joined. I remember being ten years old and playing the final trial game where the club decided whether I was good enough for Atlético or not. The nerves! That was twenty years ago and I still feel it. It makes me smile. You can see me smiling now . . .

'From that day, I did not think any of this would happen. To score one hundred goals for the club – it was too much to believe. It was so emotional, especially because of the reaction of the people. They know I am one of them. I was in the stands before and now I am lucky enough to be on the pitch. When I do not play for the club any more, I will be in the stands again.'

In 2007, a 6–0 defeat to Barcelona made Torres think about his future as an Atlético player because Barcelona was usually the one illustrious opponent Atlético found a way to beat. He was walking his two bulldogs in Madrid when the mobile phone in his pocket began to vibrate and a number he did not recognize flashed across the screen. He explains that he wouldn't usually answer to an unknown caller but, realizing the number was registered in England, he figured it might have been one of his close friends, Pepe Reina or Cesc Fàbregas. Instead, it was Rafael Benítez. Benítez had a list of five targets. They included Internazionale's Julio Cruz, Palermo's Amauri, Alberto Gilardino from AC Milan and Lisandro López of Porto. The recruitment of Torres was, however, given priority status.

'I cannot remember if he said, "Hi, it's Rafa" or, "Hi, this is Benítez,"' Torres recalls. The Liverpool manager was on holiday in Portugal a week after the Champions League final defeat to AC Milan, but his focus was already on recruiting a striker that would help propel his team towards the summit of the Premier League. 'I was surprised but did not realize the dimension of what I was hearing till I hung up. Then I thought, *Wow, this club that can get anybody in the world has rung me; they want me.*'

Benítez had complained in interviews immediately after the final in Athens in 2007 that Tom Hicks and George Gillett were not helping him move fast enough to finalize deals for new signings. Torres was in Tahiti on holiday with Olalla when another call came several weeks later, instructing him to return to Europe immediately before flying to Merseyside.

'My medical took two days and nobody knew I was in the city,' he recalls. 'The club arranged for me to stay in an apartment in the Albert Dock, supplying me with lots of DVDs and books about Liverpool's history. I knew

Liverpool was one of the great European clubs already. But it is not until you arrive that you realize really what the pressure is like – a good pressure. You are not just signing for a big football club; you are signing for a city. Millions of people across the world are watching you. I was the club's record transfer.'

If Torres was feeling the weight of expectation, he did not show it. His first goal arrived in his second league game, a 1–1 draw with Chelsea. The way he glided past his marker and the confident execution of the finish made it seem as though a matador was at work, teasing the unfortunate beast, Tal Ben Haim. Over the course of the next three seasons, he would score in all of the biggest games: against Manchester United, against Everton, against Arsenal and in the Champions League fixtures too. In 142 appearances for the club, he registered eighty-one goals, breaking all sorts of records in the process. He reached a half century of goals quicker than Roger Hunt, and the crouching Torres became a familiar sight before kick-offs, lowering himself on to his haunches and staring impassively at the opposition before him, scanning the area and familiarizing himself with the goal he was targeting. It made him look like an assassin, mentally placing his victims inside a trap before the attack.

By watching videos of Premier League matches, he familiarized himself with the opponents he would encounter and would adapt his game accordingly. Quickly, he became the player all of the boys wanted to be like and the player all of the girls wanted to be with. He darted across boxes and twisted past defenders.

He became one of the greatest strikers to ever play for Liverpool.

'I know I am never going to feel the way I felt at Anfield again, even in my dreams,' he says. 'Here at Atlético, I am home. It is where I grew up. I was a supporter in the stand, I joined the academy and then I became a player. It is normal that the people love me, because I am one of them. You can do wrong and they forgive you. At Liverpool, there was no reason for this relationship to develop the way it did. How many players have signed for Liverpool, they go there and play and pass the years but nobody remembers what they did? I was lucky. They did not have any reason to love me that way but they made me feel different to any other player.'

It helped Torres that Steven Gerrard was there, someone similarly talented, with similarly introverted personality traits. Someone, indeed, who had the same experience of captaining his local club from a very young age.

'I admire the player who gives the example by actions, not just with words. We had Carragher with the words, keeping everyone alive, which is so important. In the dressing room, he was the voice. And then on the pitch, he would support those words with actions.

'Stevie was different and more like me: leading by example. Stevie was always first in training; he could play the ball better than anyone. If he needed to kick someone, he did. When you see both of them working that way, you have to follow. If the main players give everything, you cannot give less than them. They set standards.

'Yes, Stevie in some ways is similar to me: more reserved and shy. On the pitch, it is different. There is an aura around him. You feel it as a teammate. The opponent feels it because they know what is coming. He understood everything about me. I just needed to move into the space and the first thing he would try to do is find me. And he did, whether it was with a long or a short pass. Stevie was the player that completed my game. I will never find someone like him again.'

Gerrard, Torres says, gave him the confidence to display a creative expression that had lain dormant under the burden of home expectation in Madrid.

'In 2008, I went to the Ballon d'Or gala in Switzerland. Messi won, Ronaldo came second and I came third. I could not believe I was nominated. Wow, a private jet – I was in shock. Stevie kept telling me, "Don't worry, you will win it for sure." He told me that like he really thought it. I thought he was crazy! I never once thought I'd be good enough to get invited to a gala like this. His words expressed how he felt about me at the club and the performance levels I was reaching with the help of the support. He told me I could be the best in the world and I realized this is the feeling everybody in Liverpool had about me. They made me feel anything was possible, that everything was real.'

The narrative of Torres's first two seasons at Liverpool is well documented. This was a player who came, who scored, who was adored by the Kop. Liverpool did not win the league title but they came closer than they had in any of the previous nineteen years. There were strong performances in the Champions League as well.

Torres relished life in Woolton, where he would go out for meals and be able to shop without interference. People were respectful enough to give him space. Shouting his name and waving was enough. Merseyside allowed him space to breathe and lead a relatively normal life, one that was not possible in Madrid, where it was difficult to know who to trust because everyone wanted a piece of him, where he wasn't playing for the strongest team and 80 per cent of the people were Real fans.

The story of his final eighteen months at Anfield, however, is blurred. There is an accepted version of events, especially of the last few weeks, which is that Torres asked the club to consider an offer from Chelsea before verbal and written requests forced it through. When I mention this to Torres, the shutters slowly begin to come down but then the entire window of the period is exposed for all to see, according to his memories.

He begins by telling me he cannot compare the Liverpool he joined in 2007 to the one he left three and a half years later. Torres has previously weighed all of his answers carefully. From herein, probing is unnecessary. He speaks without much interruption.

'When I decided to move to Liverpool, it was because I was sure Liverpool was very close to becoming the best team in Europe,' he says. 'But the situation changed completely . . .'

He pauses for reflection, then continues: 'At times, I believe we were the best team in Europe. We were not lucky enough to win the Premier League, though we were so close. We also lost in a Champions League semi-final. I think the team was great. You can see that by the players. One moved to Real Madrid [Xabi Alonso] and another to Barcelona [Javier Mascherano], and these players are still playing at the highest level.

'We had a team to dream about but one that still needed building. The spine was there. Providing we kept that, I knew we could compete with anyone: Reina, Carragher, Agger, Skrtel, Alonso, Mascherano, Gerrard and then me. It was strong, very powerful. We were difficult to beat and nobody wanted to play against us. We were not far away from being champions of England and champions of Europe. But we needed to keep the team.

'Everything changed when the owners started talking about selling. The mindset of the club went in a different direction. Alonso was sold, Mascherano was sold, Benítez went too. Not all of the money went into new players. The club was saying, "We still want to be the best and we want to win" but doing the opposite.'

He says that Atlético has always been *his* club.

'I left *my* club to win,' he continues. 'By the time I left Liverpool, when everybody was leaving, I did not have the feeling that I was going to win there. It was hard because I had been so happy. I'd never felt happier than during my time at Liverpool. But then I felt betrayed. That's the truth.'

Torres admits he is not blameless in what happened. And yet he ended up taking '*máximo responsabilidad*' for the outcome.

Torres reveals that in July 2010, he was aware of interest from Chelsea and Manchester City. He explains that late that month he met with Christian Purslow,

Liverpool's managing director, to discuss his concerns about the direction the club was moving in. The season before, Liverpool had finished seventh under Rafael Benítez, which contributed towards his leaving. Purslow was hired by Tom Hicks and George Gillett in 2009 in the aftermath of Rick Parry's departure, with a priority of renegotiating the £350 million loan the club had outstanding with Royal Bank of Scotland and to assume overall management of the club until a new permanent chief executive could be appointed. Purslow had emerged from Cambridge with a degree in modern and medieval languages. A career in investment banking followed.

'Benítez was not there: the club sacked him. I finished the World Cup and I talked with Purslow on holiday. He came with Roy Hodgson, who was keen to speak to me. I told them my view on what was happening at the club: that we were so close to winning and now good players were leaving. What was our future?

'Purslow explained that Liverpool were in the process of being sold to new owners and that nobody could leave in the summer because the club had a higher value with the players they had at that time. "We cannot sell you," he told me. I told them we would not win without investment and that it worried me we'd fall behind very quickly. I explained that when I joined the club, the mood was totally different and that Benítez's ambition had taken me to Liverpool. Purslow told me that nobody would leave but as soon as the club was sold he would speak to the new owner and try to find a solution. If I wanted to leave then, I could.

'Nobody ever said to me, "We want you to stay

and be like Stevie." The message was: "We'll sell the club and you can leave." That means to me the people running the club did not really care about Liverpool, only themselves. They wanted to save themselves. And then Mascherano was sold anyway.'

Torres understands that Hodgson was appointed into a difficult position, one where maybe even he did not appreciate the full facts of the bleak outlook at Liverpool. Torres says he liked Hodgson even though on the outside it may have seemed their relationship was not close.

'It was a pity because Hodgson was a great coach and a great guy,' Torres says. 'They didn't let him work. They brought in all these Australian people [a new medical team] who controlled everything: who could play, who could not. He wasn't able to use the players the way he wanted. From that pre-season to the January when I left, it was a nightmare. Not just for me but for everybody, for Hodgson too. He was not allowed to work properly – the situation was more difficult for him than it was for anyone else. Everything was a mess. We were not good enough. In the middle of that, they finally sold the club.'

Though he realizes Liverpool was rotting from the head, Torres recognizes that Hicks's and Gillett's money took him to Liverpool in the first place. He had no relationship with either of them.

'I don't think it's so important the owners are in England, in Liverpool,' he says. 'What I think is important is that they put someone in charge who is in Liverpool – the right person who understands what Liverpool means.

I am sure most owners have many businesses. The only thing they have to do in football is give the money that you need to compete with others. Whatever name you want – the president or the sporting director – they need to understand Liverpool, the feelings. He has to listen to the fans and listen to the players and do a job that is up to the level of the club, meeting the standards that have been set through history. You need someone there who understands what Liverpool is, because for the owners it is just a business and without someone telling them the right information it will fail. OK, if they are in Liverpool it will help them but if they are not, put someone in charge who is there and understands football and the club.'

Boston-based investment firm New England Sports Ventures (later to become Fenway Sports Group) acquired Liverpool in a move that Hicks described as 'an epic swindle'. Both Martin Broughton, the chairman, and Purslow stepped down from their roles at that point, though Purslow remained as an adviser for a while longer. Liverpool would be structured in a different way, with a sporting director taking on some of Purslow's responsibilities: primarily dealing with recruitment and sales. Damien Comolli, a Frenchman, was appointed to the role, having achieved varied success at Tottenham Hotspur before.

'I went to talk with Comolli and told him about my concerns and what had happened. He said the same as Purslow: "No, no, you cannot leave because we do not have any other players to play." Again, he was not telling me, "You cannot leave because we need you for the project." It was, "OK, we will find someone else, then maybe you can leave." It said to me that they did not want to keep me, really. They wanted to find someone else. But first they wanted to wait until the summer. Comolli told me Liverpool were going to buy Luis Suárez but because Suárez was not a goalscorer I needed to stay until they found one. "Suárez is the player to play behind; he is not going to score too many goals," was the message. You can see they signed Suárez thinking he could not score goals . . .'

Torres affords a light smile recalling this memory, insisting that history has since proven that Suárez deserves to be considered one of the game's best modern strikers alongside Lionel Messi and Cristiano Ronaldo.

'Comolli told me that the new owners [FSG], they had an idea of how to spend their investment. They wanted to bring in young players, to build something new. I was thinking to myself, *This takes time to work. It takes two, three, four, maybe even ten years.* I didn't have that time. I was twenty-seven years old. I did not have the time to wait. I wanted to win. Here we are five years later and they are still trying to build – around the same position in the league as when I left.'

With Liverpool mid table, FSG's next big decision was to sack Hodgson at the start of January 2011 and replace him with Kenny Dalglish until the end of the season. A reflection of Hodgson's shattered relationship with Liverpool's supporters by the end was the sound of the 'Hodgson for England' chants from the away end in a game at Blackburn Rovers. His reign proved to be the shortest of any permanent Liverpool manager in the club's history.

Dalglish, meanwhile, was viewed as the greatest Liverpool player. He had also led Liverpool to their last league title nearly twenty-one years earlier. He is someone whose status on Merseyside is at a papal level.

Torres liked Dalglish and after his appointment spoke to him about his disappointing conversations with Purslow and Comolli. At one meeting, Torres insists he did not request to leave but stressed if Liverpool were thinking about following a different path, one where investment in proven quality was not imminent 'because we needed it', it might be worth considering financially acceptable offers for him and allowing Liverpool to build with the money accrued.

In the week that followed, as Liverpool negotiated privately with Chelsea and as they inched closer to an agreement that would make Torres the subject of the highest transfer deal in English history, stories began to circulate in the press claiming that Torres had 'verbally' requested a transfer. Torres believes this came from a leak at the club, a deliberate attempt to sully his name before the conclusion of the inevitable: making him take 'maximum responsibility' for the transfer when really the club were happy to make it happen.

'When Chelsea made their first offer before the game at Wolverhampton, I spoke with Dalglish and Steve Clarke [the assistant manager]. I think Comolli wanted to be at the meeting but I told them I only wanted to speak with the coaches. Again, I told Dalglish and Clarke that I only left my club to win and now we were so far away from winning. I told them I felt as though I'd been lied to. Despite telling me they would not sell the good players, Mascherano was sold. I told them that the Chelsea offer was a good one and it would allow me to keep improving and the club would receive a huge financial reward. Dalglish told me that he did not want me to leave – he was the only one. "I need you here," he said, although he never spoke about his reasons, so they may have been the same as Comolli's.

'Before leaving the room, I thought we had an understanding. It might have been a difficult conversation but there was respect on both sides. It was *no pasa nada* [no problem]. Dalglish told me he'd always be grateful for what I'd done for Liverpool and that hopefully I'd stay.

'Whether I stayed or left, the idea was to continue as normal. I wanted to do everything the right way. I scored twice at Wolverhampton, then played OK against Fulham three days later at Anfield. Dalglish had told me he did not want me to leave but at the same time I knew Liverpool were negotiating with Chelsea, so maybe this was not the truth.

'What I did not expect was what they did with the media, changing the way it looked. They tried to show that I was the guilty one, *el único* [the only one]. I'd gone face to face with Dalglish to explain the situation so that everything was clear. I did not use my agent. He knew how I felt: I wanted to win but at Liverpool it did not seem as though that was possible for at least a few years. And you can see what happened in the few years after – I was not wrong.

'I told him City had a great team, United were still

winning things, then there was Chelsea as usual and Tottenham. We were so far from them. I told him about my conversations with Purslow in the summer and that I stayed then because I did not want to be responsible for Liverpool not being sold.

'I explained to him that nobody ever wanted me to stay for the right reasons – reasons only related to football. I told him Comolli had told me I could leave at the end of the season. He was not interested in me staying for ever. I told Dalglish I had the chance to leave then – in January – and I did not know whether Chelsea, City or Bayern Munich would come again. I knew the season was not going to be very good – we had been in the bottom half of the table. Who knows what is going to happen? I had the chance to go and it was a great offer for the club also. But if you want me to stay for ever, tell me that. If Liverpool were going to build a great team again, I wanted to stay, there would be no reason to leave, though I did not think this was going to happen, because I did not believe in Comolli's ideas. I wasn't sure whether he really cared about Liverpool at all.'

By selling Torres, Comolli would potentially have more money to play with, more money to exert influence on the club in his first few months in the job. It is Dalglish whom Torres feels most let down by, though.

'My respect for him was huge. I knew that Dalglish was one of the best players in the history of the club, that everyone loved him. But I think he had the power to change the situation. I don't know why he didn't do so. If he had asked for money for players, I think they'd have given it to him. If he had insisted to the owners that

I stay, then I would have stayed. He came and the team started playing better. I started scoring more goals. The way he wanted to play was much better for the players we had. Steve Clarke was a fantastic coach and he did a great job too.

'Stories appeared in the press about me demanding to leave, though. This made it difficult for me to stay and to trust the people at Liverpool. Someone must have told them. Because I did not.'

I remind Torres that a similar thing happened with Javier Mascherano when he left for Barcelona at the end of the previous August. After a man-of-the-match performance against Arsenal on the opening day of the season, it was reported that he had refused to play against Manchester City. I wondered whether Liverpool were in the business of discrediting a departing player's name so the club looked better and the parting of ways was made more acceptable to supporters.

'The stories that appeared in the press changed the view of everybody including myself. It was not the truth. The truth was that I moved from my home to a club that was ready to win. When I left, there was not a single piece of the winning culture left.

'What's so hard for me is that I felt the relationship between myself and the club was really close. That's why I tried to go and talk to them straight. I will say this again: I did not use my agent. I went first to Purslow, then to Comolli and after to Dalglish – all face-to-face. I tried to explain to each one of them why I left Atlético to go to Liverpool in the first place. I tried to explain that you couldn't expect to win if you sold your best players. Nobody could give me a straight answer, a football answer.

'It looked like I wanted to leave for Chelsea and I did not love Liverpool any more. It looked like I did not want to train and play and that's why I asked for a transfer request. It was presented as if I was a traitor. It was not like this in the discussion. Liverpool could not admit they were doing something wrong with the whole team. They had to find a guilty one.'

Liverpool supporters saw his choice to join Chelsea as treason. Torres viewed it as his only option.

'I feel sorry for the fans, because they are always going to love Liverpool. The club is bigger than any player. That's why it was so hard to decide to leave and why it was so hard to see the facts getting twisted, for everything to be pointed at me. I can understand the supporters, because if I read everything that was in the media and believed it, I would feel the same way. But I will tell you again: nothing will ever change my feelings for Liverpool, for the fans and for the city. From day one until the last, they were fantastic towards me.'

There is a sense from Torres that the situation either got out of control very quickly or someone at Liverpool achieved what they wanted in the end. While Dalglish had been out of front-line football for longer than a decade and was landed in a situation that was not of his making, FSG, whose principal owner is John W. Henry, had no previous experience in dealing with such political transfers. FSG have always admitted to taking council from mysterious-sounding 'pre-eminent advisers'.

During the long-running battle between Mill Financial,

former owner George Gillett and Royal Bank of Scotland, it was revealed in 2016 from a New York courtroom that back in 2010 when Mill were competing with FSG to buy the club, both Torres and Pepe Reina were viewed by FSG as being 'probably beyond their primes'.

'John Henry was the last person I spoke to and he was great to me, I cannot say anything bad,' Torres says. 'He told me he did not want me to leave. If I did want to leave, he told me that the price had to be very high. I told him that I did not want to talk about numbers; that was for him to decide and I would respect whatever decision he came to.'

The discussion with Steven Gerrard about the situation was the one he dreaded most.

'I went to him before speaking with Dalglish. We were in the dressing room at Melwood alone, sitting together. I explained there had been an offer from Chelsea and that the team was not going to be good in the years to come. I asked him what he thought I should do. Stevie told me not to go, never to leave Liverpool. But he realized too I had to do what was best for me; he understood that my situation and his were different. These were words from the best captain.

'I know that Stevie was devastated when I left. I was as well, in some ways. I remember the flight from Liverpool to London. I did not know what to feel. I was not happy, I was not angry; I was empty. I was on a helicopter and it was getting dark, flying over Liverpool below. I began to feel sad. I was so happy there, so, so happy . . .

'After a few weeks, I went back to Liverpool to get my stuff. My son was born in Liverpool. Usually, the house would be busy and he'd be greeting me at the door. But the house was silent. That was hard too . . .'

Torres struggles to describe his emotions when he made his debut for Chelsea the following weekend against Liverpool. He performed that day as if he did not want to be there.

'To play against Liverpool was never something I liked,' he admits. 'There were so many memories and feelings. The reaction of the fans was something I expected but it was still too much for me. I did not react in a good way. Again, it was so, so hard . . .'

His mind drifts to a game at Anfield in 2014 when victory for Liverpool would have put them two more wins away from the club's first league title in twenty-four years. Steven Gerrard slipped, enabling Demba Ba to score Chelsea's opener, and in injury time Torres – sent on as a substitute – raced through on goal. He could have made it 2–0 but elected to pass to Willian. During the course of this interview, it is the only question he dodges: the one where I suggest it seems as though he could not contemplate scoring, that he couldn't bear to stop Liverpool achieving a feat he never accomplished with them.

'That was the toughest day,' he prefers to say. 'I felt so sorry for Stevie and for Liverpool. [They] were so close and really deserved to win the league. If they had won, I think Liverpool would have created history. What a moment for the city. It was so hard seeing the people in the stands. I still feel the same way for them. No matter what has happened, I still love them. I know some of them are still angry but it will not change how I feel for them. Atlético is my club but I still support Liverpool and I want them to win every game, every trophy.'

He explains that he has wished for the platform to speak freely about Liverpool for some time. Being a Chelsea player made that impossible.

'Liverpool is unique. It is different to Atlético, for example,' he continues. 'I'm from here and I love Atlético because my heart is here. But as a club, at Liverpool I felt at home even though I was not from there. The relationship between the workers, the people in the offices, the people around the team and the fans – it is special.

'I never felt at Chelsea or even at Atlético the same way I did at Liverpool. At Liverpool, they made me feel like a king. I really felt like I could do anything. I remember playing my first game at Anfield. Pepe [Reina] came and said, "Look at the atmosphere – this is where you need to be. You do not get this at Atlético . . ." After the game, I told Pepe that I thought I could score in every single game at Anfield. As soon as I stepped on to the pitch: goals. I was flying. Not only because I was the best age to play football but also because of the atmosphere around the club. It was magic.'

Torres admits he reacts better when the energy towards him is positive. At Liverpool, he felt adoration. At Chelsea, he felt the need to justify a huge price tag while not being fully fit. Remorse about the manner of his departure from Liverpool lingered. From being arguably the deadliest striker on the planet for Liverpool, he was never able to reach the same level. Behind the eyes he instead appeared dead.

'Right now I do not think that winning trophies is

more important than being happy. I have realized that winning the Champions League [as he did with Chelsea in 2012], it does not change how you feel every day. I have realized the target should not be the main thing in your life; taking life day by day is key.

'When I was at Chelsea, I did not start well for a few reasons. We won almost everything I wanted to win. But maybe that was not enough for me. I was missing playing with Stevie and I missed playing for Liverpool. I thought a lot about the games with the team we had, fighting together. It really means something to me. It is something I found again at Atlético: a team together. Maybe we don't have huge names but we are a team that competes and enjoys every victory. It does not matter who scores the goal, it does not matter if at the end we cannot win, because at least we are doing something with our hearts.'

I suggest to Torres that it suits him to play for a club where there is a common cause, one that is not viewed as a representative of an establishment, like Real Madrid or, perhaps, Chelsea because they are from London.

'It is the most difficult thing in life: to choose the right moment at the right time to be in the right place,' he says. 'If you can find a club that suits you in everything, then it's going to be great, but getting there is a big challenge. You don't really know a club until you are there. And then it's too late to go back.'

This prompts me to come out and ask him: 'Fernando, do you regret moving to Chelsea?'

'No, because I won,' he insists. 'That is what I wanted at that time. I had not won anything before, only

416

promotion with Atlético and nothing with Liverpool despite a promising situation. The reason to move was to win trophies. And I did. It is silly to regret something you wanted. But maybe you realize it does not bring you contentment.'

Then he offers a different strand of thought.

'There are some questions journalists don't ask me in interviews,' he continues. 'I see Stevie leaving to go to the MLS – it was his decision. I thought, *How great would it have been for Stevie to finish his career at Liverpool, like Totti at Roma?* Maybe I should have done that here at Atlético. From the outside, you become a player to admire for ever. Everyone will always remember you as the one that stayed. Sometimes I think I should never have moved from Atlético – never. Maybe the team would have got better with me there, maybe they would still have won the trophies they won when I was not around. Now I would be nearly thirty-two – all my career at one club, winning trophies and having the respect of everyone. What could be better?

'But then I think I would never change my time in Liverpool. I needed to move. I found something great, special and different. It was my happiest time as a player. To feel the love of a community where you haven't grown up – it is hard for me to describe what this meant to me.

'I was hungry, though. I wanted trophies. When you are younger, many people are motivated by success. This was me at that moment: the next step was winning. I wanted it to be at Liverpool. But the circumstances changed.

'Chelsea was not good from the beginning, though. I did not find a team that suited me on the pitch. [There was a] good organization [off it] but the different personality [of the team] was not for me, even though I got what I wanted [by winning trophies].

'I tried in Italy with AC Milan but that was not for me either. Then I had the chance to come back to Atlético – to really enjoy every day even if I was not playing on a regular basis like I used to. I am enjoying what I'm doing. And that is more important.'

Having returned to Anfield for a charity game in honour of Steven Gerrard and Jamie Carragher in 2015, the crowd cheered when Torres's name was read out across the public address system, suggesting time has healed some old wounds. The song broke out: 'His armband proved he was a Red, Torres, Torres / You'll Never Walk Alone it read, Torres, Torres / We bought the lad from sunny Spain / He gets the ball and scores again, Fernando Torres, Liverpool's Number 9!'

'Maybe this was the happiest moment of the last five years for me,' he considers, a smile stretching across his face. 'In my last game there with Chelsea, I was booed. It was depressing. To go and hear my song again, to see the reaction of the fans – it makes me feel I am at peace now. I know I broke their hearts and in some way my heart was also broken. To have my last memory of Anfield as this one . . . I am so, so lucky.'

Torres is intelligent, introspective, sensitive and somewhat repentant. He queries the choices he has made. He does it here frequently without the need for questions. When listening to his words, there might appear to be an ambiguity to some of his conclusions. At the very end of our discussion, he makes a point of revisiting one particular subject without request.

'In my last full season with Liverpool, I had a problem in my knee,' he reveals. 'It stopped me playing and training at my best. I wanted to play in the World Cup and I was on crutches two months before the tournament started. I was so desperate, and I made it into the squad. But I was not playing well, because I could not bend my knee. Then I got injured again in the final and if you look at the pictures, you can see the pain.

'For a long time after that, I did not feel the same. Sometimes you want something so much you do not make the right decisions. I became a world champion but was it worth it? I don't know.

'Was it the right decision to think about moving away from Liverpool to Chelsea, where the chance to win trophies was greater at that time? I don't know . . .'

It is then you realize that only by looking into his dark, inky eyes can the truth really be revealed.

ACKNOWLEDGEMENTS

This book would not have been possible without the help of the following people: Brenda Kimber, my editor at Transworld, who has been consistent with her support and encouragement since we first met, along with publicist Sally Wray and my agent, David Luxton, who introduced me to Brenda in the first place. Without copy editor Ailsa Bathgate's attention to detail and inquisitive mind the finished version would not be as sharp as it needs to be.

I'd also like to thank others who have made vital contributions: Ged Rea for his knowledge and generosity; Ian Herbert for his guidance; Phil Dickinson, for being the best in the business at what he does; Jamie Carragher for vouching for me; Kevin Sampson for attempting to join the dots; James Corbett for his patience and understanding; and Mark Gilbertson for his friendship and his discretion. My dad Peter too – he's been there from the very beginning.

Finally, there is my wife, Rosalind. I'd really like her to read one of my books some day.

Red Machine

Simon Hughes

Liverpool FC in the 1980s
The players' stories

During the 1980s, Liverpool FC dominated English football, winning six league titles, two European Cups, two FA Cups and four League Cups. In *Red Machine*, Simon Hughes interviews some of the most colourful characters to have played for the club during that period. Set against the historical backdrop of both the club and the city, these candid interviews provide a vivid portrait of life at Liverpool during an era when the club's unparalleled on-pitch success often went hand-in-hand with a boozy social scene fraught with rows, fights and wind-ups.

The players featured here include John Barnes, Bruce Grobbelaar, Howard Gayle, Michael Robinson, John Wark, Kevin Sheedy, Nigel Spackman, Steve Staunton, David Hodgson and Craig Johnston, as well as first-team coach Ronnie Moran. Their candid, ribald and sometimes scathing recollections provide an antidote to the media-coached, on-message interviews given by today's players and offer a unique and fascinating insight into the greatest era in the club's history.

'An excellent, lucid journey into that
period, packed with insight'
Ian Herbert, *Independent*

'A top-class book . . . If you enjoyed *Secret Diary of a
Liverpool Scout*, you'll like this one even more'
Tony Barrett, *The Times*

Men in White Suits

Simon Hughes

Liverpool FC in the 1990s
The players' stories

In *Men in White Suits*, Simon Hughes meets some of the most colourful characters to have played for Liverpool FC during the 1990s. The resulting interviews deliver a rich portrait of life at Anfield during a decade when on-field frustrations were symptomatic of off-the-field mismanagement and ill-discipline.

Liverpool – under manager Roy Evans – displayed a breath-taking style led by a supremely talented young group of British players whose names featured as regularly on the front pages of the tabloids as they did on the back. Indeed, such was their celebrity status, they were tagged the 'Spice Boys'.

Yet despite their flaws, this was a group of intriguing individuals: mavericks, playboys, goal-scorers and luckless defenders. Wearing off-white Armani suits, their confident personalities were exemplified in their pre-match walk around Wembley before the 1996 FA Cup final (a 1-0 defeat to Manchester United). In stark contrast to the stars of today, the blunt, ribald recollections of the footballers featured here provide a rare insight into this fascinating era in Liverpool's long and illustrious history.

'A captivating book . . . essential reading
for all fans of the game'
Ian Herbert, *Independent*

'An excellent book'
Daily Mirror